I0138238

ELEVATING
Learning & Development

INSIGHTS AND PRACTICAL GUIDANCE FROM THE FIELD

Edited by **Nick van Dam**

Preface by **Elliott Masie**

Praise for *Elevating Learning & Development*

In a world of fast-paced change and radical technological advancement, I firmly believe L&D teams must play a strategic role enabling lifelong employee learning and high-impact, sustainable organizational performance. Teams that play this role will be highly valued and recognized for the benefit they bring; those that don't will be increasingly marginalized. This book helps facilitate the transformation needed in L&D in support of this strategic ambition. I would recommend it to practitioners who are serious about positioning themselves and their teams for value generation and relevance over the longer term.

—**Nic Brassey,** SVP Human Resources, Ahold Delhaize

As business leaders, it is our responsibility to provide those in our span of care with opportunities to realize their potential and know that who they are and what they do matters. How else can we help them realize their potential and elevate humanity? Let this practical yet inspiring compendium guide you on your journey to create a thriving organization.

—**Bob Chapman,** Chairman and CEO, Barry-Wehmiller Companies, Author, *Everybody Matters: The Extraordinary Power of Caring for Your People Like Family*

Built from profound insights, this important book shows what it takes to be a purposeful learner and sets the corporate agenda to inspire and motivate learning. A must-read for anyone who cares about learning.

—**Lynda Gratton,** Professor of Management Practice and Executive Education Faculty Director, London Business School

L&D professionals know better than anyone how important it is to learn from one another. In *Elevating Learning & Development*, more than 30 L&D professionals from McKinsey offer up their thoughts on a wide variety of topics, effectively catapulting the sharing of best practices in the industry ahead several years. I am impressed with the pragmatic and simple but powerful tips that the McKinsey team has shared to elevate the way training can be addressed to match the digital era and make learning a true enabler of a company's success through the development of its people.

—**Hossom Haggag,** VP of Talent and Leadership, Jumeirah

Nick van Dam has championed and diffused the latest developments in learning innovation from a unique lighthouse of knowledge and expertise: McKinsey & Company. The contributions in this volume are key to understanding how effective learning can act as the key catalyst for innovation in all organizations.

—**Santiago Iñiguez de Onzoño,** President, IE University, Spain

Foresight, agility, digital savvy, innovation, and urgency... critical capabilities for the future. Do you want more of these for your organization? *Elevating Learning & Development: Insights and Practical Guidance from the Field* provides invaluable insights for adapting your learning and development function to fuel growth.

—**Karen Kocher,** General Manager, 21st Century Jobs, Skills and Employability, Microsoft

In a knowledge economy—and particularly in professional services—it's never been more crucial to develop employees through formal and informal learning. And yet the learning-and-development function often struggles to demonstrate its impact on the organization, which stymies their efforts. This book offers a playbook, based on both theory and practical advice, for how to overcome many of the most common obstacles.

—**Peter May,** Global Chief Talent Officer, Baker McKenzie

It's never been true that 'Those who can't do, teach.' Here is the evidence: 19 chapters written by 35 L&D practitioners on how they do what they do. In *Elevating Learning & Development*, learning experts from McKinsey offer a compelling set of insights that can help their colleagues across the industry adapt to the 21st-century workforce.

—**Annie McKee,** Senior Fellow and Director of the Graduate School of Education's PennCLO Executive Doctoral Program, University of Pennsylvania

The fluidity of the current marketplace, and the certainty of the upcoming artificial intelligence wave of disruption, puts learning and development at the center of the agenda for business leaders. This book provides an extremely valuable tool kit to navigate successfully across this exciting future.

—**Guillermo Miranda,** Chief Learning Officer, IBM Corporation

Elevating Learning & Development is a fascinating look into how companies are using professional learning and development to build a global workforce that can withstand the rigors of the 21st-century economy. This book, based on substantive evidence, provides not only thought leadership but more importantly decision-making support for executives when dealing with the complexity of the strategic and operational choices that L&D faces today.

—**Maricel Perez Lovisolo,** Vice President of Global Learning and Talent Management, Jacobs Engineering S.A.

Learning-and-development functions are moving to 'center stage' within companies because they are critical to helping individuals build skills in a rapidly changing world. Nick van Dam and his colleagues provide an outstanding guide to how these L&D organizations can fulfill this critical mission.

—**Tim Welsh,** Vice Chairman Consumer Banking Sales and Support, U.S. Bank

Published by McKinsey & Company, 55 East 52nd Street, New York, New York 10022.

ISBN: 978-0-692-15081-8

Cover illustration by Hank Osuna

Contents

Preface
by Elliott Masie

When Nick van Dam, a wise learning leader, asked me to write a preface for his book on "elevating" the field of learning, I was excited and overwhelmed. The world of learning touches every organization, every employee and customer, and it is changing at the speed of technology and innovation. Yet, the art and science of learning is as old as there have been curious learners, wise teachers, and moments of need or aspiration.

As an analyst in the field of learning and a professor in learning graduate programs, I have been looking for an evidence-based book that will provide a compelling view of the current and future opportunities for learning and development. This book provides experienced learning-and-development professionals, as well as other business leaders and those just starting in our field, with a low-hype perspective on strategies that will truly elevate the learner, the learning organization, and, most importantly, the effectiveness of our organizations.

Elevating Learning & Development takes an agile and dynamic look at all the dimensions we must explore. The book creatively and pragmatically explores what we need to "elevate":

- **Elevate learning expectations:** The learner of today and tomorrow is more connected, more independent, and more bombarded by content. Elevation of learning is not just more content. In fact, it is curating the right content for the right employee at the right moment in the right format and for the right reason.

- **Elevate learning analytics and data:** We must learn about our learners. Data from our learners, from their peers, from their managers, from their performance, and from their patterns of learning can and will form a framework for analyzing real learning needs. Brave data collection can lead to brave learning decisions on what works, what does not work, and what is just "ritual."

- **Elevate and expand technology's role in learning:** Our mobile devices, the smart speakers that answer our questions, the chatbots that map to our curiosity, the growth of automation and artificial intelligence, and the promise of machine learning can form pathways to radical shifts in how, when, and what our employees learn. But cool and emerging tech must be balanced with a connection to the fundamentals of our business and a sense of design matched to real learners' experiences.

- **Elevate teaching and learning facilities:** We must find and develop the right faculty and experts, including peers who are standing right beside our learners. We must rethink our learning spaces. Our employees don't want to go back to school in replicas of their old classrooms. They want to move forward to labs, experiences, and rigorous simulations that will challenge them to learn from the expertise of our organization's best resources.

- **Elevate learning's mind-set:** I read and reread chapter 5, "Seven essentials of a lifelong learning mind-set," five times. I am deeply reflecting on the learner's opportunity to "become a serial master" and the exploration of stress and performance.

- **Elevate learning's partnerships:** Learning *does not happen* in the classroom or on a webinar. Teaching might happen there. A lecture might happen there. A discussion might happen there. But learning happens everywhere the learner is. One of my personal phrases is "Let's bring learning to the learner!" To do this, learning and development must partner with IT (to harness the tech resources of the enterprise), with the business unit (to extend the role of learning from an event to an everyday process), and with finance, HR, sales, security, and every arm of the business—to make learning an experience that is everywhere.

In addition to elevating these dimensions of the learning process, this book allows us to explore the shared governance models of learning and development.

There are hundreds of decisions that the enterprise, a line of business, a manager, and ultimately a learner will make to shape the learning experience. So many of these decisions might be made without thinking because of long-held rituals. For example, some might say that all webinars should be one hour long, even before they have defined the content, engagement, or desired outcome. Governance of learning must map to both the business strategy and to evidence-based models of choosing from a growing number of alternative learning pathways. We must blend the personal choices of a learner with the need for an enterprise commitment to current knowledge, shared competencies, and codes of conduct.

Let me throw out one more word that came to mind as I read the 19 chapters of *Elevating Learning & Development*. That word is *optimize*.

Our learners and our businesses desperately need to optimize their learning, their speed to competency, their alignment to shifting business realities, and their exploration of new technologies and knowledge bases. We want to elevate learning to optimize every dimension of the learner's processes:

- Optimize timing
- Optimize engagement
- Optimize alignment with business
- Optimize data perspectives
- Optimize teaching and faculty
- Optimize blending of learning processes
- Optimize work experience with conceptual content
- Optimize social validation and extension

- Optimize learner confidence
- Optimize curiosity
- Optimize learning excitement

The chapters in *Elevating Learning & Development* will stimulate thoughts, questions, and challenges about how we optimize.

There are shifts in marketplaces around the world:

- How we order a car to take us to a location is different since the introduction of car-sharing services.
- The role of online shopping is changing the retail marketplace.
- We can see nearby restaurants visually on our phones along with reviews from yesterday's diners.
- Ordering goods and services has become personalized and "just in time."

So, how will the learning marketplace shift for our employees? This is not a question about tomorrow. Let's look closely at our learners and we will see these seismic shifts already in place and growing:

- Learners have high-powered curiosity devices in their hands and pockets. Mobile devices and search engines allow them to be curious at their exact moments of need, pain, confusion, aspiration, or curiosity.
- Learners no longer need or want to memorize much. They want navigational wisdom to get and return to the data, resources, or process steps they will need, but they don't want to memorize something they might never use or that could change quickly.
- Learners want validation of knowledge from multiple perspectives. They want to know the *context* as well as the

content. They want to have the backstory and want their sources to validate it.

- Learners want to engage deeply and even fail safely–if they can. Give them a game, simulation, or experience rather than a 24-slide PowerPoint deck. Let them "fail forward and upward."

- Learners don't want to go to a specific webpage or site to find knowledge. They want it around them, both digitally and among their colleagues who are physically and virtually connected to their work spaces.

- Learners want recommendations to help them curate their learning content and process choices. They want to avoid the low-value options and rapidly find the best and most personally applicable knowledge chunks.

- Learners want to be optimized!

Finally, I want to add some context to this preface. Dozens of new books about learning are published every year. This one, *Elevating Learning & Development*, is deeply credible because of its editor and primary author. Nick van Dam has led learning for some of the largest organizations in the world, has championed the availability of no-cost e-learning for children around the globe, and is a chief learning officer committed to the value and preciousness of learning and employee energy. Nick loves technology and avoids the hype cycle of innovation. He challenges learning designers to deeply align with real learners and real business requirements. Most importantly, he is a learning leader who is an authentic learner himself.

Elevating Learning & Development is a much-needed strategic and practical look at the future of our field, our learners, and our businesses.

Elliott Masie
Chair of The Learning CONSORTIUM
www.masie.com

Foreword and acknowledgments
by Nick van Dam

A little more than 30 years ago—at the time when the first microcomputers arrived in the workplace—my career began in learning and development (L&D). It was very exciting to experience the first generation of computer-based training solutions and even the computer-based "management games" that were introduced for leadership development. In those days, the L&D function was called "training," and most efforts were mandated for the workforce and focused on technical skills and training initiatives.

Almost all training was delivered in a classroom or conference center, and research on people-capability building and corporate training was at a preliminary stage. People involved in training mostly had a technical or business background (or sometimes both) that enabled them to bring expertise to a training event. The head of the training department was typically a senior leader with rich business experience who was given the role as a last step before retirement. During this era, most people in the workforce enjoyed long-term or even lifetime employment. Being loyal and continuing to bring the best of yourself to your job contributed in a significant way to a successful career, which was often spent at a single organization or, at most, a limited number of organizations.

Fast-forward to today. We are at the beginning of the Fourth Industrial Revolution, which is fueled by advancements in technologies, such as the Internet of Things, machine learning, robots, the autonomous car, 3-D printing, and the mobile internet, to name a few. All these technologies have already had tremendous impact on what is required of people capabilities in organizations. The world and the workplace have changed dramatically. The good old personal computer has been replaced by the smartphone. It seems like the internet has always been around: people work virtually from a variety of locations, technology has introduced and disrupted many business models, and IT has gained dominance over the way we work.

During this time, training has evolved into L&D. Organizations that want to stay in business have realized they must continually invest in the development of their human capital, and about 45 percent of all today's formal learning is delivered through digital solutions.[1] In many cases, these channels have replaced traditional classroom programs. Technology enables learning to be even more personalized and self-directed. The classroom of the 21st century is enabled by technology and provides people with immersive-learning experiences. The future is about high-tech and high-touch learning. Young professionals and leaders have told us that they benefit tremendously from time away from daily work, where they can collaboratively solve wicked problems, practice new skills, receive coaching, connect and learn from others, get inspired by new insights, and reflect on their own work and personal development. Additionally, individuals have realized that they need to embrace lifelong learning mind-sets to remain relevant and that their careers will involve multiple employers and roles.

Research in multiple fields has contributed significantly to the L&D profession. Thanks to cognitive neuroscience we know more about how the brain works and how people learn. This research has provided evidence that because of the brain's neuroplasticity, people can continue to learn and grow throughout their lifetime. Many universities have performed groundbreaking research in the broader field of adult learning, and L&D professionals benefit tremendously from these insights on how to design the most effective and efficient learning solutions. We also have a better understanding from developmental psychology research on what it takes to change people's behaviors. Finally, the very promising field of positive psychology looks at what enables organizations and people to flourish, and these insights have been incorporated into the design of learning programs.

I am very gratified that over the past 30 years L&D has also matured as a profession. There are now several bachelor's, master's, and doctorate university degrees offered in this field, and a growing number of companies have acknowledged that L&D is a vital profession, akin to accounting, IT, and marketing. In these organizations, the role of a chief learning officer has become accepted, and the people appointed to lead L&D are specialists in this broad field of knowledge and expertise.

It has been an amazing personal journey to watch the L&D profession make such an impact over the years. At McKinsey I have the honor of working with a group of the most talented L&D professionals I've encountered in my career. Over the past five years, we have collaborated on a new L&D strategy, aligned the organization, advanced learning governance, recruited and developed learning experts, designed amazing learning solutions and programs, and achieved major progress on learning measurement.

As I am passionate about how I can advance the profession, I reached out to my colleagues and invited them to coauthor this book with me, focusing on a variety of learning topics that matter for every L&D professional. This book includes 19 chapters with terrific perspectives from leading McKinsey L&D practitioners and thought leaders. I couldn't be prouder or more appreciative of all the amazing work that this team has accomplished, and I am delighted to present this book to you. I'm excited about the contribution this book, along with another forthcoming book from McKinsey called *Leadership at Scale*, will make to the profession's discussion of how to develop leaders.

This book would not exist without the unwavering engagement and contributions of a great many people. The entire project hinged on the tireless efforts of Laura Soto, who did a fabulous job in managing this project in addition to all her other responsibilities related to learning communications and reach and relevance. The incredible members of my McKinsey Learning

Leadership team—Mary Andrade, Tonya Corley, Gina Fine, Liz Gryger, Matthew Joseph, Gene Kuo, and Larry Murphy—were engaged throughout the effort and helped inspire their colleagues to be part of this initiative.

And of course, I thank 34 of my McKinsey Learning colleagues for taking time out of their busy schedules to spend the better part of a year writing and revising their chapters: Mary Andrade, Maria Eugenia Arias, Carissa Bell, Kim Blank, Jacqueline Brassey, Janine Carboni, Lisa Christensen, Katie Coates, Tonya Corley, Sara Diniz, Gina Fine, Karen Freeman, Stephanie Gabriels, Sarah Gisser, Terrence Hackett, Gene Kuo, Duncan Larkin, Maeve Lucey, Barbara Matthews, Karen J. Merry, Larry Murphy, Stephanie Nadda, Nick Pappas, James Pritchard, Ron Rabin, Brodie Riordan, John Sangimino, Lois Schaub, Janice Steffen, Allison Stevenson (now at Kirkland & Ellis), Allison Thom, Gina Webster, Ashley Williams, and Cathy Wright.

In addition, I would like to acknowledge the following individuals:

- My McKinsey partners Rik Kirkland, Mary Meaney, Nicolai Nielsen, Charlotte Relyea, and Ramesh Srinivasan for reading the manuscript and your ongoing support.
- My dear friend Elliott Masie who has written a preface for this book and who I admire as an amazing leader in our profession. I have learned so much from you, Elliott.
- The members of our editorial and design team at Leff, including Scott Leff, Heather Ploog, Alia Samhat, Brittany Williams, Justin Durkin, and Delilah Zak, as well as freelancer Margaret Currie, for supporting all the authors as they developed their chapters. I'd also like to acknowledge Mike Borruso, an editor with McKinsey's Global Editorial Services, for his terrific feedback at a crucial stage in the book's development, which made the book so much stronger.

- My former colleague and friend Tim Welsh, who gave feedback on the initial proposal of this book and has been a big champion of this project.
- The McKinsey partnership for allowing us to write this book and supporting my e-learning for kids foundation by donating all proceeds from its sales.

I am grateful to a number of special friends and family members who have had a huge impact on my professional career, including Dominic Barton, Scott Beardsley, Bob Chapman, Jos Marcus, Peter May, Annie McKee, Santiago Iñiguez de Onzoño, Michael Pehl, Doug Ready, Jan Rijken, Eileen Rogers, Juergen Sattler, Kathy Scholz, and James (Jim) Wall. I dedicate this book to the memory of my beloved father, Nic van Dam (1939–91), who taught me to care for people in organizations, and to my mom, Wilma, for her unconditional love and optimism.

Finally, most of my work for this book occurred during late evenings, weekends, and even vacations. I want to thank my wife, Judith Grimbergen, who has been a source of inspiration in my life, and my son, Yannick van Dam, for putting up with me in my relentless effort to have an impact on the L&D profession and for supporting my passion for developing better leaders and sustainable organizational cultures. ■

[1] *2017 state of the industry,* ATD Research, December 2017, td.org.

INTRODUCTION:

Components of a successful L&D strategy

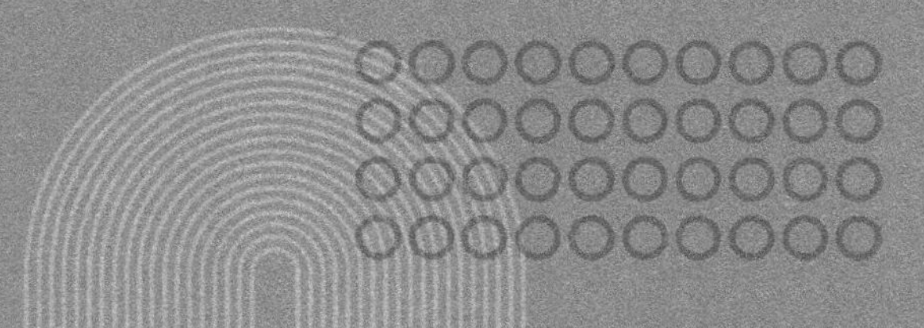

AUTHORS
Jacqueline Brassey
Lisa Christensen
Nick van Dam

The ACADEMIES framework is a useful tool for conceptualizing learning strategy.

Over the past decade, the global workforce has been continually evolving due to a number of factors. An increasingly competitive business landscape, rising complexity, and the digital revolution are reshaping the mix of employees. Meanwhile, persistent uncertainty, a multigenerational workforce, and a shorter shelf life for knowledge have placed a premium on reskilling and upskilling. The shift to a digital, knowledge-based economy means that a vibrant workforce is more important than ever: research suggests that a very significant percentage of market capitalization in public companies is based on intangible assets—skilled employees, exceptional leaders, and knowledge.[I]

All of these trends have elevated the importance of the learning-and-development (L&D) function. To get the most out of investments in training programs and curriculum development, L&D leaders must embrace a broader role within the organization and formulate an ambitious vision for the function. At McKinsey, we use a variety of frameworks to help companies set up and manage their corporate academies. One such structure is the ACADEMIES© framework, which encompasses nine dimensions that can help to strengthen the L&D function and position it to serve the organization more effectively.

The strategic role of L&D

One of L&D's primary responsibilities is to manage the development of people—and to do so in a way that supports other key business priorities. L&D's strategic role spans five areas (Exhibit A).[2]

Exhibit A: **The learning function of an organization has a strategic role in five areas.**

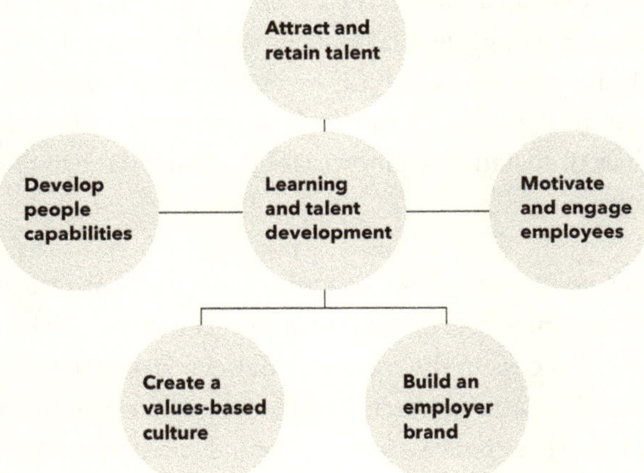

Source: Adapted from Nick van Dam, *25 Best Practices in Learning & Talent Development*, Raleigh, NC: Lulu Publishing, 2008

1. *Attract and retain talent.* Traditionally, learning focused solely on improving productivity. Today, learning also contributes to employability. Over the past several decades, employment has shifted from staying with the same company for a lifetime to a model where workers are being retained only as long as they can add value to an enterprise. Workers are now in charge of their personal and professional growth and development—one reason that people list "opportunities for learning and development" among the top criteria for joining an organization. Conversely, a lack of L&D is one of the key reasons people cite for leaving a company.

2. *Develop people capabilities.* Human capital requires ongoing investments in L&D to retain its value. When knowledge becomes outdated or forgotten—a more rapid occurrence today—the value of human capital declines and needs to be supplemented by new learning and relevant work experiences.[3] Companies that make investments in the next generation of leaders are seeing an impressive return. Research indicates that companies in the top quartile of leadership outperform other organizations by nearly two times on earnings before interest, taxes, depreciation, and amortization (EBITDA). Moreover, companies that invest in developing leaders during significant transformations are 2.4 times more likely to hit their performance targets.[4]

3. *Create a values-based culture.* As the workforce in many companies becomes increasingly virtual and globally dispersed, L&D can help to build a values-based culture and a sense of community. In particular, millennials are particularly interested in working for values-based, sustainable enterprises that contribute to the welfare of society.

4. *Build an employer brand.* An organization's brand is one of its most important assets and conveys a great deal about the company's success in the market, financial strengths, position in the industry, and products and services. Investments in L&D can help to enhance company's brand and boost its reputation as an "employer of choice." As large segments of the workforce prepare to retire, employers must work harder to compete for a shrinking talent pool. To do so, they must communicate their brand strength explicitly through an employer value proposition.

5. *Motivate and engage employees.* The most important way to engage employees is to provide them with opportunities to learn and develop new competencies. Research suggests that lifelong learning contributes to happiness.[5] When highly engaged employees are challenged and given the skills to grow and develop within their chosen career path, they are more likely to be energized by new opportunities at work and satisfied with their current organization.

The L&D function in transition

Over the years, we have identified and field-tested nine dimensions that contribute to a strong L&D function. We combined these dimensions to create the ACADEMIES framework, which covers all aspects of L&D functions, from setting aspirations to measuring impact (Exhibit B). Although many companies regularly execute on several dimensions of this framework, our recent research found that only a few companies are fully mature in all dimensions.

1. Alignment with business strategy

One of an L&D executive's primary tasks is to develop and shape a learning strategy based on the company's business and talent strategies. A learning strategy seeks to support professional development and build capabilities across the company, on time,

Exhibit B: **The ACADEMIES framework includes nine components.**

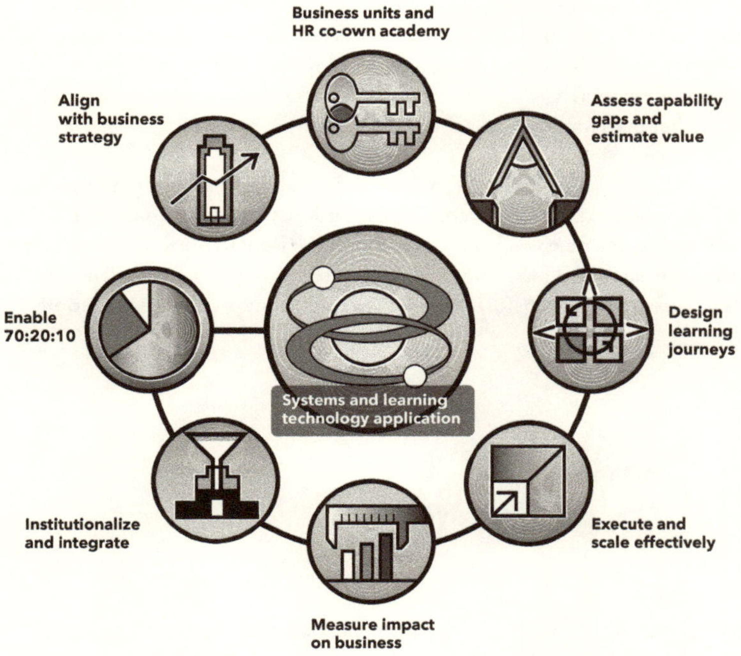

Source: McKinsey & Company

Learning and development—From evolution to revolution

To understand trends and priorities in L&D, we undertook several phases of research. We began in 2014 by surveying 1,500 executives about capability building. In 2016, we added 120 L&D leaders at 91 organizations to our database, gathering information on their traditional training strategies and aspirations for future programs. We also interviewed 15 chief learning officers or L&D heads at major companies.[1]

Historically, the L&D function has been relatively successful in helping employees build skills and perform well in their existing roles. The main focus of L&D has been on upskilling. However, the pace of change continues to accelerate; McKinsey research estimates that as many as 800 million jobs could be displaced by automation by 2030.[2] Employee roles are expected to continue evolving, and a large number of people will need to learn new skills to remain employable. Unsurprisingly, our research confirmed our initial hypothesis: corporate learning must undergo revolutionary changes over the next few years to keep pace with constant technological advances.[3] In addition to updating training content, companies must increase their focus on blended-learning solutions, which combine digital learning, fieldwork, and highly immersive classroom sessions. With the growth of user-friendly digital-learning platforms, employees will take more ownership of their professional development, logging in to take courses when the need arises rather than waiting for a scheduled classroom session.

Such innovations will require companies to devote more resources to training: our survey revealed that 60 percent of respondents plan to increase L&D spending over the next few years, and 66 percent want to boost the number of employee-training hours. As they commit more time and money, companies must ensure that the transformation of the L&D function proceeds smoothly.

[1] Richard Benson-Armer, Arne Gast, and Nick van Dam, "Learning at the speed of business," *McKinsey Quarterly,* May 2016, McKinsey.com.

[2] For more information, see "What the future of work will mean for jobs, skills, and wages," McKinsey Global Institute, November 2017, on McKinsey.com.

[3] Benson-Armer, Gast, and van Dam, "Learning at the speed of business."

and in a cost-effective manner. In addition, the learning strategy can enhance the company culture and encourage employees to live the company's values.

For many organizations, the L&D function supports the implementation of the business strategy. For example, if one of the business strategies is a digital transformation, L&D will focus on building the necessary people capabilities to make that possible.

Every business leader would agree that L&D must align with a company's overall priorities. Yet research has found that many L&D functions fall short on this dimension. Only 40 percent of companies say that their learning strategy is aligned with business goals.[6] For 60 percent, then, learning has no explicit connection to the company's strategic objectives. L&D functions may be out of sync with the business due to outdated approaches or because budgets have been based on priorities from previous years rather than today's imperatives, such as a digital transformation.

To be effective, L&D must take a hard look at employee capabilities and determine which are most essential to support the execution of the company's business strategy. L&D leaders should reevaluate this alignment on a yearly basis to ensure they are creating a people-capability agenda that truly reflects business priorities and strategic objectives.

2. Co-ownership between business units and HR

With new tools and technologies constantly emerging, companies must become more agile, ready to adapt their business processes and practices. L&D functions must likewise be prepared to rapidly launch capability-building programs—for example, if new business needs suddenly arise or staff members require immediate training on new technologies such as cloud-based collaboration tools.

L&D functions can enhance their partnership with business leaders by establishing a governance structure in which leadership from both groups share responsibility for defining, prioritizing, designing, and securing funds for capability-building programs.

Under this governance model, a company's chief experience officer (CXO), senior executives, and business-unit heads will develop the people-capability agenda for segments of the enterprise and ensure that it aligns with the company's overall strategic goals. Top business executives will also help firmly embed the learning function and all L&D initiatives in the organizational culture. The involvement of senior leadership enables full commitment to the L&D function's longer-term vision.

3. Assessment of capability gaps and estimated value

After companies identify their business priorities, they must verify that their employees can deliver them—a task that may be more difficult than it sounds. Some companies make no effort to assess employee capabilities, while others do so only at a high level. Conversations with L&D, HR, and senior executives suggest that many companies are ineffective or indifferent at assessing capability gaps, especially when it comes to senior leaders and midlevel managers.

The most effective companies take a deliberate, systematic approach to capability assessment. At the heart of this process is a comprehensive competency or capability model based on the organization's strategic direction. For example, a key competency for a segment of an e-commerce company's workforce could be "deep expertise in big data and predictive analytics."

After identifying the most essential capabilities for various functions or job descriptions, companies should then assess how employees rate in each of these areas. L&D interventions should seek to close these capability gaps.

4. Design of learning journeys

Most corporate learning is delivered through a combination of digital-learning formats and in-person sessions. While our research indicates that immersive L&D experiences in the classroom still have immense value, leaders have told us that they are incredibly busy "from eight to late," which does not give them a lot of time to sit in a classroom. Furthermore, many said that they prefer to develop and practice new skills and behaviors in a "safe environment," where they don't have to worry about public failures that might affect their career paths.

Traditional L&D programs consisted of several days of classroom learning with no follow-up sessions, even though people tend to forget what they have learned without regular reinforcement. As a result, many L&D functions are moving away from stand-alone programs by designing learning journeys—continuous learning opportunities that take place over a period of time and include L&D interventions such as fieldwork, pre- and post-classroom digital learning, social learning, on-the-job coaching and mentoring, and short workshops. The main objectives of a learning journey are to help people develop the required new competencies in the most effective and efficient way, and to support the transfer of learning to the job.

5. Execution and scale-up

An established L&D agenda consists of a number of strategic initiatives that support capability building and are aligned with business goals, such as helping leaders develop high-performing teams or roll out safety training. The successful execution of L&D initiatives on time and on budget is critical to build and sustain support from business leaders.

L&D functions often face an overload of initiatives and insufficient funding. L&D leadership needs to maintain an ongoing discussion with business leaders about initiatives and priorities to ensure the requisite resources and support.

> **After companies identify their business priorities, they must verify that their employees can deliver them—a task that may be more difficult than it sounds.**

Many new L&D initiatives are initially targeted to a limited audience. A successful execution of a small pilot, such as an online orientation program for a specific audience, can lead to an even bigger impact once the program is rolled out to the entire enterprise. The program's cost per person declines as companies benefit from economies of scale.

6. Measurement of impact on business performance

A learning strategy's execution and impact should be measured using key performance indicators (KPIs). The first indicator looks at business excellence: how closely aligned all L&D initiatives and investments are with business priorities. The second KPI looks at learning excellence: whether learning interventions change people's behavior and performance. Last, an operational-excellence KPI measures how well investments and resources in the corporate academy are used.

Accurate measurement is not simple, and many organizations still rely on traditional impact metrics such as learning-program satisfaction and completion scores. But high-performing organizations focus on outcomes-based metrics such as impact on individual performance, employee engagement, team effectiveness, and business-process improvement. We have identified four lenses for articulating and measuring learning impact:

1. *Strategic alignment:* How effectively does the learning strategy support the organization's priorities?

2. *Capabilities:* How well does the L&D function help colleagues build the mind-sets, skills, and expertise they need most? This impact can be measured by assessing people's capability gaps against a comprehensive competency framework.

3. *Organizational health:* To what extent does learning strengthen the overall health and DNA of the organization? Relevant dimensions of the McKinsey Organizational Health Index can provide a baseline.[7]

4. *Individual peak performance:* Beyond raw capabilities, how well does the L&D function help colleagues achieve maximum impact in their role while maintaining a healthy work-life balance?

Access to big data provides L&D functions with more opportunities to assess and predict the business impact of their interventions.

7. Integration of L&D interventions into HR processes

Just as L&D corporate-learning activities need to be aligned with the business, they should also be an integral part of the HR agenda. L&D has an important role to play in recruitment, onboarding, performance management, promotion, workforce, and succession planning. Our research shows that at best, many L&D functions have only loose connections to annual performance reviews and lack a structured approach and follow-up to performance-management practices.

L&D leadership must understand major HR management practices and processes and collaborate closely with HR leaders. The best L&D functions use consolidated development feedback from performance reviews as input for their capability-building agenda. A growing number of companies are replacing annual performance appraisals with frequent, in-the-moment feedback.[8] This is another area in which the L&D function can help managers build skills to provide development feedback effectively.

Another example is onboarding. Companies that have developed high-impact onboarding processes score better on employee engagement and satisfaction and lose fewer new hires.[9] The L&D function can play a critical role in onboarding—for example, by helping people build the skills to be successful in their role, providing new hires with access to digital-learning technologies, and connecting them with other new hires and mentors.

8. Enabling of the 70:20:10 learning framework

Many L&D functions embrace a framework known as "70:20:10," in which 70 percent of learning takes place on the job, 20 percent through interaction and collaboration, and 10 percent through formal-learning interventions such as classroom training and digital curricula. These percentages are general guidelines and vary by industry and organization. L&D functions have traditionally focused on the formal-learning component.

Today, L&D leaders must design and implement interventions that support informal learning, including coaching and mentoring, on-the-job instruction, apprenticeships, leadership shadowing, action-based learning, on-demand access to digital learning, and lunch-and-learn sessions. Social technologies play a growing role in connecting experts and creating and sharing knowledge.

9. Systems and learning-technology applications

The most significant enablers for just-in-time learning are technology platforms and applications. Examples include next-generation learning-management systems, virtual classrooms, mobile-learning apps, embedded performance-support systems, polling software, learning-video platforms, learning-assessment and -measurement platforms, massive open online courses (MOOCs), and small private online courses (SPOCs), to name just a few.

The learning-technology industry has moved entirely to cloud-based platforms, which provide L&D functions with unlimited opportunities to plug and unplug systems and access the latest functionality without having to go through lengthy and expensive implementations of an on-premises system. L&D leaders must make sure that learning technologies fit into an overall system architecture that includes functionality to support the entire talent cycle, including recruitment, onboarding, performance management, L&D, real-time feedback tools, career management, succession planning, and rewards and recognition.

■ ■ ■

L&D leaders are increasingly aware of the challenges created by the Fourth Industrial Revolution (technologies that are connecting the physical and digital worlds), but few have implemented large-scale transformation programs. Instead, most are slowly adapting their strategy and curricula as needed. However, with technology advancing at an ever-accelerating pace, L&D leaders can delay no longer: human capital is more important than ever and will be the primary factor in sustaining competitive advantage over the next few years.

The leaders of L&D functions need to revolutionize their approach by creating a learning strategy that aligns with business strategy and by identifying and enabling the capabilities needed to achieve success. This approach will result in robust curricula that employ every relevant and available learning method and technology. The most effective companies will invest in innovative L&D programs, remain flexible and agile, and build the human talent needed to master the digital age.

These changes entail some risk, and perhaps some trial and error, but the rewards are great. ■

A version of this chapter was published in TvOO Magazine *in September 2016.*

1 Intangible Asset Market Value Study, Ocean Tomo.

2 Nick van Dam, *25 Best Practices in Learning & Talent Development,* Raleigh, NC: Lulu Publishing, 2008.

3 Gary S. Becker, "Investment in human capital: A theoretical analysis," *Journal of Political Economy,* 1962, Volume 70, Number 5, Part 2, pp. 9–49, jstor.org.

4 "What successful transformations share: McKinsey Global Survey results," March 2010, McKinsey.com; and "Economic Conditions Snapshot, June 2009: McKinsey Global Survey results," June 2009, McKinsey.com.

5 John Coleman, "Lifelong learning is good for your health, your wallet, and your social life," *Harvard Business Review,* February 7, 2017, hbr.org.

6 Human Capital Management Excellence Conference 2018, Brandon Hall Group.

7 For more information, visit the Organizational Health Index on McKinsey.com.

8 *HCM outlook 2018,* Brandon Hall Group.

9 *HCM outlook 2018,* Brandon Hall Group.

Mapping the ACADEMIES framework to the book chapters

Chapter 1
Enabling agile learning organizations: Structuring options for L&D

Chapter 2
L&D governance: The key to earning a seat at the table

Chapter 3
Optimizing the partnership with IT

Chapter 4
Learning-needs analysis: Cracking the code

Chapter 5
Seven essential elements of a lifelong-learning mind-set

Chapter 6
Shaping individual development along the S-curve

Chapter 7
Maximizing learning impact: The role of authentic confidence

Chapter 8
Curation: Moving beyond content management

Chapter 9
How to improve employee engagement with digital learning

Chapter 10
Changing mind-sets and behaviors: Our role in personal and organizational change

Chapter 11
Marketing the idea of lifelong learning

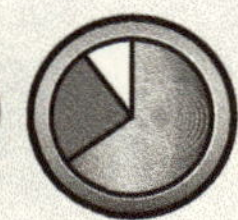

Chapter 12
Harnessing analytics to shape the learning-and-development agenda

Chapter 13
Reinvigorating blended learning

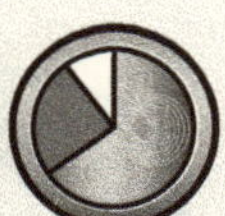

Chapter 14
Proven strategies to integrate immersive learning into your organization

Chapter 15
Maximizing the impact of feedback for learning and behavior change

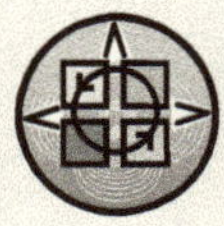

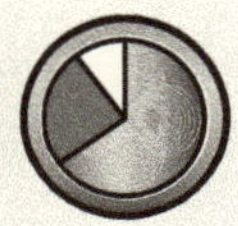

Chapter 16
Developing an organizational coaching strategy and culture

Chapter 17
Finding the right faculty: Teaching excellence means classroom success

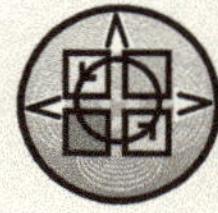

Chapter 18
The learning facility of the future

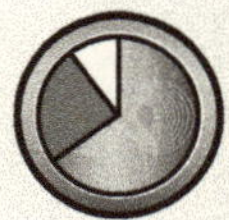

Chapter 19
Migrating learning to the cloud

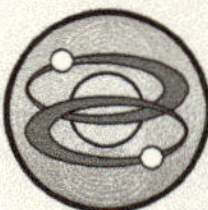

CHAPTER

01/

ENABLING AGILE LEARNING ORGANIZATIONS:

Structuring options for L&D

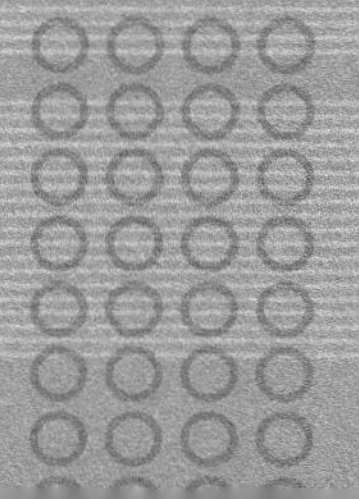

AUTHORS
Lisa Christensen
Karen Freeman
Nick van Dam

Learning-and-development functions are at a pivotal moment, as the need for new kinds of talent requires organizations to foster a culture of learning. A stable structure paired with agile processes can be foundational for success.

Learning-and-development (L&D) functions need to enable learning at the speed of business—and business is moving faster than ever. The pace of innovation leads to the emergence of new roles, capabilities, and techniques, raising the bar for L&D to meet fast-changing learning needs.

Digital talent is a prime example: in a 2017 Capgemini and LinkedIn survey of 1,250 employees, recruiters, and leadership teams, half of those surveyed acknowledged the digital talent gap is widening. Fully 29 percent of employees said their skill sets are already redundant or will be soon, and another 38 percent said their skills will be redundant in four to five years. Even more troubling, almost half are not satisfied with their organization's current L&D offerings, and 43 percent said they would be willing to move to another company if they felt their digital skills were stagnating.[1]

In response, L&D functions are working on all fronts to close the gap: developing shorter, just-in-time learning; improving user experience of programs; and adopting new learning technologies and platforms. And yet they are still struggling; McKinsey surveys of executives, senior L&D officers, and chief learning officers (CLOs) found that only 57 percent of respondents believe their learning functions are "very or fully aligned" with business priorities, and just 52 percent said that these functions enable their companies to meet strategic objectives. Of the CLOs we surveyed, about 40 percent said their learning initiatives are either "ineffective" or "neither effective nor ineffective" in assessing employees' capabilities and skills gaps.[2]

Where to start? This book covers a variety of topics, including how to engage learners in both digital and in-person learning, how to design learning journeys, and the science of learning itself. But before L&D leaders can develop a culture of learning or implement cutting-edge teaching technologies, they must look inward at their own structure, processes, and governance, and develop a stable yet flexible framework for delivering learning.

In this chapter, we review the three basic options for L&D structural organization—centralized, decentralized, and hybrid—each of which offers advantages and disadvantages tied to the parent organization's characteristics, the mandate of L&D, the needs of learners, and the need for scale or resource efficiency. Once a decision is made about the structural backbone of the learning function, leadership must stabilize the function with an agile overlay—the processes that complement the function's structure and best support the company's unique situation. This overlay will help the L&D function stay relevant to business needs, scale learning and maintain quality, and improve cohesion and the adoption of central services. Good L&D governance, which is discussed in the following chapter, is also an essential component of designing your L&D function.

Before L&D leaders can develop a culture of learning or implement cutting-edge teaching technologies, they must look inward at their own structure, processes, and governance, and develop a stable yet flexible framework for delivering learning.

Constant organizational flux is unsustainable

Businesses today face an ongoing temptation to tinker with organizational structure in response to a variety of pressures. Indeed, a McKinsey survey of global executives suggests many companies are in "a nearly permanent state of organizational flux. Almost 60 percent of the respondents, for example, told us they had experienced a redesign within the past two years, and an additional 25 percent said they experienced a redesign three or more years ago."[3]

Given the rapid pace of change, reorganizing L&D support in response to every change in the business is a fool's errand for learning leaders. Indeed, only 23 percent of the redesigns assessed in the McKinsey survey were considered successful by respondents; often, these frequent redesigns fail to deliver as promised, leading employees to reject or undermine them in anticipation of another (unsuccessful) redesign in a few years. Part of the problem, the survey authors determined, is executives' false assumption "that they must choose between much-needed speed and flexibility on the one hand, and the stability and scale inherent in fixed organizational structures and processes on the other."

In truth, the authors write, agile organizations—those that can withstand the speed of business and achieve growth—"learn to be both stable (resilient, reliable, and efficient) and dynamic (fast, nimble, and adaptive). To master this paradox, companies must design structures, processes, and governance with a relatively unchanging set of core elements—a fixed backbone. At the same time, they must create looser, more dynamic elements that can be adapted quickly to new challenges and opportunities."

Mastering the agility paradox in L&D

Building on the work of our colleagues, we suggest that a strong organizational structure forms the stable backbone of an L&D function, while a deliberate overlay of flexible elements, including team, process, and goal creation, ensures the agility needed in today's dynamic environment.

Choosing a backbone

The learning backbone is fundamentally about where the learning people sit in the organization. In the decentralized model, learning personnel are dispersed throughout a variety of business units. In the centralized approach, learning sits in HR or in its own freestanding space. A hybrid function, sometimes referred to as a federated structure, is a mix of both.

Weighing pros and cons

Our research indicates that 23 percent of L&D functions are completely centralized, 46 percent are hybrid, and 27 percent are decentralized, while 4 percent of respondents didn't know their L&D structure.[4] Each backbone has advantages and disadvantages.

Centralized functions offer strong coordination through the central learning team, whose members report to a single learning or HR executive, which helps to avoid duplication of learning efforts and offers economies of scale. The function is clearly accountable for enterprise-wide budget, resources, L&D talent, external partnerships, vendor management, and standards and guidelines. However, there is a risk that centralized learning teams will be less attuned to the specific needs of business units.

Decentralized functions give ownership of learning initiatives to individual business units, enabling them to tailor initiatives to their specific functions, needs, and people. In this model, however, the learning function has limited oversight, and learning programs don't have a clear connection with the C-suite. Programming may lack cohesion as a result.

Hybrid functions are becoming the norm in larger organizations. In this model, a central team develops professional and leadership-development programs, sets and enforces standards, and manages learning platforms and tools, while business units are responsible for technical learning (and, often, delivery of enterprise programs). This structure allows for better connections with business units while enabling more economies of scale, especially in systems. However, hybrid models can create communication and coordination challenges by blurring lines and causing confusion about who is in charge of what.

Agile elements help overcome the natural deficiencies of each approach—but every company needs to decide for itself which backbone is the best fit.

Four factors to determine the right backbone

The ideal place for the learning function in an organization is determined by four factors:

The parent organization. In principle, the L&D function serves the organization as a whole, no matter where it sits. The determination of whether it is centralized, decentralized, or a hybrid depends on the broader organization's structure and size, and the locations of adjacent functions.

- *The company structure:* If power is held in decentralized units, a centralized learning function will find itself usurped or centralized in name only.

- *The size of the organization:* The largest organizations often take a hybrid approach, creating different backbone structures in response to business needs. Smaller businesses are more likely to be focused on building technical skills, requiring L&D professionals to be closer to the functions they support, such as in a decentralized model.

- *The locations of adjacent functions:* Collaboration is easier if the learning team is aligned structurally to the functions it supports. So if L&D's mandate includes onboarding or organizational effectiveness, then it stands to reason that the L&D function should be aligned with the recruiting or organizational design functions.

The mandate of L&D. The responsibilities and outcomes ascribed to the learning function also have implications for its organizational structure. A 2018 LinkedIn survey found that executives, people managers, and talent developers believe soft skills such as leadership, communication, and collaboration are a top priority—even over role-specific skills.[5] The relative importance of these learning goals has implications for the learning function's organizational backbone. A focus on leadership development, for example, would require the function to be aligned with corporate leadership—likely centralized within HR—while a strategy to develop role-specific, technical skills would need to be more aligned with individual business units.

The needs of learners. To deliver effective learning, L&D functions must understand the learners' business context well enough to determine the real issues underlying a request; for example, "we need communication training" might mean "employees are resisting a change because they don't know how to manage a critical process." Indeed, L&D professionals are often tasked with challenging and shaping business units' understanding of skill development and how to deliver learning. They must also understand the more technical aspects of business units' needs so they can accurately translate their needs and deliver learning that directly addresses those needs. The more technical the background, the more alignment is required between the L&D function and the various business units—which may require a hybrid or fully decentralized model.

The need for scale or resource efficiency. As noted above, centralized L&D functions can more easily avoid duplication of effort and can take advantage of economies of scale. In an organization where learning has limited funding relative to the number of employees, a centralized structure is more cost effective, though it may also be less responsive to emerging needs in business units.

It should be noted that all organizations, regardless of backbone, retain certain centralized capabilities—such as learning-technology platforms and digital content. For example, most organizations would choose not to maintain several learning-management-system platforms.

Stabilizing the backbone with an agile overlay

Once the structure of the learning organization has been chosen, the next step is to build an agile overlay to overcome the challenges inherent in that backbone.

- *For an HR-aligned or centralized L&D function,* the major challenges are aligning learning content with business needs and understanding the business context.

- *For a business-aligned or decentralized L&D function,* there are challenges in finding scale and efficiency, and maintaining learning expertise and quality.

- *For a hybrid L&D function,* the challenges are persuading business units to adopt central services, maintaining cohesion across learning programs, and keeping an eye on long-term goals as project teams form and disband.

With these challenges in mind, we sought out examples of companies that have successfully mitigated the downsides of each type of organizational structure.

Addressing centralized L&D challenges: Staying relevant to business needs

Centralized learning functions can take several steps to ensure that business context is built into learning programs and that employees engage with learning—and avoid rogue efforts that distract from the company's learning goals.

- *Improve mechanisms to gather information about emerging skill needs.* The L&D function at one technology company uses a social-learning platform that empowers employees to chart their own career course by arming them with insights on the capabilities and skills that will increase their value to the business. This portal also helps the L&D team identify experts across the

While decentralized L&D functions are becoming less prevalent, they may still be the best choice for some organizations, particularly those that teach very technical content.

company and enables employee learning through peer-to-peer communication, thus democratizing learning to a degree while also maintaining a centralized L&D function.

- *Embed learner context into the design process.* When developing new programs, one Australian bank systematically collects information about the learner experience and the organizational context, including creating a learner-empathy map to understand what triggers learner concerns. This approach keeps the bank's learning programs up to speed on barriers to learning on an individual level.

- *Hold learners—and their peers—accountable.* After recognizing that employees would need to perform differently to meet the company's global growth goals, one food manufacturer redesigned its performance-review program to include learning as a key component of employee performance. The program now lists "develops self and others" as one of the six behaviors expected of all salaried employees; this behavior specifically includes "enables a learning environment" to reinforce the need to learn and to support the learning of others. By setting this expectation, the company fosters learner motivation and creates a safer, less risky space for the application of learning. (For more on helping employees adopt a lifelong-learning mind-set, see chapter 5.)

- *Identify evangelists for learning.* One IT company recruits respected individuals in other departments to share information about learning opportunities and help reinforce the value of learning. These individuals wield the credibility they've earned in their own functions, and their informal affiliation with L&D can serve to both influence colleagues and communicate information on business needs to the L&D function.

Addressing decentralized L&D challenges: Finding scale and maintaining learning quality

While decentralized L&D functions are becoming less prevalent, they may still be the best choice for some organizations, particularly those that teach very technical content. However, decentralized learning has a few pitfalls, including redundant efforts and inconsistent learning quality across business units. Decentralized functions can overcome the challenges of scale and learning quality in a couple of ways.

- *Audit learning and create common standards.* One financial corporation audits L&D activity across the organization and then works with stakeholders to divide responsibility appropriately. And an electronics company crowdsources standard learning processes to ensure they are relevant across the learning community.

- *Educate business units on best practices in learning.* One airline developed formal programs to teach the principles of learning design, such as needs analysis and learning measurement, to those interested in creating learning programs within their various business units. Those learners then become certified and act as advocates for improving the quality of learning throughout the organization.

Addressing hybrid L&D challenges: Improving cohesion and the adoption of central services

Learning organizations often opt for hybrid structures to avoid the challenges inherent in purely centralized or decentralized approaches. But depending on the tasks offered as shared services, hybrid structures may experience the same challenges noted above. They also face the challenge of "selling" their services and bringing cohesion to a learning function spread throughout the company but held to common standards. Talent is critical in a hybrid structure, as is governance; organizations looking to strengthen these areas can implement a few proven techniques.

- *Ensure your L&D professionals understand the business.* Most learning functions need to upskill learning professionals to understand the business and its challenges—for example, by role-playing tough interactions or delaying the solution-generation phase when a need arises. By complementing their capability-building expertise with both business proficiency and advisory skills—a mix that Gartner has found to be increasingly crucial for L&D professionals[6]—learning professionals are better able to push back when appropriate against unreasonable business-unit requests or proposed solutions.

- *Create channels for learning teams to interact.* Deliberately mixing up teams for each learning design project builds a team-wide sense of community. The learning function can further build community by supporting the teams with specific channels such as real-time messaging, monthly calls sharing vendor experiences, and meetings of subcommunity members intended specifically to share best practices.

- *Establish strong governance models.* Hybrid L&D functions are inherently complex, with many individuals throughout the organization playing a variety of roles. To manage the nexus, L&D can use business-unit sponsors and advisory committees to track each department's priorities, which aids strategic prioritization in shared-services functions such as the design and digital teams. In addition, L&D should complete its budgeting process early and in conjunction with strategic planning, ensuring that the L&D function's budget reflects the following year's strategic priorities and that it can be used to influence decision-making.

■ ■ ■

Looking beyond organizational structure

As the L&D function strives to meet the growing need for new skill sets and foster a culture of learning, leadership needs to determine the best option for a stable backbone and put in place agile processes that can help overcome the chosen structure's deficiencies.

In the next chapter, our colleagues expand on the nonstructural elements that constitute L&D governance—and how, regardless of structure, good governance is a prerequisite to developing the credibility and resources that L&D needs to ensure the organization can keep up with the speed of business. ■

1 "The digital talent gap–Are companies doing enough?," Capgemini and LinkedIn, October 26, 2017, capgemini.com.

2 Richard Benson-Armer, Arne Gast, and Nick van Dam, "Learning at the speed of business," *McKinsey Quarterly*, May 2016, McKinsey.com.

3 Steven Aronowitz, Aaron De Smet, and Deirdre McGinty, "Getting organizational redesign right," *McKinsey Quarterly*, June 2015, McKinsey.com.

4 McKinsey Academy Survey 2015.

5 *2018 workforce learning report: The rise and responsibility of talent development in the new labor market*, LinkedIn, 2018, learning.linkedin.com.

6 *CEB Blogs*, "3 steps to build a better L&D staff," blog entry by CEB HR, June 24, 2015, cebglobal.com.

CHAPTER

02/

L&D GOVERNANCE:

Aligning for organization-wide impact

AUTHORS
Karen Merry
Ashley Williams

Strengthening the learning-and-development governance model and aligning it with the organization's business strategy can provide long-term credibility to the learning function.

Good learning-and-development (L&D) governance practices are shaped by aligning stakeholder interests, while ensuring that learning initiatives map back to, and are in support of, organizational goals. It sounds simple, yet many L&D functions struggle with governance—and some don't have a defined governance model at all.

In a recent McKinsey survey of L&D professionals, just 57 percent of respondents said their function is "very or fully aligned" with the company's strategic priorities.[1] This disconnect means that L&D functions struggle to gain credibility and resources. Of the 200 L&D senior decision makers surveyed by the Open University Business School in 2017, 42 percent said they "lack direction from the top and the leadership team does not value learning." The result is succinctly articulated by Bernd Vogel, director of Henley Centre for Leadership at Henley Business School: "L&D is often seen as a 'token' activity and that is the underlying philosophy that top managers have about it."[2]

Paradoxically, McKinsey research has found that capability building is consistently a top priority of the C-suite.[3] According to a 2017 McKinsey Global Institute (MGI) report, "62 percent of executives believe they will need to retrain or replace more than a quarter of their workforce between now and 2023 due to advancing automation and digitization."[4]

L&D is the obvious choice to address these challenges—but many L&D functions face steep barriers in defining a clear vision that ties in to the overall business, securing resources to develop those programs, and thus building institutional capabilities. Good governance processes and bodies are crucial to gain greater alignment with organizational goals. But what does good governance look like, and how do we get from here to there?

In short, to strengthen learning governance and establish strong foundations for growth, transformation, and credibility, L&D functions must identify the specific elements that leadership perceive L&D is lacking—and address them accordingly. To do this, learning leaders must establish linking mechanisms that engage L&D professionals in strategy setting; develop a learning, prioritization, and planning process; define, adopt, and regularly review robust key performance indicators (KPIs); and establish effective governing bodies.

Defining governance

Learning governance can be defined as the mechanisms, processes, and relationships that control and direct L&D. As with broader corporate governance, L&D governance and its principles identify the distribution of rights, responsibilities, and decision-making parameters among different participants in the organization and help align and engage important stakeholders around the strategic learning agenda. Good learning governance, when implemented with the right organizational structure, people, and processes, can bolster efficiency and clarity within L&D and help the function boost its reputation as a driver of business value, earning the resources that many learning functions currently lack.

A number of factors can lead to poor L&D governance, including the use of outdated governance models and a failure to recognize that existing governance is insufficient. Poor governance can affect not only the effectiveness and efficiency of the learning function but also the company's ability to reach its overall goals. Top indicators of poor governance include unclear process, roles, and responsibilities;

Exhibit 2A: **Poor L&D governance can lead to several key problems.**

Challenge	Result
Unclear processes, roles, and responsibilities for determining most critical short- and long-term capability gaps for driving business impact, and how to address those gaps	Wasted time and resources, given lack of focus on topics where expertise is needed; redundant L&D efforts occurring in multiple functions across the company
Insufficient senior leadership involvement and support in L&D	Fleeting or spotty sponsorship of core capability-building efforts; inability to engage core subject matter experts in development; continued deprioritization of L&D efforts in budget and strategic plans across business units
Inability to manage the end-to-end curriculum and associated budget effectively	Curriculum becomes outdated or expands beyond the scope of core priorities; lack of learning prioritization and budget; inability to effectively show return on curriculum

insufficient senior leadership; and inability to manage end-to-end curriculum and budget (Exhibit 2A).

Keys to redefining and improving governance

For a learning organization to be successful, it needs to demonstrate value to the company. As such, capability-building priorities and programs need to be integrated into the organization's overall business priorities; for example, if digital transformation is a core priority for the organization, then L&D priorities should focus on building the capabilities to make this happen. In the following sections, we lay out several steps L&D leadership can take to bolster learning governance and align priorities with those of the overall organization.

Establish linking mechanisms that engage L&D professionals in strategy setting

Organizations should begin by ensuring that capability needs are an integral part of overall organizational strategy discussions, not an afterthought. This approach doesn't require an established reporting line; it can be tackled with linkage mechanisms—that is, intentional actions or activities that bring L&D professionals to the table early and often. Examples of linkage mechanisms include annual strategy sessions, learning networks, and subteams.

Annual strategy sessions

If the company hosts annual strategy sessions for a particular region, business unit, or product group, L&D professionals should actively participate. Their role at such gatherings is to inform their non-L&D colleagues, including business-unit and executive leadership, on the capability building that will be required to implement the organization's strategic agenda.

Learning networks

Some organizations have informal internal networks, or communities of shared interests or practice. Aligning with these networks gives the L&D function a way to connect to specific topics, projects, or skill sets so it can support the capability-building agenda for core priority project teams.

Subteams

Many organizations create subteams within the L&D function that are aligned with business units. Depending on the size of the organization and the function, these teams may consist of one or several learning professionals with skills that span learning architecture, instructional design, and project management. It is critical that these professionals have both L&D expertise and business-unit experience so they can build credibility with other functional leaders and be seen as potential strategic partners.

Charged with managing the L&D needs and priorities of a specific business unit or portfolio, subteams partner with business-unit leadership to identify capability and performance gaps, build custom learning products, and measure short-term and long-term impact. For example, a subteam might include a head of functional learning in the centralized L&D department who aligns with the functional leadership across the globe. While this individual might not report directly to the functional leadership, he or she would be integrated into local leadership teams, engaged in strategic priority setting, and empowered to translate those priorities into specific capability-building requirements.

Linkage mechanisms can exist outside of the specific L&D structures discussed in chapter 1 (centralized, decentralized, and hybrid). The goal of these mechanisms is to develop operating models that connect L&D professionals to business units, strategic projects, product launches, or broad transformational efforts in meaningful ways. Success requires early and consistent engagement, agreement, and, ultimately, a champion beyond the walls of HR or L&D.

Develop a learning, prioritization, and planning process

A learning, prioritization, and planning (LPP) process can help learning functions identify capability gaps, develop appropriate learning solutions, and then prioritize and plan the build-out of those solutions. By implementing an LPP, an L&D organization can ensure consistency in how business units make learning requests and assess whether these requests fit into the company's overall business objectives. Several questions can help determine if the request directly supports a strategic program or initiative:

- Would the learning solution address a core capability gap—that is, one that is tied to value creation? Does it appear on a learning-journey map, or in support of it?

- What is the size of the target audience? Will the solution reach enough people to trigger a pivot point for impact or behavior change?

- Where are the targeted learners located geographically?

- What is the expected investment per learner, and what is the expected return on that investment?

We developed a sample LPP process to provide a road map for L&D leaders (Exhibit 2B). The process is not revolutionary; rather, it

Exhibit 2B: **A sample learning, prioritization, and planning (LPP) process includes three phases.**

Learning (need) →	Prioritization →	Planning
Identify capability gaps (short and long term) Test capability gaps with stakeholder to ensure alignment to broader company strategy Craft business case and proposed learning intervention(s) with related estimated spend for application process Submit application to leadership for review/ approval	Prioritize approved applications against a set of standard criteria–example criteria may include: • Core offer (large flagship programs) • Capability tied to learning journey • Target audience size • Type of innovation Submit prioritized projects to production pipeline for planning purposes	Assign budget and resources to projects

asserts that L&D prioritization should be as rigorous as any other business planning process—starting with assessing needs, then building out the business case for impact, prioritizing identified needs according to organizational value drivers and priorities, and developing a plan. Ideally, this process should be adapted to align with other business-planning processes in the organization to increase credibility, buy-in, and efficiency.

Define, adopt, and regularly review a robust set of KPIs

L&D leaders tend to make three core mistakes when developing solutions and managing curricula. The first mistake is waiting until the solution (or set of solutions) is complete before asking how success will be measured. Second, the answer to that question is often quite narrow, relating not to business impact but to operational or efficiency metrics on the program itself—such as number of participants, participant satisfaction, and

For more on learning-needs analysis, see chapter 4.

suitability of venue and technology. Third, metrics are often monitored by L&D professionals, not incorporated in the broader scorecard for a business unit or a business leader's individual success metrics. According to the learning research firm Towards Maturity, only 36 percent of organizations work with business leaders to identify the metrics that need to be improved through learning—and less than half of those businesses go back to review progress against the agreed-upon metrics.[5]

It is imperative to break this cycle by connecting learning initiatives to the organization's overall objectives and ensuring that they have an impact on the entire organization. Organizations can assess impact across a range of measures, including financial metrics (such as revenue or cost savings) and nonfinancial metrics (such as satisfaction and process improvements).

Some organizations break the cycle by developing an annual learning plan that outlines the company's core capability-building objectives—ensuring that the plan is mapped to all activity in the business unit, down to an individual's performance. This approach might feel overly prescriptive, but it yields great success when determining organizational goals, measuring business impact, assessing individual performance, and tracking whether the organization is closing skill and capability gaps and driving desired behavior change.

But looking only at organizational impact is not enough. As previously noted, good governance requires a balanced scorecard that includes metrics addressing behavior change, clear measurement

An L&D governing body should engage senior executives who will challenge the status quo and embrace innovation in capability building.

of knowledge proficiency, financial and operational efficiency, and learner reactions, attendance, and engagement. In addition, L&D should create a performance-management cadence through which scorecards are discussed with relevant target groups, including governing bodies, L&D leadership, managers, and practitioners. Without discussion and review, even the most meaningful scorecards can't build the buy-in, credibility, and engagement that L&D needs.

Chapter 12, which focuses on learning analytics and measurement, addresses this subject in more detail.

Establish effective governing bodies for L&D

Regardless of reporting structure, an engaged, influential L&D governing body and an executive learning council are crucial to ensure alignment between L&D and the organization. Depending on the overall structure of L&D, the function may also benefit from a learner advisory group, an external advisory board, or an operational steering group.

L&D governance board

The function of an L&D board is to provide leadership and strategic and financial oversight of L&D efforts across the organization. It does so by developing strategic learning initiatives, shaping the budget and making major investment decisions, ensuring regular review of performance scorecards, and providing important bridges to organizational leaders and structures.

An L&D governing body should engage senior executives who will challenge the status quo and embrace innovation in capability building. These individuals must be well respected, have a strong network in the organization, and serve as role models for lifelong learning. (For more on developing a culture of lifelong learning, see chapter 5.) This body is accountable to the executive learning council, other core governing bodies in the organization, or both.

> **Regardless of reporting structure, an engaged, influential L&D governing body and an executive learning council are crucial to ensure alignment between L&D and the organization.**

Executive learning council
This council works with the L&D governance board to oversee the strategic direction of the learning function and ensure that L&D is meeting the organization's highest-priority needs. Its responsibilities might include identifying and prioritizing business needs; approving decision gates for new L&D solutions; reviewing and providing feedback from the business on the strategic plan and budget; providing regular (for example, quarterly) feedback from the business on progress against capability-building goals; and, importantly, helping to remove roadblocks. This council typically includes senior executives from the learning function and from business units.

Learner advisory group
It is essential to consider the learner's perspective, especially with today's increasing focus on personalization and the customer experience. One way to do this is to create an advisory group consisting of learners from various levels across the organization. The group can take on a variety of responsibilities, but its overall mission is to support L&D by keeping leaders informed about the latest thinking in learning technology and innovation, providing a detailed picture of learner populations and their preferences, and facilitating learner input on both the overall learning agenda and specific learning solutions. An internal learner advisory group (or its equivalent) supports a design-thinking approach to L&D that relies

on research and observation to inform learning solutions from the perspective of the learner.

External advisory group

Given the pace of change in L&D, external advisers with content expertise can play a powerful role in advancing the agenda and building the L&D function's credibility. The group can provide best-practice insights and external content expertise, facilitate contacts and introductions for new partnerships, and validate existing L&D practices.

Operational steering group

A steering body that oversees day-to-day operations can provide valuable support for decentralized L&D functions. Among other responsibilities, this group could review performance and learning scorecards, support new partnerships, manage and guide the review of specific L&D initiatives, and support L&D leaders in managing the L&D function. Of course, the need for such a group is highly dependent on the broader management and organizational structure of L&D. In centralized L&D structures, the leadership team may support this remit without the need for another steering committee.

It is important to note that the various governing bodies described here are not essential in every organization, and they can be configured in different ways to meet the needs of a variety of organizational structures. The point is that nearly every organizational structure needs some sort of governing body or bodies to support oversight and connections beyond the formal L&D function structure. Each organization should thus design governing bodies that link L&D with the business, engage at an appropriately senior level, allow for connections outside the organization, account for learner preferences, and ensure that learning is tied to operational and performance management.

■ ■ ■

Other chapters in this book speak to the rapidly changing ecosystem in L&D: the lines between knowledge management and learning are blurring; advancements in neuroscience demand that we move learning closer to the front lines; and rapid advancements in learning technology require an agile approach. In the face of constant change, the imperative to elevate the function is clear.

L&D functions that fortify their governance model and align it with the organization's overall strategy gain long-term credibility and stability. With that, they can also find the funding and resources needed to spur the workforce growth and organizational impact to which they aspire. ■

1 Richard Benson-Armer, Arne Gast, and Nick van Dam, "Learning at the speed of business," *McKinsey Quarterly*, May 2016, McKinsey.com.

2 Karen Higginbottom, "Learning and development not valued by organizations," *Forbes*, May 5, 2017, forbes.com.

3 "Building capabilities for performance," January 2015, McKinsey.com.

4 For more information, see "Retraining and reskilling workers in the age of automation," McKinsey Global Institute, January 2018, on McKinsey.com.

5 *Aligning learning to business*, Towards Maturity, 2015, towardsmaturity.org.

CHAPTER

03/

OPTIMIZING THE PARTNERSHIP WITH IT

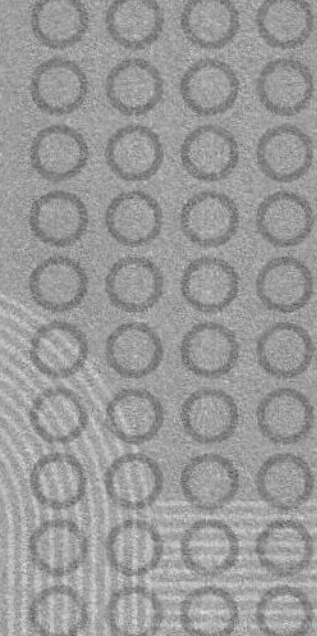

AUTHORS
James Pritchard
Stephanie Nadda

Small but deliberate steps can improve the relationship between learning and IT and make both teams function better and more efficiently.

Much of the learning we do today happens on a digital platform. Many of us in the learning-and-development (L&D) profession have never experienced a time when digital learning didn't exist or wasn't on the rise. Sure, your organization may still put instructors in front of a classroom, but today these teachers ask learners to take out their phones to respond to a real-time survey, or the lesson is video-recorded so employees around the world can play back lessons long after the actual event. In fact, 45 percent of learning today is delivered via technology.[1] Digital solutions provide great reach and great efficiency, bringing huge savings in learning budgets. They also make learning more effective: the experience application programming interface (xAPI, also known as TinCan) can tell us more than ever before about how our learners are consuming and learning from our content, while learner-experience platforms (LXPs) are enabling an unprecedented level of personalization that helps learners find exactly what they need.

These digital solutions depend on the strategic delivery of underlying technologies. And therein lies the rub. Implementing digital learning means working closely and well with your partners in IT. Digital-learning resources today involve a lot of complexity. Technology advances at a breakneck speed—every year brings new buzzwords and concepts to be absorbed, understood, and integrated into your road map—but that's not all. Different types of learners require different types of content modalities. One individual might learn better from a digital primer at home after work, while another might thrive on hearing directly from a trusted coach via video. Different use cases for learning require wildly different apps, sites, modules, and tools. A learner on the go, for example, may be catching up on a topic in a taxi via microlearning on a mobile device, or a learner may receive performance support in a moment of need through a digital resource that sits on the desktop ready for quick information retrieval.

Delivering personalized, technology-enabled learning isn't for the faint of heart or the technically inexperienced. Whatever your particular company structure, a strong partnership with IT is essential. In our research, we heard from one fast-food company whose learning department historically had no relationship with IT, only pulling them in as a last-ditch effort to save a technology project. With both teams working in a vacuum, bad assumptions were often made, leading to poor, costly decisions. If your relationship with IT is struggling, so too will your learning organization. And if your relationship with IT is succeeding—well then, your learners are likely to be learning better, more, and in their own preferred way.

To better understand how L&D can optimize its relationship with IT, we spoke with a range of professionals, from long-time veterans to brand-new hires, in a variety of industries, from fast-food companies to higher-learning institutions (see sidebar, "About the research"). These conversations yielded great insights and a surprising number of common themes. We distilled our findings into four recommendations:

- *Speak the same language.* Just as learning professionals need to understand the basics of technology implementation, from access to security to support, IT partners need to understand the unique aspects of learning technology, from enrollments to completions to SCORM (Sharable Content Object Reference Model).

- *Assemble a dedicated IT team and give it ownership.* To really soar, you'll want a committed technology team assigned to learning, with a broad-based skill set and clearly defined specialization.

- *Know who's driving and plan the trip accordingly.* Whether L&D or IT is ultimately responsible for driving projects forward, embrace that reality to optimize for success.

- *Put structures in place for regular communication.* Good communication doesn't happen by accident, especially when teams are siloed and geographically dispersed. Being proactive about communication will help build partnership and trust.

Both L&D and IT have many tasks and projects vying for their attention. Optimizing the relationship between the two will benefit both—and relieve some of the stress and frustration. Small but deliberate steps can make both your teams function better and more efficiently.

Recommendation 1: Speak the same language

Language is one of the greatest gifts of humanity, enabling us to communicate and—crucially—minimize misunderstandings. The language of learning and technical aptitude is no different. We have

About the research

In the fall of 2017, we conducted a series of interviews with experienced learning-technology leaders representing global fast-food companies; an institution serving the needs of specialized physicians; and an organization providing performance-improvement, training, and talent-management solutions for the public sector. Together, these organizations provide digital-learning solutions and platforms for more than 500,000 diverse learners.

observed frustration, anger, and disconnection when team members don't speak the same language and don't have a translator. To succeed, you need a learning team that understands technology and a complementary team in IT that understands the business of learning.

Learning technology originated in the early 1990s as the personal computer was expanding into the workplace. Tools such as e-learning, e-books, learning-management systems (LMSs), and content-creation systems emerged alongside WordPerfect and MS-DOS—and the need for understanding on both sides was born. Traditional learning professionals were "learning" people. They understood Kirkpatrick levels of evaluation, the ADDIE instructional systems design model, and instructional design theories, but they didn't necessarily understand the world of software development and implementation. IT considered learning to be "training," which took place inside a classroom. As learning technologies expanded and became more sophisticated, need grew for professionals who could understand the world of learning and translate it into technical requirements.

All of the organizations we interviewed have dedicated learning teams or individuals who can communicate in technical language. One digital-learning leader with whom we spoke spent his early career working directly with system engineers, so he was comfortable using IT terminology to communicate with IT. Another, a director at a large, global company, spent his entire career in the learning-technology space, implementing, managing, and administering learning-management systems. All of the learning-technology leaders we spoke with had deep exposure to technology at some point in their careers, but there was no single formula for success. While work experience isn't the only way to develop a deep understanding of technology, speaking and understanding the language is essential. As such, creative thinking, an ability to synthesize information, and a fundamental understanding of technology and learning are critical.

At the same time, our most successful IT partners have a deep understanding of the learning industry. They know that you can't just set up an LMS and call it done—there are other learning-delivery mediums, and they all need to work together across browsers and platforms and devices. These professionals work closely with the business team too—researching API capabilities, for example, to support the push toward personalization and customization. On the other hand, if your organization is faced with an IT team that doesn't have the time or the desire to dive deep into the learning industry, then your L&D group must impart that knowledge to the best of its ability. Invite IT team members to planning meetings, include them in structured training opportunities, and facilitate knowledge transfer between the two teams.

As you move ahead, the skill profiles of the two functions may remain distinct, but they will always need to speak the same language. Work together to map methodologies and processes to deliver successful projects—carve out half a day for an in-person collaborative workshop. Call out challenges and questions on both sides. The ultimate goal is to share a strong common language.

Recommendation 2: Assemble a dedicated IT team and give it ownership

A dedicated IT contact or team can successfully bridge the divide between learning and IT. This dedicated team would be charged with accumulating critical knowledge, incorporate the perspective and expertise of IT in key decisions, and ensure structures are in place to naturally support cross-team communications. In the absence of a dedicated team, decisions can be disjointed, communication becomes siloed, and the learning organization might even "go rogue" and avoid looping in IT.

Indeed, many of the more successful organizations we interviewed had IT teams dedicated to learning. One professional-services company had an IT portfolio manager dedicated solely to learning. This role oversaw the LMS product owner, and both reported to the director of portfolio management for human resources. In this example, the learning and IT teams worked closely together to plan for the upcoming year's projects and expenditures. A major fast-food company followed a similar model, with a dedicated director of IT people systems and individual product owners, including one for the company's LMS. Similarly, the L&D group at an organization focused on advocating excellence in medicine relied on a dedicated business relationship manager in IT. Finally, another fast-food company employed a manager of human resource management systems whose direct area of oversight included learning. Once a dedicated team or individual is identified, the learning and IT functions can clarify ownership of different activities. Some activities will naturally fall to one group due to the specific skills required—security and disaster recovery, for example, should sit with IT. Other activities are not as well defined and will require conversations about roles and tasks to ensure teams aren't stepping on each other's toes; an example of how to divide roles and responsibilities is displayed in Exhibit 3A.

There are also important strategic activities that require the two groups to collaborate. For example, implementation and ongoing support and maintenance are easier when the IT team or point of contact is included in annual planning, budgeting, and strategy sessions.[2] This partnership helps eliminate surprises arising from unexpected gaps in budget or capacity and fosters a sense of common ownership in the overall vision. In general, we recommend erring on the side of collaboration, communication, and syndication. The better your IT partners understand your objectives, the better able they'll be to help you reach them.

Although we recommend a dedicated IT team or individual, not every organization has the resources to make this work. If your organization is small or stretched thin, try to find empathetic partners in IT who understand your challenges and can help you navigate their world. You might also train someone on the learning team to better understand technology challenges, enabling him or her to partner more efficiently with IT.

Exhibit 3A: **Key digital-learning responsibilities involve learning, IT, or both.**

Activity		Owner
Tool solution assessment, review, selection, and implementation	IT, Learning	**Shared**
Custom solution definition and development (includes requirements, user research, iterative development, testing, and deployment)	IT, Learning	**Shared**
Hardware (if needed), including load-balancing	IT	**IT**
System administration and configuration	Learning	**Learning**[1]
Security and permission management	IT, Learning	**Shared**[2]
Single sign-on and user authentication	IT	**IT**
Integrations with internal and external systems, eg, HRIS, vendor content, data warehouse	IT	**IT**
External content implementation and integration	IT, Learning	**Shared**
Quality assurance and system testing	IT, Learning	**Shared**[3]
Product support (tier 1)	IT	**IT**–Centralized help desk
Product support (tier 2+ escalations–technical or content)	IT, Learning	**Shared**
Disaster recovery and business continuity	IT	**IT**
Standard reporting	Learning	**Learning**
Custom reporting	IT, Learning	**Shared**
Contract negotiations with vendors (LMS, content, other learning tools such as content creation)	IT, Learning	**Shared**
Annual budgeting	IT, Learning	**Shared**

1 We found in our research that system administration generally resides within learning. However, at one fast-food company we spoke to, this function resides within IT. This does require up-front clarification of roles, responsibilities, process, and a strong partnership to be successful.

2 In our research, we found some organizations in which learning owns and controls user administration, security, and permissions for digital-learning technology; in others, that task is assigned to IT.

3 As organizations move toward cloud-based learning solutions, it is important to establish clear testing processes and roles. Cloud-based solutions generally enforce a regular cadence of mandated releases that must be thoroughly reviewed and tested in the organization's environment.

Recommendation 3: Know who's driving the car and plan the trip accordingly

Anyone who has been part of a team without clearly defined leadership knows how chaotic a leadership vacuum can be. It's no different in the learning/IT dynamic. As discussed, both functions have specific areas of responsibility, and the skills each function has may dictate which side takes strategic ownership. However, to enable a digital-learning strategy and build out a robust learning ecosystem, we recommend that one function drive the vision and decisions, with one senior leader clearly at the helm. We have seen both IT and learning play this role successfully. Most important is to be clear about who's driving and strategize accordingly.

At one fast-food company, the director of learning technologies reports to the chief learning officer (CLO). With his experience and technical aptitude, the CLO champions and helps drive key learning-technology initiatives and positions them strategically. At a talent-management company, the executive director of learning technologies sits in the IT organization and reports to the chief technology officer. He has a strong relationship with IT and enjoys the department's full support. This arrangement also ensures that both teams' goals are aligned to business objectives, minimizing conflicts and disconnections. Finally, at a professional-services company, the director of digital learning reports to both the CLO and the director of digital people systems in IT. This structure ensures that the learning vision adheres to learning's strategic direction and fits well with the various people-related IT systems.

Smaller learning organizations may face greater challenges, especially when the power center lies with IT. For example, they may compete with other groups for limited IT dollars. Since learning is a cost center (not a revenue-generating one), extra effort may be needed to prove value and return on investment. Building strategic partnerships with other HR functions may help strengthen the business case for a new learning-technology solution. The more areas of your company that can expect positive impact from a solution, the stronger the potential ROI. Another fruitful strategy

> **A common mistake is getting lured in by a shiny new technology without truly thinking through the business need the technology is intended to solve.**

is to identify an executive-level champion who understands digital technologies and their huge potential boost to learning and development. A champion can articulate the value of digital solutions and the need for a comprehensive ecosystem to key decision makers. This in turn can result in funding, resources, and the ability to move forward with key initiatives.

Recommendation 4: Put structures in place for routine communication

Aligning closely with your IT partners lays the groundwork for good communication. Working together over time builds trust, relationships, and communication—each of which is essential in completing complex projects. As one learning professional shared with us, "In the end, it's all people dynamics, and you need to have conversations to make it successful."

One fundamental strategy for effective communication is to bring learning and IT together at the same table—or put another way, to set up the necessary meetings, calls, chats, emails, and social-media posts so that the two teams can compare notes and share key updates on a consistent basis. This is especially important in modern business organizations, where a globally distributed workforce means the shared table is often a virtual one. Spontaneous discussions at the proverbial water cooler aren't a reality anymore; instead, team members keep up to speed through video conferences, virtual meetings, and screen-shares. The daily scrum of agile methodology can lock regular communication into the schedule, just as a nightly family dinner provides an opportunity to catch up on the day.

> **Just being in the room gives IT team members access to the information they need to identify a technical roadblock in an otherwise flawless plan.**

However you approach it, you must make a concerted effort so the communication happens.

When it comes to large projects, we've learned to bring IT in at the very start. The planning and discovery stages of a project will be more focused on learning needs than on technical problem solving, but these meetings can provide critical context for the team that will eventually develop the solution. At the same time, IT's input may help learning realize that the timeline needs to be extended due to unforeseen technical complexities.

Indeed, making decisions in a vacuum is a danger. Just being in the room gives IT team members access to the information they need to identify a technical roadblock in an otherwise flawless plan, or realize that another group in the company has just achieved what you're trying to do. A common mistake is getting lured in by a shiny new technology without truly thinking through the business need the technology is intended to solve. When both teams are in the room from the start, it's easier to focus on the goals without getting distracted by the technology. IT should be deeply involved in defining project objectives and the metrics for success. As our colleague from a learning consultancy said, "If you can't measure it, you can't manage it." (For more on using analytics to measure learning success, see Chapter 12.)

■ ■ ■

L&D and IT can build a cohesive collaboration devoid of stress and frustration. It may take time to establish a good working relationship, and you may need to change the way you work together, but those changes need not be complex. They can be as simple as instituting weekly interdepartmental meetings or daily stand-ups or shifting ownership of key repeated tasks. These steps can improve the functioning and efficiency of both teams, and they can also make the work itself more pleasant and rewarding. The outcome is an organization that can stay a few steps ahead of the ongoing digital revolution and provide more innovative ways to learn. ■

1 *2017 state of the industry*, ATD Research, December 2017, td.org.

2 One company we spoke with has a dedicated VP in IT who sits on the HR leadership team. This position gives her a direct line of sight to what HR and learning want to accomplish, saving considerable time aligning on expectations and priorities.

CHAPTER

04/

LEARNING-NEEDS ANALYSIS:

Cracking the code

AUTHORS
Mary Andrade
Karen Merry

L&D professionals sometimes face pressure to skip a learning-needs analysis, but the insights from this step are vital to ensure that investments in training pay off.

Learning professionals understand that learning-needs analysis (LNA) is a critical first step in developing effective training programs and courses. Despite this realization, they often skip the LNA and move directly to course development. In some cases, the push for shorter design and development cycles leads companies to eliminate perceived unnecessary activities, with LNA first on the chopping block. In others, LNAs fail to elicit actionable insights and are perceived as a waste of time and money. And when senior leaders identify a development need and request a course, their wishes often supersede any LNA results, making the analysis seem superfluous. For all these reasons, organizations can find it too easy to skip LNAs.

What's at stake? Unfortunately, the credibility and effectiveness of your learning organization. CEB (now Gartner) estimates that for a typical company, the average rate of scrap learning—knowledge that is delivered but not applied by learners—is 45 percent.[1] In other words, companies regularly throw nearly half of their learning budgets down the drain. When learning professionals and stakeholders ignore LNAs, quality suffers, and content is neither directly relevant to the learner nor aligned with business strategy. Since ineffective training and learning programs undermine the C-suite's confidence in L&D, it's in the interest of every learning professional to take a more objective, analytical approach to course design. In addition, LNAs create transparency into the process and help to bring key stakeholders on board.

Companies must not only recognize that LNAs are an essential element of effective learning programs but also actually perform them as part of the development process. For LNAs to produce valuable insights, problems must be properly defined and scoped. To accomplish these twin goals, L&D professionals must first understand what a good LNA process looks like. Then they must recognize and address common barriers that have the potential to derail LNA efforts. Doing so will directly improve the quality and relevance of learning programs and dramatically reduce the frequency of scrap learning. For companies, the benefits include cost savings, improved workplace performance, and learning data that can demonstrate efficacy. Such tangible data can lend credibility to LNA efforts and also give learning professionals a voice at the decision-making table.

LNA frameworks and impact

The utility of LNAs in developing learning programs and courses is well established. They can provide invaluable information on learners' capability gaps, desired performance, and internal and external factors that influence learning. Many learning functions are still using the ADDIE (analysis, design, development, implementation, and evaluation) or other instructional models for their development efforts, and LNA fits neatly into the analysis phase. However, there is no one right way to conduct an LNA. Rather, the planning process and steps to execution should reflect the organization's culture and approach to problem solving. At a very high level, most LNA processes seek to define the problem, identify performance and capability gaps, and select an appropriate learning intervention. LNAs can also help isolate the root cause of

Such tangible data can not only lend credibility to LNA efforts but also give learning professionals a voice at the decision-making table.

a problem—and determine whether a nonlearning intervention might be a better solution.

A best-practice approach is to pursue LNA in two rounds connected by a go/no-go decision gate (Exhibit 4A). In the first round, we focus on defining the business context, clarifying the problem to solve, and conducting a high-level analysis of performance dimensions that may include, but are not limited to, learning solutions. At the end of the first round (which should consume around 40 percent of the total time invested in performing an LNA), we stop to evaluate whether a learning solution will have an adequate impact on the problem. If the answer is *yes*, we then proceed to perform a detailed analysis focused on informing the learning solution. The staging process ensures that L&D professionals don't get stuck conducting a lengthy assessment focused on the wrong issues or performance areas.

Exhibit 4A: **A best-practice approach to learning-needs analysis involves a two-round process.**

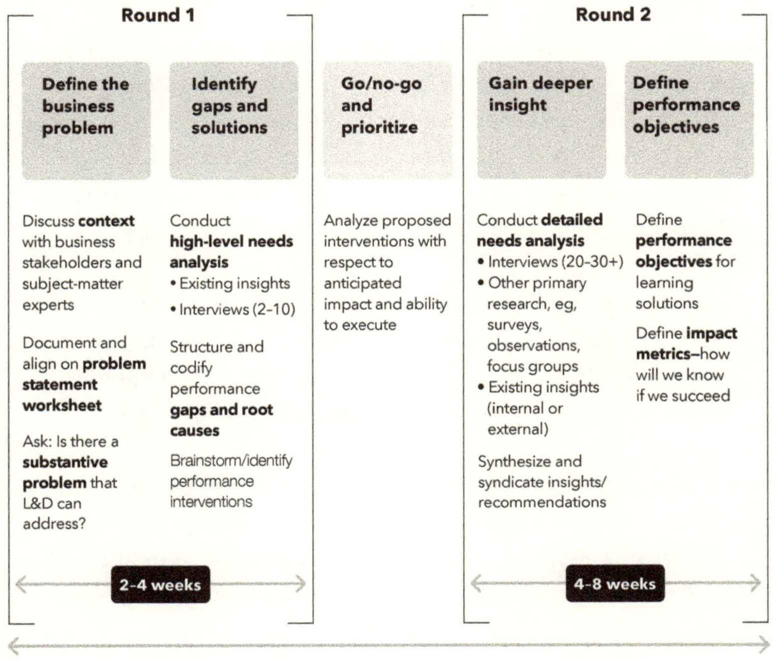

The two-round process helps elevate the L&D function from taking orders to participating as a strategic decision-making partner on short- and long-term capability building. With objective analysis, learning professionals can drill down to the source of the problem—for example, can the problem be addressed with learning, or would incentives and operational measures be more effective remedies? Further, by providing concrete data, LNA outcomes give L&D professionals greater leverage and influence.

LNAs also ensure that L&D stays aligned with the strategic needs of the company, so that learning solutions not only have the most positive impact on business objectives but also enjoy key leadership support. By contrast, forgoing a thorough LNA can have a negative impact on the delivery of effective learning solutions that promote positive mind-sets and behaviors. The following strategies can help L&D professionals prepare for and conduct LNAs:

- *Identify the purpose of the LNA before starting to collect information.* Know how the LNA's data and findings will be used to support decision-making.

- *Collect information from multiple sources.* Use a variety of techniques for data gathering, such as focus groups, surveys, interviews, and data collected for other reasons (for example, performance management). To augment these techniques, teams can also borrow approaches from consumer insights, such as diagnostics, observation, digital journals, and additional data analysis.

- *Remain objective.* Keep your perspective, and try not to get too close to the data or overemphasize findings that resonate with you personally. The needs analysis might confirm your hypothesis, but it also might contradict it. The point is to follow the data.

- *Keep the analysis phase concise.* It is better to survey a small sample of high and low performers than to attempt to analyze the entire workforce. A good rule of thumb is that a basic needs assessment can be completed in as little as four weeks; a comprehensive assessment can take up to eight weeks.

Again, bear in mind that although your initial charge is to develop a training program, you may discover that nonlearning interventions are also required for an effective solution. (For more information on effective approaches that complement training and professional development, see chapter 10 for a discussion of the influence model.)

Common LNA pitfalls and mitigation strategies

We have identified three common pitfalls that often sidetrack LNA efforts. If you find yourself mired in analysis quicksand, the following points to consider and mitigation strategies, along with some real-world examples, can help.

Common pitfall #1: Leadership wants a solution now

Points to consider: With the pressure from leadership, you may feel that there's no time or resources to conduct an LNA. But ask yourself, can you afford *not* to conduct an analysis? Companies that choose not to perform an LNA run a higher risk of rework, a costly process that includes wasted effort by not only the learning team but also subject-matter-expert stakeholders. An LNA provides a touchstone that guides iteration of design and content and bridges gaps in stakeholder perspectives.

Mitigation strategy: Do a quick mini-LNA. And yes, we said *quick*. This solution may not be ideal (or the approach recommended by instructional-design purists), but some learner insights are better than none. You can conduct such an analysis by seeking out existing data (people analytics) and getting input from a few learners and subject-matter experts. This sample won't be all-inclusive, but it will give you enough information to form an early hypothesis on which you can build. Plan on two to three weeks to complete your mini-analysis and accommodate for scheduling and synthesis time.

Example: One organization sought to design a program to help its new executives enhance their client-management capabilities. Under a tight deadline, the L&D team initially envisioned a module that included videos featuring experienced leaders sharing best practices, process templates that the new executives could use to manage their teams and clients, and techniques for inspirational leadership. When the team conducted an LNA, one of the key takeaways was that the new leaders needed a clearer baseline expectation of the job—how to transition onto a project, clarify the client's challenges, and direct colleagues to ensure outcomes that would meet the client's expectations. With insights from the LNA, the L&D team crafted a module that directly addressed these development needs.

Common pitfall #2: Stakeholders aren't aligned on the learning objective

Points to consider: If you didn't get stakeholders aligned on the learning objective up front, you may have trouble getting the necessary buy-in. Your course may have a solid design and great content, but it could still get stuck in stakeholder review. You need to confirm (and sometimes reconfirm) the problem you are addressing with your stakeholders. Alignment is critical.

Mitigation strategy: Invest time up front to define the specific issue, explore the business context, and determine if it is aligned with strategy. Stage-gating helps to avoid drift and keep the effort focused. Often, clarifying the success criteria, the expected results, and the constraints will help build consensus with stakeholders.

Example: Sometimes various business leaders have different perspectives on the needs the learning solution should address. At one organization, the LNA pointed to four learning needs for people moving into more senior leadership roles: advanced stakeholder-facing skills, adjustment in day-to-day focus and activities, the ability to lead a team, and appreciating the opportunities the new role offered. The L&D team crafted a blended-learning approach that would address the tactical needs through digital solutions, the interpersonal skills through a live simulation, and the shift to an owner mind-set by simulating a key leadership process. When one stakeholder disagreed with this approach, data from the LNA was used to highlight what learners wanted and needed. Although achieving alignment took many conversations across several weeks, the thorough LNA was instrumental in achieving consensus.

Common pitfall #3: Dozens of interviews haven't pinpointed learning needs

Points to consider: Getting the right answers starts with asking great questions and knowing how to dig deeper. More interviews don't necessarily lead to better findings. It's all about quality, not quantity, so don't overdo it. Instead, plan carefully, investigate thoroughly, use existing sources where possible, and focus your research on actual needs in day-to-day work.

Mitigation strategy: Craft your interviewee list thoughtfully—target articulate employees who have a deep understanding of the organization's talent-development needs, challenges, or both. The LNA should seek to determine the ecosystem of potential interview subjects before homing in on the critical participants. Ensure the group includes a diverse range of individuals who will provide a balanced perspective (various regions, business units, management levels, or roles). How many people should you interview? Exhibit 4B offers a good rule of thumb.

Next, write an interview guide to help you zero in on observable behaviors. Questions should be tailored to the role and experience of the interview subject. Don't be satisfied with generic responses—

Exhibit 4B: **Determining the right number of interview subjects helps to ensure diversity.**

Total population served	Interviewees	Number of interviewees at the manager and oversight level
<100	10-20 people	2-4
>100	20-50 people	10-20

Note: These figures are guidelines; the goal is simply to conduct enough interviews to identify patterns.

It's all about quality, not quantity, so don't overdo it. Instead, plan carefully, investigate thoroughly.

probe to understand the struggles facing employees and why certain tasks are challenging.

Finally, before you interview anyone, don't forget to tap existing company surveys. These sources can provide quick and easy insight. Consider alternative ways to test and learn against an identified need instead of starting from scratch. For instance, you could adapt a learning solution that was built for another population.

Example: At one company, the L&D team started the process by asking senior leaders what the program should focus on. The leaders felt that aspiring managers needed to become conversant in digital technologies and analytics. This insight was shared with the design team, which had broad and varied interpretations of this information and a host of questions about how to proceed. The team conducted subsequent interviews with the same senior leadership group, but these discussions didn't provide the necessary clarity on objectives.

To augment the high-level, senior-leader perspective, the L&D team also talked to the aspiring managers. What were their experiences with digital technologies and analytics to date? What was hard for them in this space? What did they wish to gain from the learning experience? This group expressed a variety of needs, from resetting foundational knowledge to understanding application nuances by industry and type of service. Using this information, the L&D team created a phased-learning approach to provide aspiring managers with a solid foundational understanding of digital technologies and analytics. The program started with monthly launches of digital solutions, progressed to cover nuances specific to each aspiring manager's circumstances, and culminated in a lab focused on how helping them increases impact for clients.

■ ■ ■

Needs analysis is a critical component of identifying performance issues and informing learning design: it ensures focus on the right problem, supports multiple dimensions of the performance process, helps prioritize where learning solutions can have the most impact, and ultimately informs the definition of focused performance objectives and metrics.

We all want our learning solutions to help our learners grow and develop. Too often, we find ourselves under the gun to simply "create something now," which leads to courses that don't adequately address capability gaps or an issue's root causes. It's time to recognize the value and impact of LNAs and collectively raise the perception of its worth among our peers and our stakeholders. Investing time on the front end can create effective solutions, increase credibility during times of stakeholder resistance, and support learner development. ■

The authors would like to acknowledge the valuable contributions made by Sara Diniz in the development of this chapter.

1 "Confronting scrap learning: How to address the pervasive waste in talent development," CEB, 2014, cebglobal.com.

CHAPTER

05/

SEVEN ESSENTIAL ELEMENTS OF A LIFELONG-LEARNING MIND-SET

AUTHORS
Jacqueline Brassey
Katie Coates
Nick van Dam

In a rapidly changing workplace, employees need to keep learning to remain relevant and in demand. Here's some advice for them.

Organizations around the world are experiencing rapid, sweeping changes in what they do, how they do it, and even why they do it. Increasing globalization and new technologies demand new modes of working and talent with new and diverse skills. In addition, a continually increasing life expectancy—since 1840 life expectancy has increased three months for every year—means that people will stay in the workforce longer.[1]

To flourish in this environment, individuals must keep learning new skills. In fact, studies show that people who maintain their ability to learn outpace others professionally.[2] The people who will thrive in the 21st century will be those who embrace lifelong learning and pursue knowledge for personal or professional reasons throughout their lives—continually increasing their knowledge, skills, and competencies.[3]

Building a workforce of such lifelong learners is critical for organizations to keep pace. To ensure they have the required skills and talent, businesses must create a learning-for-all culture in which people are encouraged and inspired to continue learning new skills.

But even within a learning-for-all culture, it's up to the individual to seize the opportunity to get ahead. Here are seven distinctive practices designed to help you become a lifelong learner and remain relevant in today's business environment (Exhibit 5A).

Exhibit 5A: **A lifelong-learning mind-set consists of seven essential elements.**

Source: Nick van Dam, *Learn or Lose*, Nyenrode Publishing, November 2016

1. Focus on growth

Learning starts and ends with the individual. But is there a limit to how much a person can learn? Is intelligence fixed at birth, or can it be developed?

In 2008, researchers asked the ten best chess players in the world—people who had spent 10,000 to 50,000 hours mastering the game—to take an IQ test.[4] They discovered that three out of ten had a below-average IQ. Since playing chess at the top level in the world is associated with extreme intelligence, they wondered how this was possible.

Many studies have confirmed that it is not intelligence that creates expertise but effort and practice—that is, hard work.[5] The most successful people devote the most hours to deliberate practice, tackling tasks beyond their current level of competence and comfort, observing the results, and making adjustments.[6]

Such studies show that intelligence can be developed and that there are no limitations on what we can learn throughout our lives. As the psychologist Jesper Mogensen discovered, the brain is like a muscle that gets stronger with use, and learning prompts neurons in the brain to grow new connections.[7]

Over the past 30 years, Carol Dweck, a psychologist at Stanford University, has studied learners intensively.[8] She has determined that people generally fall into one of two categories when it comes to how they view their ability to learn: a fixed mind-set or a growth mind-set. And she has concluded that mind-set has a significant impact on the effort you put forward, your perception of criticism, your willingness to accept failure, and ultimately, how much you will learn.

If you have a fixed mind-set, you believe that your learning potential is predetermined by your genes, your socioeconomic background, or the opportunities available to you. You might have thoughts like, "I'm not good at public speaking, so I should avoid it."

If you have a growth mind-set, however, you believe that your true potential is unknown because it is impossible to foresee what might happen as a result of passion, effort, and practice. You appreciate challenges because you see them as opportunities for personal growth. Ultimately, you may achieve more of your potential than someone with a fixed mind-set.

Dweck also suggests that a person may have a growth mind-set in some situations or subjects and a fixed mind-set in others.

To become a lifelong learner, you need to believe that you have a lifetime of opportunities and unlimited capacity to learn and grow. And organizations can encourage employees to tackle new challenges and learn new skills by assigning them new and different tasks.

To develop a growth mind-set, you can take the following actions:[9]

- Determine whether you have a fixed mind-set, and if you do, figure out why.

- Recognize that you have a choice in how you approach and interpret new tasks, ideas, or situations.
- Learn to hear and reject the fixed mind-set voice.
- Refocus with a growth mind-set.

2. Become a serial master

London Business School professor Lynda Gratton, in her book *The Shift,* argues that the age of the shallow generalist is over. Businesses no longer need employees who know a little about a lot of different topics.[10] After all, a company that needs a particular skill at a given time can hire a freelancer. In fact, sociologist Richard Greenwald estimates that up to half of all workers may be freelancers in the next decade.[11] To succeed as a lifelong learner and stay relevant in the workforce, you will need to master multiple domains over the span of your career, as opposed to learning a little about various topics.[12]

Traditionally, workers developed deep expertise in one discipline early in their career and supplemented this knowledge over the years with on-the-job development of integrative competencies. This kind of knowledge can be represented by a T-shape or T-profile (Exhibit 5B).

But now that people are living and working longer, you need depth in different areas of expertise, supplemented with targeted on-the-job development, to stay relevant. Today, your knowledge should fit the M-shape or M-profile (Exhibit 5C).

Let's say you have a master's degree in journalism and start your career working at a publication. During your 30s, you find yourself specializing in financial journalism, so you decide to pursue a master's degree in business economics. As you proceed into your 40s and 50s, you might continue to grow by taking in-depth master classes on related topics, such as digitization.

Relevant skills have become currency in the workplace. Using the M-profile as a guide and achieving mastery in a few topics will set you

Exhibit 5B: **Workers have traditionally accumulated knowledge in a T-shaped profile.**

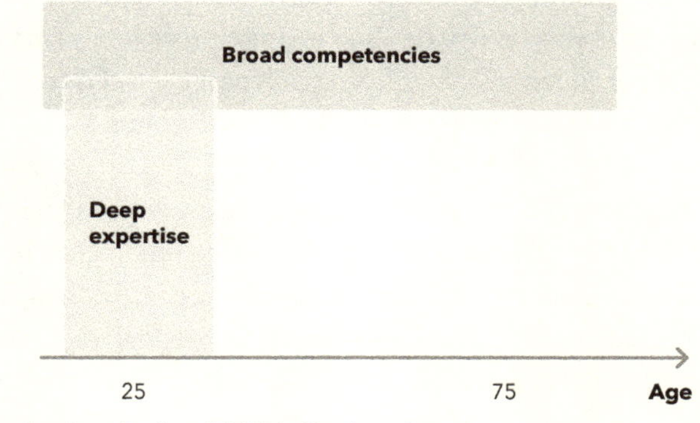

Source: Nick van Dam, *Learn or Lose*, Nyenrode Publishing, November 2016

Exhibit 5C: **Today's workers need M-profle knowledge.**

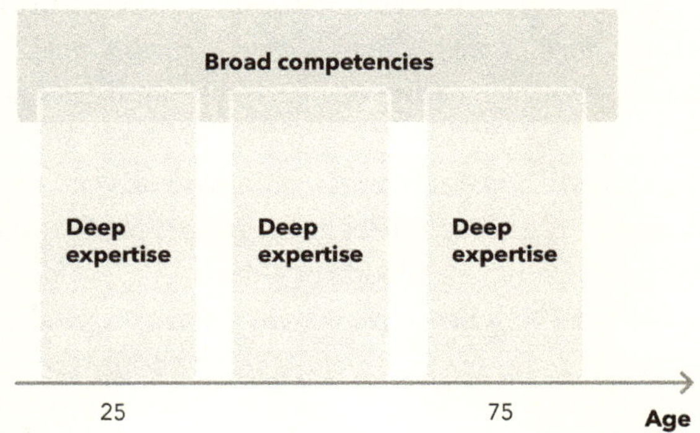

Source: Nick van Dam, *Learn or Lose*, Nyenrode Publishing, November 2016

apart. Organizations, for their part, can support workers in this development by offering stipends for coursework and suggesting master classes and professional development sessions.

3. Stretch

Many researchers have suggested that learning takes place only when you stretch outside your comfort zone[13] "a behavioral space where people's activities and behaviors fit a routine and pattern that minimize stress and risk."[14]

When you work on tasks that aren't entirely comfortable, you are in your learning zone, where you acquire new knowledge and develop and practice new skills (Exhibit 5D). Once you have spent time learning a new skill, you will develop enough proficiency that it becomes part of your comfort zone. At that point you can turn your attention to a new task and return to the learning zone.[15]

The learning zone exposes you to risk and stress, which can be either helpful or detrimental to your efforts. Harvard psychologists Robert Yerkes and John Dodson conducted research on comfort zones. Their findings helped create the Yerkes–Dodson Law, which describes the relationship between an increase in stress (which they term "arousal") and the enhancement of performance (Exhibit 5E).[16] When you first encounter a new task, according to Yerkes–Dodson, you experience "good" stress, leading to a higher level of performance. However, too much stress can cause anxiety ("bad" stress) and have a negative impact on performance. So when you set out to expand your comfort zone, be sure to choose the right tasks and the right pace. Of course, these vary from one person to another.

The personal growth and stretching that individuals experience from continued exposure to the learning zone typically follows a standard progression represented as an S-curve.[17] Developed in the 1960s, the S-curve shows how, why, and at what rate ideas and products spread throughout societies.[18] Organizations can adapt

Exhibit 5D: **Stretch beyond your comfort zone into the learning zone.**

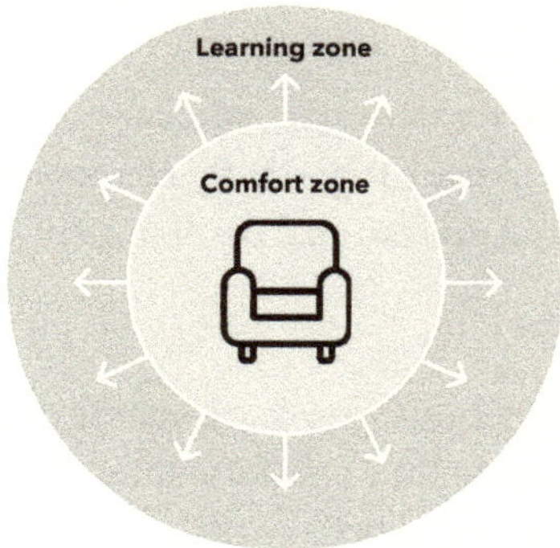

Source: Nick van Dam, *Learn or Lose*, Nyenrode Publishing, November 2016

Exhibit 5E: **The Yerkes-Dodson Law describes the relationship between arousal and performance.**

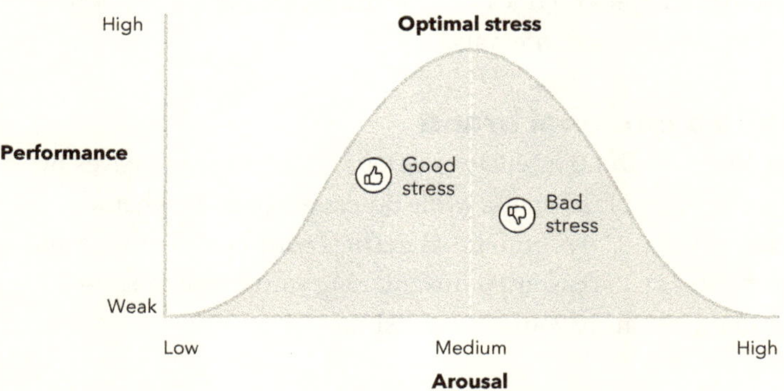

Source: Robert M. Yerkes and John D. Dodson, "The relation of strength of stimulus to rapidity of habit-formation," *Journal of Comparative Neurology and Psychology*, November 1908, Volume 18, Issue 5, pp. 459–82, doi.org/10.1002/cne.920180503

this model to support their L&D agendas, their performance dialogues, and the career progression of employees. (For more on S-curves in L&D, see chapter 6.)

When you try something new, such as starting a new job, you are at the beginning of a new S-curve. You experience a steep learning curve in which your knowledge and skills increase rapidly. During this first stage of the S-curve, your progress and the business impact of your performance are limited.

After a time, you reach an inflection point where your understanding, competence, and confidence suddenly accelerate very quickly, and you have an increasing impact on the business.

Continuing in the role for a bit longer, you will reach the upper, flat part of the S-curve. At this stage, the excitement of the new role has worn off, personal learning and development have stalled, tasks and activities have become automatic, boredom has kicked in, and your impact on the business has slowed down significantly.

If you stay in a role in which you are no longer excited or motivated, your performance may suffer, and you might be replaced. If you're a lifelong learner, though, you can avoid this downfall and find new ways to stretch by starting a new S-curve. And organizations can help keep employees on track by providing learning and stretching opportunities at timed intervals.

4. Build a personal brand

Henry Wadsworth Longfellow once said, "We judge ourselves by what we feel capable of doing, while others judge us by what we have already done."[19] A brand that defines your best elements and differentiates you is essential in achieving your career goals—and in demonstrating your accomplishments.

Everyone has a professional brand, whether it's a carefully crafted expression of who they want to be or simply the impression they make on others. A brand communicates your value and provides a focus for personal learning and development. Key elements of a personal brand include authenticity, a clear value proposition, a story, expertise, consistency, visibility, and connections.

In *Leadership Brand: Developing Customer-Focused Leaders to Drive Performance and Build Lasting Value,* authors Dave Ulrich and Norm Smallwood describe the following five steps for shaping a personal brand:

- Determine the results you want to achieve in the next year.
- Decide what you wish to be known for.
- Define your identity.
- Construct your personal brand statement and test it.
- Make your brand identity real.

Your personal brand should evolve over the course of your career. Since you likely will develop new skills and play different professional roles, you will need to rebrand yourself multiple times.

Social media tools are helpful in conveying a clear brand and skill set. For example, you can earn digital badges for your LinkedIn profile through online learning vendors such as Coursera, edX, Lynda.com, and Udemy. Such badges demonstrate not only your skills but also your commitment to continued growth.

But building a clear brand is important within your current role as well. Your colleagues need to know who you are, what they can count on you to handle, and what unique capabilities you bring to the table. With this knowledge they will be more likely to give you interesting new assignments, and they may even consider you first for new positions.

Lifelong learners use the opportunity of building a brand to think through what skills they have and which ones they should develop to make themselves more marketable—both within the company and beyond. L&D professionals can counsel people in this process and provide a way for them to develop the necessary skills.

5. Own your development

Lifelong employment no longer exists, so people today expect to work for many organizations throughout their careers—and maybe even for themselves at times. To maintain forward motion in an environment that lacks continuity, you need to own your development and take charge of your learning through the following actions (Exhibit 5F).

Create and execute learning goals

To become and stay successful, you need to ask yourself, "How can I ensure that I'm more valuable at the end of a year than I was at the beginning?" Create learning goals by assessing your current knowledge and expertise and identifying competency gaps. You should also plan to pursue the most important learning goals relentlessly because this is a competitive advantage. Unfortunately, too many people focus only on quick wins.[20]

Exhibit 5F: **Have a plan for owning your development path.**

Source: Nick van Dam, *Learn or Lose*, Nyenrode Publishing, November 2016

Measure progress

Periodically reflect and assess your progress. Learning journals or logs, in which you track what you learn, have proved to be extremely valuable.

Work with mentors and seek feedback

A mentor is someone who shares insights and experience with more junior colleagues in an effort to offer guidance and model positive behaviors. Mentors are invested in supporting the long-term personal and professional development of their colleagues. Feedback from supervisors, peers, direct reports, customers, and clients is another critical component of professional development. You can forge a relationship with a mentor by letting different stakeholders know that you are open to feedback and setting up formal check-ins to review your work and collect feedback.

Make personal investments

As discussed previously, the required level of learning for individuals who want to retain a market-relevant skill set exceeds the amount of formal and informal learning hours that most organizations offer their employees. Therefore, people need to make (more) personal time and financial investments in their growth and development.

Harvard professors Robert Kegan and Lisa Lahey, in their book *Immunity to Change: How to Overcome It and Unlock the Potential in Yourself and Your Organization,* suggest that you can demonstrate ownership of your development if you can answer the following questions:

- What is one thing you are working on that will require that you grow to accomplish it?
- How are you working on it?
- Who else knows and cares about it?
- Why does this matter to you?

6. Do what you love

"Your time is limited, so don't waste it living someone else's life. Don't be trapped by dogma—which is living with the results of other people's thinking. Don't let the noise of others' opinions drown out your own inner voice. And most important, have the courage to follow your heart and intuition."

—Steve Jobs (Stanford University commencement address, 2005)

Most people are in the workforce for 40 to 50 years, and they spend a lot of their waking hours at work. Your work has a huge impact on your health and well-being, so it's imperative that you do what you love.

A sense of purpose is essential for a well-lived life. In Japan, the term *ikigai* means "reason for being," and it encompasses all elements of life—including career, hobbies, relationships, and spirituality. The discovery of one's *ikigai* brings satisfaction and imbues life with meaning.[21] A study of more than 43,000 Japanese adults showed that the risk of mortality was significantly higher among subjects who did not find a sense of *ikigai* than among those who did.[22]

To find *ikigai,* start by answering four questions (Exhibit 5G):[23]

- What do you love?
- What does the world need?
- What can you be paid for?
- What are you good at?

The intersection of these questions is where you will find *ikigai*. Of course, everyone's journey of discovery will be different. What's more, the meaning of work depends on how we view our work—our motivation as well as the objective of the work. Exhibit 5H shows three different ways to look at the meaning of work.

Exhibit 5G: **The reason you get up in the morning is your *ikigai*.**

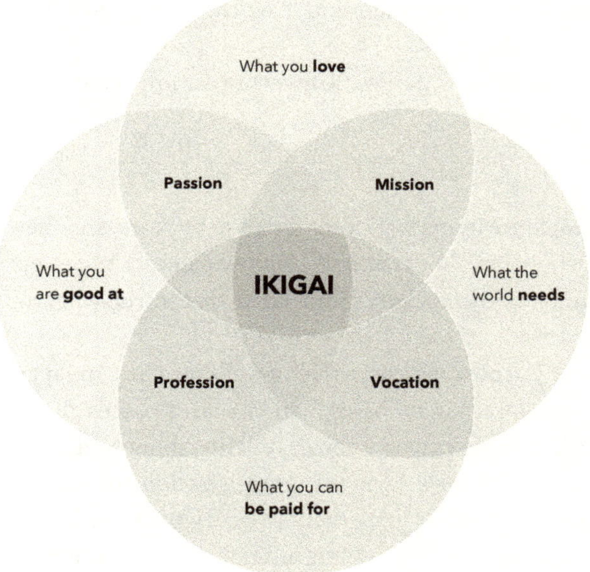

Source: Toshimasa Sone et al., "Sense of life worth living (ikigai) and mortality in Japan: Ohsaki study," *Psychosomatic Medicine*, August 2008, Volume 70, Number 6, pp. 709–15

Exhibit 5H: **Employees can view their jobs through three different lenses.**

Meaning of work	Motivation	Objective
A job	Financial and material rewards	Obtain financial resources to engage in another activity, eg, "I want to purchase a new car."
A career	Success	Achieve personal growth, recognition, and capability development, eg, "I want to publish a book."
A calling	The work itself	Work for a greater good or cause beyond personal benefit or reward, eg, "I care deeply about what I am doing."

Source: Eileen Rogers and Nick van Dam, *You! The Positive Force in Change*, Lulu Publishing, 2015

Although organizations have a great responsibility to provide a context for meaning, individuals can do much to create a calling for themselves.

Exploring your career purpose, meaning, and passion is not easy. It takes intentional reflection and planning. You can also seek guidance from a career counselor, or explore life design—an emerging field that can help you articulate your identity and design a meaningful life. Life design is a concept emerging from career choice and development theories as a method to help people explore and develop their identity and deliberately design a life that will give them meaning.[24]

Today, academic institutions are teaching learners to apply design principles to life and career planning. For example, Bill Burnett and Dave Evans created a popular "Designing Your Life" program at Stanford University. Intended for juniors and seniors looking for career guidance, the course typically has a waiting list. Participants learn about five mind-sets: be curious, try stuff, reframe the problem, know it's a process, and ask for help. They learn about a range of different tools, from design thinking and a daily gratitude journal to decks of cards featuring problem-solving techniques and life-design interviews. Instead of taking a final exam, learners present three radically different five-year "odyssey" plans to their peers. Alumni of the program report that they repeatedly refer back to the tools and their odyssey plans as they evaluate and redesign their lives. Burnett and Evans have made their philosophy and tools available to everyone in their book *Designing Your Life: How to Build a Well-Lived, Joyful Life.*[25]

7. Stay vital

The ability to stay vital can contribute significantly to your development. This goal demands that you make health and well-being a priority. Pay attention to exercise, nutrition, sleep, and relaxation (for example, mindfulness and yoga), and develop good, sustainable habits. The impact of such personal care and self-nurturing can be far-reaching: sufficient sleep has a huge impact on our ability to acquire, retain, and retrieve knowledge. Sleep also affects attention and concentration, creativity, development of insight, pattern recognition, decision-making, emotional reactivity, socioemotional processing, the development of trusted relationships, and more.[26]

Longevity in the workforce requires reinvention and growth. A reservoir of energy to support this hard work can help set you on the path to lifelong learning and give you the resilience to sustain these efforts. ■

A version of this chapter was published in Nick van Dam, Learn or Lose, *Nyenrode Publishing, November 2016.*

1 Lynda Gratton and Andrew Scott, *The 100-Year Life: Living and Working in an Age of Longevity,* London, UK: Bloomsbury, 2016.

2 Barbara Mistick and Karie Willyerd, *Stretch: How to Future-Proof Yourself for Tomorrow's Workplace,* Hoboken, NJ: John Wiley & Sons, 2016.

3 Hae-du Hwang and Daesung Seo, "Policy implication of lifelong learning program of EU for Korea," *Procedia–Social and Behavioral Sciences,* 2012, Volume 46, pp. 4822-9, doi.org/10.1016/j.sbspro.2012.06.342.

4 Nicholas Mackintosh, *IQ and Human Intelligence,* New York, NY: Oxford University Press, 1998.

5 Geoffrey Colvin, "What it takes to be great," *Fortune,* October 19, 2006, fortune.com.

[6] Edward T. Cokely, K. Anders Ericsson, and Michael J. Prietula, "The making of an expert," *Harvard Business Review,* July–August 2007, hbr.org.

[7] Jesper Mogensen, "Cognitive recovery and rehabilitation after brain injury: Mechanisms, challenges and support," *Brain Injury: Functional Aspects, Rehabilitation and Prevention,* Croatia: InTech, March 2, 2012, pp. 121–50, doi.org/10.5772/28242.

[8] Carol S. Dweck, *Mindset: The New Psychology of Success,* New York, NY: Random House, 2006.

[9] Jim Thompson, *Mindset: Powerful Insights from Carol Dweck,* Stanford University Athletic Department, Positive Coaching Alliance, 2010, positivecoach.org.

[10] "Turn education into a lifelong experience," *Chief Learning Officer,* August 12, 2013, clomedia.com.

[11] Richard Greenwald, "A freelance economy can be good for workers: Let's make it better," *The Atlantic,* November 16, 2012, theatlantic.com.

[12] "Turn education into a lifelong experience," *Chief Learning Officer.*

[13] Andy Molinsky, "If you're not outside your comfort zone, you won't learn anything," *Harvard Business Review,* July 29, 2016, hbr.org.

[14] Alan Henry, "The science of breaking out of your comfort zone (and why you should)," *lifehacker,* July 3, 2013, lifehacker.com.

[15] Molinsky, "If you're not outside your comfort zone, you won't learn anything," *Harvard Business Review.*

[16] John D. Dodson and Robert M. Yerkes, "The relation of strength of stimulus to rapidity of habit-formation," *Journal of Comparative Neurology,* November 1908, Volume 18, Number 5, pp. 459–82, doi.org/10.1002/cne.920180503.

[17] Whitney Johnson, "Throw your life a curve," *Harvard Business Review,* September 3, 2012, hbr.org.

[18] Johnson, "Throw your life a curve," *Harvard Business Review.*

[19] Dorie Clark, "Reinventing your personal brand," *Harvard Business Review,* March 2011, hbr.org.

[20] Dorie Clark, "Plan your professional development for the year," *Harvard Business Review,* January 7, 2016, hbr.org.

[21] Gordon Mathews, *What Makes Life Worth Living?: How Japanese and Americans Make Sense of Their Worlds,* Berkeley and Los Angeles, CA: University of California Press, 1996.

[22] Toshimasa Sone et al., "Sense of life worth living *(ikigai)* and mortality in Japan: Ohsaki study," *Psychosomatic Medicine,* August 2008, Volume 70, Number 6, pp. 709–15, doi.org/10.1097/PSY.0b013e31817e7e64.

[23] *Alyjuma,* "Ikigai: The reason you get up in the morning," blog entry by Aly Juma, alyjuma.com.

[24] Mark L. Savickas et al., "Life designing: A paradigm for career construction in the 21st century," *Journal of Vocational Behavior,* 2009, Volume 75, Number 3, pp. 239–50, doi.org/10.1016/j.jvb.2009.04.004.

[25] Bill Burnett and Dave Evans, *Designing Your Life: How to Build a Well-Lived, Joyful Life,* New York, NY: Alfred A. Knopf, 2017.

[26] Nick van Dam and Els van der Helm, "The organizational cost of insufficient sleep," *McKinsey Quarterly,* February 2016, McKinsey.com.

CHAPTER

06/

SHAPING INDIVIDUAL DEVELOPMENT ALONG THE S-CURVE

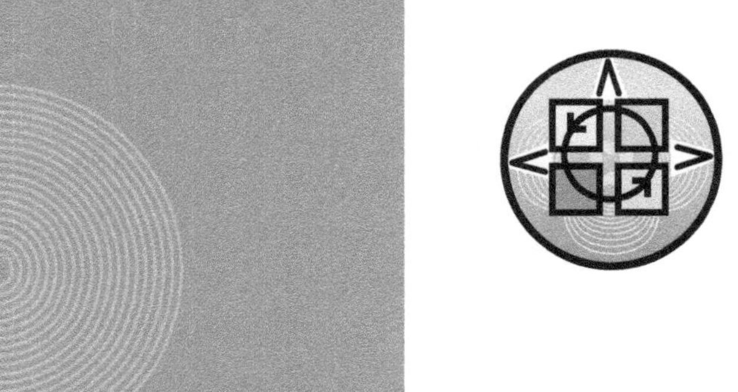

AUTHORS
Jacqueline Brassey
Gene Kuo
Larry Murphy
Nick van Dam

An S-curve that shows growth mapped against time is a useful framework for enabling L&D to intervene at the right time, with the right support.

Career development is not a linear proposition for the vast majority of the 21st-century workforce. Careers today progress in widely diverse ways, increasing the challenge for learning-and-development (L&D) leaders to meet learners when and where they need support. As a result, most L&D functions struggle to determine how to support the personal and professional growth and satisfaction of their learners over time.

Of course, in the context of an organization, learning encompasses much more than formal programs. L&D leaders are charged with helping individuals weave together the experiences and investigations that support their continued development. And those experiences take place throughout the organization, not just in formal learning programs provided by L&D. To navigate this new age of learning and provide the best possible learning experiences, L&D professionals must make connections between the "what" (the kind of support to provide, whether emotional or intellectual) and the "how" (ways to deliver that support). They also need to understand where a learner is in his or her individual journey.

The S-curve framework—used in various disciplines to represent the beginning, rapid growth, and maturity of something via an S-shaped curve—can help L&D leaders understand the what and how for individual learners in a given role. These insights can help them design and tailor learning for various audiences, improve the learner experience, and ensure that once an employee has reached mastery of their role, they are primed to make the leap to the next.

The S-curve framework is not a new concept. The management thinker Charles Handy first applied it, also known as life-cycle thinking or the "sigmoid curve," to organizational and individual development in the mid-1990s.[1] Applying this thinking to the L&D context, however, is a new, innovative, and powerful way to describe cycles of learning and development and link them over time.

How the S-curve can enable learning at the speed of business

In a September 2012 article in *Harvard Business Review,* author Whitney Johnson uses the S-curve to illustrate the development of competence in a new domain of expertise—the very essence of professional learning.[2] During the initial phase of a personal learning curve, she writes, progress is slow. With further practice, though, "we gain traction . . . accelerating competence and confidence" (Exhibit 6A).

Exhibit 6A: **An S-curve follows a learner's journey from unfamiliarity to mastery.**

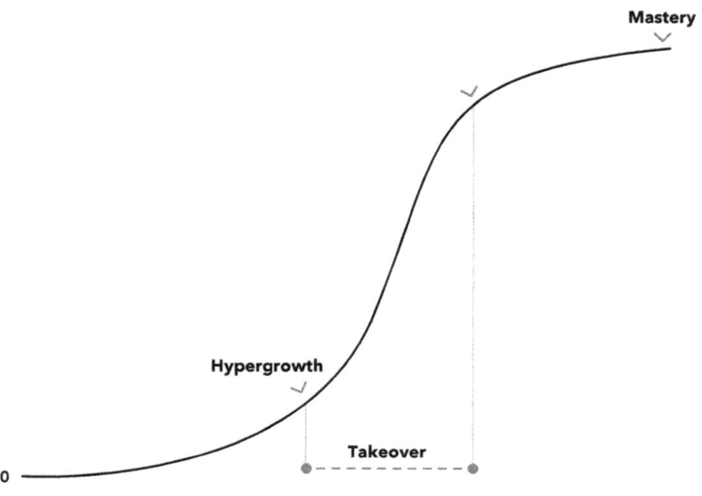

This middle phase can be followed by a phase during which we plateau, becoming too comfortable with our processes. When we do our jobs in the same way over and over, tasks become automatic, and we often forget the importance of learning new things and keeping up with new developments. Eventually, our skills become out of sync with organizational or market needs. That is when it becomes crucial to leap to the beginning of a new S-curve.

If the S-curve illustrates how a particular competence might develop over time, then it stands to reason that one's portfolio of competencies is simply the cumulative or serial sum of specific S-curves of development. Johnson encourages readers to disrupt themselves—to jump from one learning curve onto another and string together a series of S-curves to navigate a long-term journey of development and professional impact. However, each time we make a jump, it can be one of the most challenging and risky professional maneuvers we make. The next S-curve might involve changing your role or function within an organization—or changing companies altogether. And we can never be assured of a successful outcome.

It is important to note that moving from one S-curve to the next does not necessarily involve a hierarchical progression in the organization. S-curve leaps can also mean broadening a skill set or moving between functional areas (for example, expertise areas within the function) while staying at the same level of hierarchy.

It may seem safer, easier, and more comfortable *not* to make those leaps. But to grow beyond our comfort zones and develop sustainable careers, we must—and L&D has a key support role to play.

Each time we make a jump, it can be one of the most challenging and risky professional maneuvers we make.

Encouraging development with opportunities and rewards

We have identified four elements that determine whether professionals will successfully navigate from one S-curve to another. Two of these elements, mastering the skills of lifelong learning and developing the confidence to approach challenges in a constructive way, are up to the learner to embrace and are examined in detail in chapters 5 and 7. The L&D function has more direct influence over the remaining two, providing opportunities and recognizing and rewarding performance, because L&D is part of the organization's overarching talent management system (which also includes recruiting and onboarding, HR, and essentially all management). L&D leaders have an important opportunity and responsibility to align with their colleagues from related functions to reinforce value drivers within their talent system.

Providing opportunities

Companies create both formal and informal processes for growth and development. Examples include:

- Mobility—Providing talent-development opportunities across functions or geographies
- Secondments—Allowing employees to take temporary placements in another department or function
- Job shadowing—Encouraging employees to follow, and learn from, experts and leaders of the organization
- Project work—Providing special projects outside the employee's day-to-day work that may or may not relate to current responsibilities
- Sabbaticals—Permitting leaves of absence aimed at personal development and growth
- Mentoring—Encouraging experienced colleagues to share knowledge and experience with more junior colleagues

- Networking—Developing contacts with other professionals to explore opportunities and get new insights

- Formal learning—Offering structured classes on the necessary skills and knowledge to move along the learner's current S-curve and prepare for the next

The degree to which L&D leaders are involved in the development of these various types of offerings can vary among—or even within—organizations, but they should be involved. Of course, to create these opportunities, organizations need effective collaboration among related functional areas. In addition to leading formal learning, the learning function can also support, inspire, and advocate for individual and organizational investment by increasing learners' awareness of opportunities, fostering self-reflection, and serving as a forum for helping employees find the opportunities that are right for them, at the right time. The more opportunity there is for profes-sional growth, the more growth there will be—as long as a complementary reward system is in place (more on that below).

L&D professionals can achieve greater impact by taking a thoughtful approach, with the S-curve in mind. But at the same time, learners also have to be in the right mind-set to make the most of opportunity systems within an organization.

Rewarding performance

Like opportunities, rewards vary in type and are managed and influenced by several functional areas across an organization. The L&D leader's role in contributing to the creation and maintenance of reward systems is perhaps less direct, but no less significant, than in the development of opportunities.

Business line managers within an organization's talent system may be primarily responsible for rewards that drive performance—such as compensation, ratings, and promotions. But in many cases, it's the acquisition of new skills that drives the performance improvement that entitles people to the rewards. For this reason, it is extremely valuable to have regular conversations with people to discuss where they are on their S-curve and what can be done to help them continue to learn and grow. That is where learning leaders come in. They support the talent system by helping line leaders become better coaches and managers. They can also help learners develop greater self-awareness and get motivated to do the work that is most fulfilling to them and enables them to reap rewards. By being aware of how the talent systems in the organization work, L&D leaders can better design and develop solutions that support these systems.

If we think about an individual's progressive series of S-curves over time as linked cycles of a professional's L&D journey, opportunities and rewards are what encourage movement along and among those curves. Opportunities support the learner's individual progress, and rewards provide motivation for making progress. An organization's learning culture can, in fact, be described quite handily with reference to how widely these two factors are made available to employees (Exhibit 6B).

Exhibit 6B: **The presence of opportunities and rewards make a learning culture possible.**

If a learner has reached the top of his or her S-curve and there's no next curve visible on the horizon, he or she may become bored and lose momentum, resulting in mediocre performance and the types of attitudes described in the bottom boxes of Exhibit 6B.

Even when further opportunities are available, learners at the top of an S-curve might choose to forgo the leap to the next, staying in their current roles even though they are technically ready to move on. All kinds of factors can play into the decision to stay too long in a role, including a lack of opportunities elsewhere, inadequate rewards, and intolerance for risk. In some cases, this is not a problem as long as the employee continues to perform.

If the employee is stagnating and the work suffers as a result, however, L&D leaders must collaborate with their colleagues across the organization's talent system to find solutions. When those solutions are found, benefits accrue to both the learners and the organization. Learners are fulfilled, personally and professionally, and the organization benefits from having more capable and engaged employees.

S-curves in action: Learner archetypes

The implications of S-curve-based thinking for L&D are perhaps best illustrated by looking at tangible archetypes and examples, each covering different attempts to move along a role-based S-curve—or across curves.

Archetype 1: Starting a new S-curve

Rae joined a highly regarded professional services firm 18 months ago, and now she's been promoted from associate to project leader. While excited, Rae is also anxious. She knows the promotion means that she'll face higher expectations. Although she's read the competency grid for her new role and has a general sense of the job from observing project leaders in the past, she's not sure how to make the transition. Moreover, her new role is a lonely one: project leaders don't usually work in the same vicinity, and although Rae technically has a boss, the two of them won't work closely together over sustained periods.

Archetype 1: **Learning and development can support employees like Rae at the beginning of a new S-curve.**

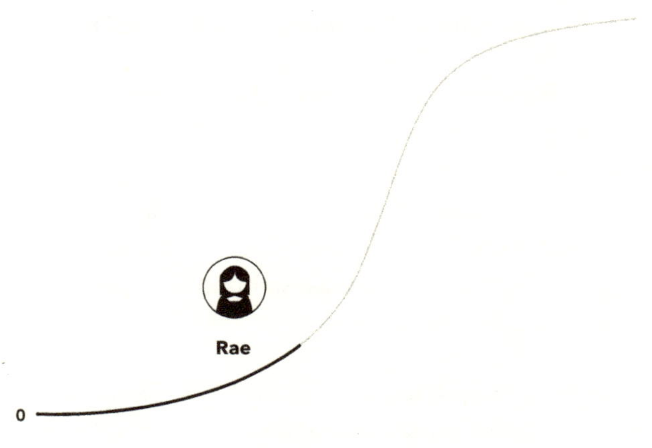

How L&D can support Rae

Rae has made the leap from her previous S-curve and now sits at the bottom of a new one. L&D's role is perhaps obvious in this case, but a deliberate application of S-curve thinking can significantly sharpen the L&D strategy for supporting employees who are starting a new role over the "here's a crash course in your new role" approach. A sharpened L&D strategy here might include:

Offering experiential learning that lets Rae practice the role in a risk-free way. It is not sufficient to hand Rae a description of the new role's responsibilities. L&D can offer all new or promoted hires the opportunity to practice new responsibilities through highly experiential live workshops and immersive simulations. (For a more in-depth discussion on how to guide successful immersive learning, see chapter 14.)

Shifting mind-sets and mental models—not just building skills. As L&D professionals know, any role change or move up the corporate ladder requires more than skill development—it requires a change in mind-set. In a move to management, for example, the technical skills that helped Rae succeed as an individual contributor are less important than the ability to think strategically, see the bigger ecosystem, and develop her team. Simulations, again, are useful in encouraging reflection, as are techniques such as reverse role plays and small-group discussions with peers. (For a more in-depth discussion of shifting mind-sets, see chapter 10.)

Mapping role requirements to Rae's existing strengths and weaknesses. As Rae transitions to her new role, L&D can make a huge contribution to launching her into the S-curve through honest, one-on-one conversations about which skills she needs to develop and what she might need to leave behind. Rae has reached a new level where the attributes that helped her succeed in her prior S-curve no longer apply. She may have previously underused strengths that L&D professionals can now help her to emphasize. Going from what might be considered a generic role to a more tailored one requires analysis and self-reflection—and it reinforces the value of authentic confidence and emotional flexibility to offset the natural anxiety associated with embarking on a new curve.

Archetype 2: Ascending the current S-curve

Gustavo supervises a team of claims adjusters for a large property and casualty insurer—a position he's held for the past nine months after spending four years as a claims adjuster. After some initial struggles,

Archetype 2: **Learning and development can support employees like Gustavo who are ascending their current S-curve.**

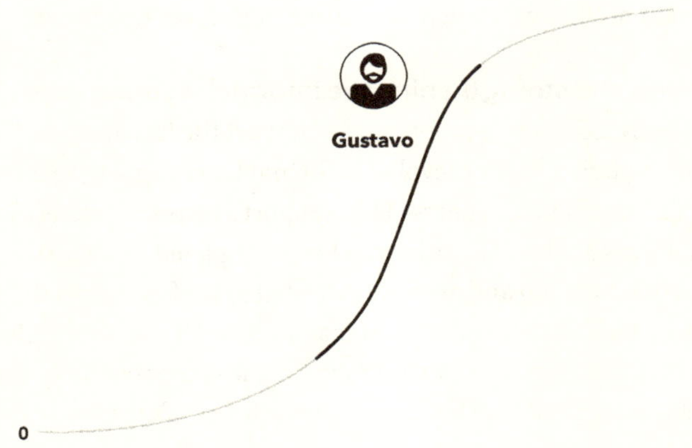

Gustavo feels increasingly confident in his role and is performing it competently. However, both he and his manager recognize that he has untapped potential—and a chance for Gustavo to exhibit truly distinctive performance in the role in the year or two ahead.

How L&D can support Gustavo

Conventional L&D approaches often underserve people like Gustavo on this part of the S-curve—partly because learners themselves may not express much need, and partly because the employee is not explicitly changing roles. But employees at this juncture are often in need of more tailored, on-the-spot support as they seek to consolidate gains and fully apply what was learned at the start of the S-curve. Specific, S-curve-aligned L&D strategies to support employees like Gustavo include:

Providing robust on-the-job performance support. As a dedicated discipline of L&D, performance support—learning aids available at the point or moment of need while someone is performing a job—is burgeoning. The "front-middle" part of the S-curve is an ideal point for performance support and working to offset the forgetting curve—described by psychologist Hermann Ebbinghaus as exponential memory loss during the 30 days following learning.[3] L&D can also employ tactics to change behavior in many ways, including digital platforms that seamlessly integrate with the claims-processing applications on Gustavo's mobile device, stand-alone apps or chatbots, or lower-tech means such as laminated placards offering step-by-step help, job aids, and pointers to reference material. (For an in-depth discussion of BJ Fogg's behavior change model, see chapter 9.)

Activating and strengthening the informal learning ecosystem. Increasingly, L&D's role is not only to support the learner directly but also to elicit a higher level of informal learning support from managers, coaches, and peers. This support is especially useful for employees such as Gustavo who have completed initial orientation and new job training and are now expected to perform. Specific L&D actions include doubling down on coaching and leadership training for managers, creating internal marketplaces for coaching support and help, and providing flexible platforms for employees to engage with people in similar roles and with subject-matter experts for social learning and knowledge sharing. (For more on creating a coaching culture, see chapter 16.)

Offering Gustavo opportunities to define a vision of himself in the role. It is only after Gustavo has weathered the initial transition to his supervisor role that he can define what his peak performance in the role could look like. At this point, Gustavo is no longer focused on simply keeping his head above water; he has enough experience to determine how his existing strengths fit with role requirements. L&D can help Gustavo work through the necessary reflection, accompanied by tools and forums to help gather feedback from others and to create an action plan that complements formal reviews. These tools can increase individual commitment to learning and accelerate ascension of the S-curve.

Archetype 3: Preparing to leap to the next S-curve

For the past six years, Julia has been distinctive in her role as a process engineer for a global technical services firm serving the energy industry. She knows through conversations with leaders

Archetype 3: **Learning and development can support employees like Julia in making the leap to a new S-curve.**

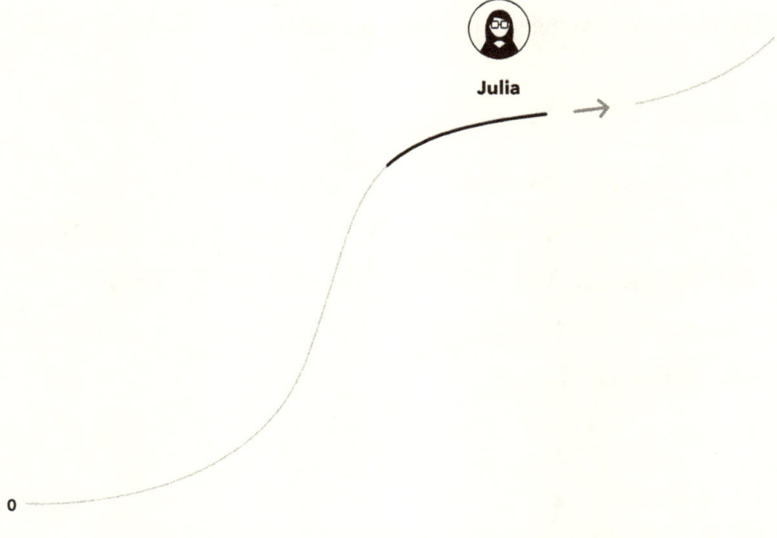

in her office that she's seen as a terrific candidate for a senior management role in the coming 12 to 18 months—which in her company would mean taking on new responsibilities related to business development, as well as a likely move to another continent.

How L&D can support Julia

L&D can play a vital role in helping employees like Julia, who are at or near the top of their current S-curve, explore and then transition to new roles and paths. As L&D professionals, we often make the critical mistake of either leaning in too late—when the person has already been thrust onto their next S-curve via promotion or transfer—or not engaging at all. In either case, the result is increased risk that the employee plateaus, grows bored, and even regresses in performance.

The reality is that if employees get continual support while navigating their current curve—especially when it complements other talent-management levers such as secondments, rotations, or mobility programs—they will experience fewer growing pains when they transition to the next.

As previously noted, L&D should create shorter learning journeys to support various stages of growth: an S-curve covering a longer period of time (for example, five years) can be built out of a series of shorter S-curves (for example, six months or a year). These journeys consist of a mix of group learning programs and individually tailored learning solutions that meet at-the-moment needs of the employee. These

The reality is that if employees get continual support while navigating their current curve, they will experience fewer growing pains when they transition to the next.

journeys can also be supported with digital-learning solutions that learners can access at their own pace. This strategy helps to minimize the gaps between one S-curve and the next and makes the transition as smooth as possible.

Examples of L&D strategies that help achieve smooth transitions between S-curves include:

Building capabilities for the next role in the context of the current role. When an employee's potential next S-curves are known or can be predicted, as in Julia's case, there are benefits to focusing on building capabilities she will need in the future. Learning can provide the triggers and forums for this to happen by making employees like Julia more aware of the specific skills she will need in the future; providing safe, risk-free opportunities to begin developing these skills; and offering advice for how to hone these skills in her current role. For example, a program might specifically focus on topics such as gravitas, empathy, and team-based problem solving—some of the most common stumbling blocks facing new managers. Learners could participate in this program 6 to 18 months prior to making the transition to manager, giving them time to practice these skills in the context of their current position.

Catalyzing reflection and exploration of future S-curves. One of the most popular courses at Stanford University is "Designing Your Life," which applies design principles to questions of career development and life paths.[4] Across organizations, career tracks are becoming far less linear or predictable. L&D can offer employees opportunities to step back and reflect on their strengths and areas of passion; gather input and advice from peers, coaches, and senior colleagues; identify potential new roles they would like to explore; and design near- and midterm strategies for testing and prototyping these roles for themselves.

■ ■ ■

Strategic S-curve thinking for the broader organization

The value of S-curve-driven L&D actions is exponentially higher when they support professional development, talent management, and organizational strategies that also follow an S-curve.

Such a strategy would include:

- Mobility—providing talent-development opportunities across functions or geographies
- Flexible competency frameworks and consistent language across all career paths in the organization
- Rewards and recognition that encourage employees to seek out the next S-curve when they have reached the top of the current one
- Regular conversations with employees to discuss where they are on their S-curve, where they would like to go, and what can be done to continue their growth

And from an overall organizational standpoint, CEOs and heads of HR can create S-curve-friendly organizations by:

- Emphasizing a culture of continual learning and self-development (for more on developing a lifelong-learning mind-set, see chapter 5)
- Acknowledging that the time it takes to go from one S-curve to the next has gotten shorter than it was even five years ago—and encouraging the mind-set that this is exciting rather than scary or daunting

The S-curve offers a simple but effective framework for supporting learners at every stage of their careers in conjunction with the talent system of the organization. L&D has a crucial role to play at each stage—but leaders must understand existing (and ideal) rewards and opportunities, know where each learner stands, and offer the right support at the right time. Simultaneously, there is huge value for learners in understanding their own learning journeys and taking responsibility for their learning and development.

This new dynamic also requires L&D professionals to develop new skills. Conceptualizing learning and development through the lens of S-curves means thinking about learning as a journey and designing solutions as such. ■

1 Charles B. Handy, *The Empty Raincoat: Making Sense of the Future,* New York: Arrow Books, 1995.

2 Whitney Johnson, "Throw your life a curve," *Harvard Business Review,* September 3, 2012, hbr.org. Johnson also wrote a book that discusses the topic: *Disrupt Yourself: Putting the Power of Disruptive Innovation to Work,* New York and Abingdon: Routledge, 2016.

3 Margie Meacham, "Don't forget the Ebbinghaus Forgetting Curve," Association for Talent Development, January 20, 2016, td.org.

4 "ME104B: Designing your life," accessed May 31, 2018, lifedesignlab.stanford.edu/dyl.

CHAPTER

07/

MAXIMIZING LEARNING IMPACT:

The role of authentic confidence

AUTHORS
Jacqueline Brassey
Barbara Matthews
Nick van Dam

Anxiety affects productivity and well-being, but emotional flexibility can give employees the confidence to approach challenges in an engaged and constructive way.

The world is increasingly unpredictable. The accelerating pace of change—from changes in climate to digitization—has created a volatile, uncertain, complex, and ambiguous (VUCA) environment.[1] Our workforce isn't prepared to deal with this VUCA world: constant, rapid change can leave organizations struggling to respond. Add typical workplace factors such as leadership changes, poor management, and frequent reorganizations, as well as potential challenges that employees face in their home lives, and the average worker today is dealing with a lot of stress.

Stress disrupts the human system. Uncertainty evokes fear, and fear causes employees to respond in irrational and ineffective ways. Too much stress and uncertainty can lower performance and increase emotional distress and may eventually lead to burnout and depression.[2] The negative effects are undeniable. In the United Kingdom, workers miss nearly 70 million workdays a year, and poor mental health (for example, anxiety, depression, and stress-related conditions) is the number-one factor contributing to illness-related absence.[3] Based on current predictions, depression will be the primary health-related burden worldwide by 2030.[4]

Despite this bleak picture, there is hope. A recent study by Tupperware, in collaboration with Georgetown University, found a correlation between employee confidence and success at work. Workers with more confidence have a 17 percent greater chance of being innovative, are 24 percent more likely to rise above obstacles on the job, and are 16 percent more likely to come up with better ways of getting things done.[5] The study showed that employees who are confident have the emotional strength and flexibility to thrive regardless of change.

Unfortunately, our ongoing research shows that many workers lack confidence. Almost 50 percent of professionals think they could perform better if they were less worried about making mistakes: 24 percent of these employees spend a significant amount of time worrying about their performance or their inability to measure up. An additional 18 percent have these worries constantly.[6]

This dearth of confidence is negatively affecting the bottom line, according to the Tupperware study. Our own research shows that when people don't feel confident, they avoid engaging. They don't take on challenges or opportunities that push them out of their comfort zones, which has a negative impact on their personal growth, and they don't share their viewpoints or ideas for fear of making mistakes or being negatively evaluated by peers and senior leaders.

In today's VUCA world, we need a workforce that can handle insecurity and uncertainty. We suggest that organizations help their employees develop what we call authentic confidence—defined as acknowledging your insecurities regarding your capabilities and dealing with them in an action-oriented and skillful way. Authentic confidence is inner peaceful awareness about your true capabilities, your values, and your purpose.

With an understanding of the origins and neuroscience of confidence—and tools for developing emotional flexibility—individuals can gain authentic confidence and be better, more productive members of the workforce. They must also understand and overcome the barriers to building this type of confidence.

The neuroscience of anxiety and fear

> "Many people believe that certain situations are the cause of their anxiety, but anxiety always begins in the brain, not with the situation."
>
> —Elizabeth Karle and Catherine Pittman, authors of *Rewire Your Anxious Brain: How to Use the Neuroscience of Fear to End Anxiety, Panic, & Worry*

Confidence is directly influenced by the level of anxiety we feel in situations. Anxiety can be helpful or harmful. If you are in danger, it can be a helpful warning sign. Often, however, when we feel anxiety (and thus worry) we "have a sense of dread or discomfort but aren't, at that moment, in danger."[7] Anxiety usually results from thinking we are either not qualified or not good enough, combined with fear of failing or being evaluated negatively. This anxiety (conscious or unconscious) influences our choices, our performance, how we grow and learn, and our overall feeling of well-being.

But where does anxiety come from? To understand what happens in the brain when we experience emotions such as fear and worry, we can examine the function of a few elements, including the prefrontal cortex,[8] thalamus, and amygdala.[9] The brain systems that are most obviously relevant to confidence are the fear system, the reward system, and the habit system. In this chapter we will focus on the fear system since it is at the heart of how we regulate our fears and worries.

One of the central structures to the fear system is the thalamus. The thalamus is a structure in the middle of the brain, located between the cerebral cortex and the midbrain, that serves as a kind of "air traffic control system." It is critical in relaying sensory information to the brain; when we feel, hear, see, or taste something, this sensory data goes to the thalamus. In fact, all the senses besides smell have a relay station in the thalamus. (Smell goes directly to its destination in the brain.) The thalamus sends the data it receives on to many other parts in the brain, including the amygdala (where emotions are regulated) and the prefrontal cortex (where rational thinking occurs).

There are two roads that fear can travel in the brain: the low road and the high road (Exhibit 7A).[10] When we see someone who makes us fearful, this image is registered by the eye, then it travels through the thalamus and numerous parts of the cortex before the amygdala processes this emotion and we respond with anxiety (high road). However, when this fear is extreme, the cortex is bypassed or hijacked. The image goes from the eye to the thalamus and then the amygdala, which responds accordingly (low road). It's faster, though probably less accurate.

Route A: The low road, or direct pathway

If the fear is extreme, it travels the "low road" or the "direct pathway" as visualized in Route A of Exhibit 7A. If the amygdala registers immediate danger, its activation may lead to the release of cortisol and adrenaline. Cortisol increases blood sugar levels, helping us to use our muscles in an emergency, while adrenaline gives us energy, serves as a painkiller, and increases our heart rate. The information will eventually reach the cortex, but by that time, you have already

Exhibit 7A: **There are two roads fear can travel in the brain: The low road and the high road.**

The low road or direct pathway

The high road or indirect pathway

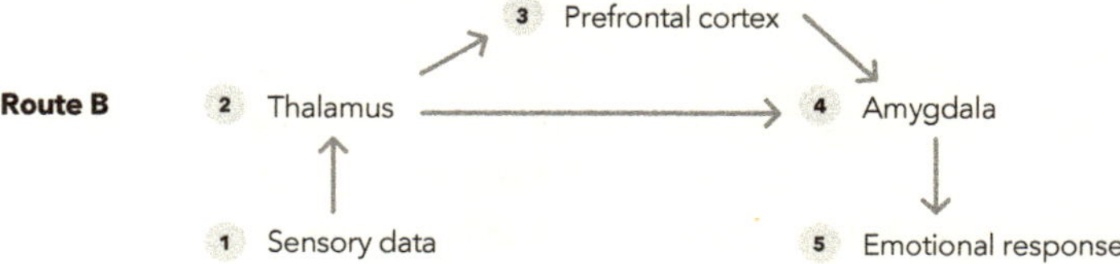

Source: Adapted from Srinivasan S. Pillay, *Life Unlocked: 7 Revolutionary Lessons to Overcome Fear*, New York: Rodale Books, 2011

responded. It's too late. When an amygdala hijack occurs, the responses we often see are fight, flight, or freeze.[11]

For example, consider an employee we'll call Jack. He is about to present to the executive board on the progress of a large-scale transformation that is happening at his company. He worked for many long nights to create thorough slides and put together a folder with colored sticky notes structured by question and topic. When he enters the boardroom, he feels his stomach churning and his heart racing. Once in front of the room, he drops his pen and accidentally tips over a glass of water. He feels his nervousness increasing and his hands are shaking, but he thinks to himself, "I prepared well; nothing can go wrong." But a few minutes in, the CFO asks him how much money this transformation will save the company. Jack panics because he was not able to calculate this figure and doesn't have a great hypothesis. He is scared to make something up—he already had a few difficult conversations with this CFO—and he freezes. He is standing in front of the room and is not able to respond, even as colleagues ask him if he is feeling OK. After a few seconds, he becomes aware he is just standing there silent. Embarrassed, he asks a colleague to finish the presentation for him.

Jack just experienced an extreme case of amygdala hijack, which led to a "freeze." His cortex was not given a chance to assess the situation properly. Other examples are when people suddenly become very angry and react extremely emotionally (fight) or decide to withdraw from a situation (flight). Reactions from an amygdala hijack are almost always regretted afterward because they are purely an emotional response to a threat experience. In this case, the person's experience does not reflect factual truth, and emotional responses as described above are not rationally controlled.

Route B: The high road, or indirect pathway

Anxiety can also take the "high road," or the indirect pathway through the brain. This route may be triggered by an external event that a person interprets a certain way or an internal event, such as a thought or mental image.

Triggered by an external event, interpretation based

Sometimes an external event may not be interpreted by the amygdala as immediately dangerous, so the data reaches the cortex on the high road. But if the cortex, which takes past experiences into consideration, processes the data in a way that creates worry, eventually, if this keeps going on, the amygdala may be signaled, setting off the stress response. For example, if someone takes on a new project at work, that information may not trigger immediate concern in the amygdala. But because the cortex is a major player in rational thought, it can anticipate many possible outcomes of the project, including potentially negative ones. These thoughts could cause worry,[12] which would trigger the amygdala, creating an emotional response.

Triggered by internal events, thoughts or imagery based

Two other routes to anxiety via the cortex are possible. In these routes, an external trigger does not cause a stress reaction. Instead, people create the anxiety themselves.

One way anxiety might start to influence our confidence is through thoughts we have, for example, when we start ruminating about something. This likely starts in the areas in our brain where our logical and rational thinking is based. Our thoughts can be very powerful. They can lead to anxiety that can ultimately become so challenging that this process triggers the amygdala, with a subsequent emotional response. For example, we may start worrying about something we said in a meeting, rehashing others' reactions and how they may have been interpreted our words, as well as how the interaction could affect the way our work is perceived. This anxiety is the result of something that was not triggered by an external event but rather started from within our own minds.

Another way to create anxiety is through our imaginations, such as images or visualizations of what might happen. This anxiety is more likely to originate from the area in our brain where we visualize—where our imagination and intuition comes alive. To give an example: I might be sitting behind my desk and suddenly imagine myself failing during a presentation I'm scheduled to give. This visualization might make me so anxious that I want to cancel my participation because I start believing it won't go well.

Both of these routes, thoughts or imagery based, can trigger the amygdala and cause an emotional reaction that is uncomfortable—initially perhaps not as strong as with the amygdala hijack, however if these reactions become extreme, they might cause an amygdala hijack.

Stress and its effects

Regardless of the path anxiety takes, it is a by-product of excess stress. In 1908, Robert Yerkes and John Dodson identified a curvilinear relationship between stress and performance called the Yerkes–Dodson law (Exhibit 7B). According to this law, explained in a simplified way, stress is a requirement for optimal performance; however, too much stress can lead to anxiety and cause a decline in performance.

The relationship between stress and performance as described by the Yerkes–Dodson law is intuitive and easy to understand, but the law lacks an explanation for why too much stress leads to lower performance. Also, this simple inverted U-shaped relationship has

Exhibit 7B: **The Yerkes-Dodson law charts the relationship between stress and performance.**

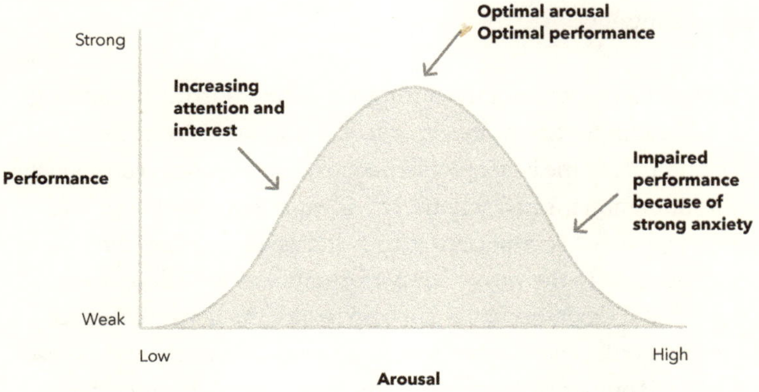

Source: Robert M. Yerkes and John D. Dodson, "The relation of strength of stimulus to rapidity of habit-formation," *Journal of Comparative Neurology and Psychology*, November 1908, Volume 18, Issue 5, pp. 459–82, doi.org/10.1002/cne.920180503

turned out to be an oversimplification, since the relationship between stress and performance can vary in different situations. The fear system of the brain and the three pathways provide a useful alternative lens through which to examine the effect of fear on performance.

In the workplace, stress can create a variety of emotional, physical, and psychological responses (or signals). To illuminate the range of possible responses, we have described three distinct scenarios: plain sailing, bumpy ride, and crash (Exhibit 7C).[13]

Plain sailing

In the plain sailing scenario, we are at our best. Our thoughts are not holding us back. We are focused and present, and our heart rates and blood pressures are normal. These conditions enable us to be fully engaged in our work, and the quality of our output reinforces how the absence of stress and anxiety contributes to productivity and performance.

Bumpy ride

In this scenario, our inner critic comes to visit. We think negatively about ourselves or worry (high road), and our biofeedback reflects this worry: we might blush or stutter during a meeting, feel our heart rate increase and our eyes becoming tense, and get cold hands. As stress begins to build, our performance slips, which can result in a variety of potential actions. We might stay quiet in a meeting or decline a job offer or opportunity because we don't want to leave our comfort zone.

It's common to experience the bumpy ride when starting something new—for example, a new project or role. Being in this zone for a short amount of time is not problematic as long as we can consciously change our emotions and actions. If this experience starts keeping us away from what is important to us (what we value), then the bumpy ride gets in the way of our performance as well; developing our emotional flexibility skills can help reduce the negative impact of our inner critic and the stress we experience. If we stay in this space too long or if our stress continues to increase, we might enter the crash zone.

Exhibit 7C: **Different levels of worry affect the relationship between mind, body, and action.**

■ **Learning effectiveness reduces**

Examples of mind: Thoughts feedback

- Extreme fear/anxiety
- Completely irrational thoughts
- Inner critic
- Self-talk
- Worry
- Anxiety
- Messy/fog
- Fused
- Normal emotions
- Aware
- Present
- Anxiety
- Emotionally flexible

Crash

Bumpy ride

Plain sailing

Examples of behavior: Action feedback

- Can't move
- No control
- Shaking
- Bad performance
- Withdrawal behavior
- Not speaking up
- Avoid plenary session in team
- Decline job offer
- Decline opportunity for public speaking
- Suboptimal performance
- Fully engaged in the task
- Engaging
- Optimal performance

Examples of body: Bio feedback

- "Normal" heart rate
- "Normal" blood pressure

- Blushing
- Stuttering
- Increased heart rate
- Eyes stressed
- Cold hands

- Freeze
- Brain blocks
- Severe sweating
- Heart pounding
- Jaw clenching

Source: Jacqueline Brassey, Nick van Dam, and Arjen van Witteloostuijn, 2017

Crash

The crash zone, which corresponds to the far right of the Yerkes–Dodson curve, is where the amygdala hijack might happen (low road), and stress impedes performance. In a crash, we may find ourselves shaking or frozen and thinking completely irrationally. Our hearts may pound, our jaws may clench, and we may sweat.

The good news is that emotional flexibility skills can enable us to decrease the amount of time we spend in the crash zone or avoid it altogether, giving us true authentic confidence to lean into our jobs and careers.

Developing authentic confidence through emotional flexibility

We can actually train ourselves in how we react to amygdala activation. We can "rewire" the connection between the cortex and the amygdala through, for example, meditation. We can also manage the overall "sensitivity" of the amygdala to stress by ensuring we get enough sleep and exercise. When we are in an immediate stress situation, we can apply deep belly breathing to calm our system down. For anxiety that is influenced by interpretation of events, tools that help us to look differently at the situation in context (reframing or identifying the rest of the "iceberg," that is, getting an understanding of what drives your behavior by exploring your underlying thoughts, feelings, mind-sets, and needs) might be very helpful. For other cortex-originated anxiety (high road), tools that help us explore our thoughts and emotions (acceptance and defusion tools) might be very helpful. And for overall feeling of direction and focus of what is important to us in work, basic reflection tools about our goals and values will be helpful—and this is where the concept of emotional flexibility comes in.

Emotional flexibility, also known as acceptance and commitment theory (ACT), is an evidence-based concept derived from cognitive psychology.[14] ACT consists of six interactive elements that help us build and maintain authentic professional confidence: purpose and values, committed action, self in context, defusion, acceptance, and mindfulness (Exhibit 7D). By paying attention to all of these elements and the practical tools for each, we can strengthen our ability to deal with stressful situations. With this self-empowerment and confidence, we will no longer avoid opportunities out of fear of failure but rather we may choose to actively pursue them with excitement.

Purpose and values: Ground it

There is no prescribed sequence of where to start developing emotional flexibility, but our experience has found it is helpful to start with purpose and values that can serve as a foundation of authentic confidence. A strong sense of purpose—having a

Exhibit 7D: **Gain authentic confidence using these six processes of emotional flexibility.**

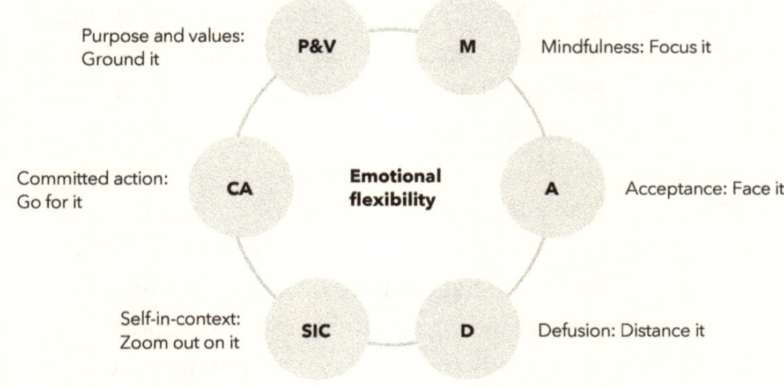

Source: Jacqueline Brassey, Nick van Dam, and Arjen van Witteloostuijn, 2017

reason to get out of bed, setting a clear direction, and knowing what is important to you—can act as an anchor when you experience challenging times. Behind this purpose are values, or guiding principles. For example, if your key value is to be healthy, including getting sufficient sleep and eating well while working, you might decide to forgo a new role that requires excessive traveling because it could compromise your values.

Conscious reflection on purpose and values fosters the development of an inner compass. By engaging the brain's cortex, this reflection deflects our attention from the fear center (the amygdala) and helps us remain calm when things become challenging.

The tools in this dimension primarily address anxiety that "originates" in the cortex (high road), since they engage the rational-thinking part of the brain.

Mindfulness: Focus it

Mindfulness means being fully present and aware of your emotions and surroundings or immersing oneself completely during daily activities. Even just a few minutes a day of being mindful while exercising, meditating, breathing, or even listening to music builds the mental muscle needed for focus and peak performance. This mind-set helps address anxiety resulting from an amygdala hijack (low road) as well as in the cortex (high road). Mindfulness is a great tool for maintaining overall mental health, helping to both prevent and ease strong emotional reactions in challenging situations.

Acceptance: Face it

We often avoid challenges for fear of making mistakes or failing. While this behavior is understandable, authentic confidence is impossible if we are avoiding situations that are important to us. To become authentically confident, we need to face our fears, consciously step out of our comfort zone, and learn from the experience. When we hit the bumpy ride or crash scenarios, acceptance will help us acknowledge our fear and observe it in a nonjudgmental way, thus reducing its negative impact tremendously. If the ability to present in front of large groups is important to you but you dread speaking in public, for instance, consider practicing in safer contexts to build up the skill and courage. The tools in this dimension address anxiety traveling both the high and the low road.

Defusion: Distance it

This element is all about awareness of factors that trigger anxiety. For example, an angry board member, a dissatisfied client, or a nasty email from a colleague can cause worry and anxiety. Defusion is learning how to keep those potential dangers at a distance. Practicing defusion (through detached observation of our thoughts) doesn't mean ignoring potential dangers or thoughts; it means acknowledging that they are just thoughts, not identifying ourselves with them, so we can focus on the task at hand and stay calm. The tools in this dimension are helpful in addressing anxiety or fear that travels via the high road but also for recovery after an amygdala hijack.

Self-in-context: Zoom out on it

The ability to look at challenges from a distance and in context, instead of ignoring them, is an essential skill in developing authentic confidence. Often, we are so caught up in busy operations and day-to-day activity that we don't have a high-level view of what is happening or what we are feeling. Zooming out helps us understand the causes of our feelings. Keeping in mind who we are as people—our purpose, values, and goals—provides perspective. Renowned educator Ronald Heifetz refers to this perspective as being on the dance floor and on the balcony at the same time.[15]

Committed action: Go for it

Developing authentic professional confidence through emotional flexibility requires us to think through the changes we want to make in our daily lives. This process is not about defining intentions but rather about creating a very clear plan and integrating it straight away. For example, you might develop a personal operating model to face a particular challenge that you have been avoiding by deciding to practice daily meditation.

The tools in this dimension focus on bringing all the other elements together and embracing challenges to reach maximum potential. Depending on where the key challenges lie, the activities in this step will focus on either preventing an amygdala hijack or reducing the impact of fear traveling the high road.

Overall emotional flexibility: How to bring it all together

This model for developing greater emotional flexibility is not a step-by-step process. It was originally built for therapeutic practice and offered to therapists and coaches in cognitive psychology practice. However, the clear framework makes it possible to include practical steps and tools along the journey. Some of us already have a great awareness of our purpose and values and hence might benefit more from learning mindfulness or dealing with worries in the moment (acceptance and defusion). Others might be very good at facing their fears or taking a step back to gain perspective but have never thought through what is really important to them, leaving them directionless. This approach is about moving toward our goals, purpose, and values while dealing with fears and anxieties along the journey in a way that has proved to lead to better performance and well-being (Exhibit 7E). It provides the context through which we can reach our maximum potential.

Exhibit 7E: **Manage emotional flexibility on the journey to authentic confidence.**

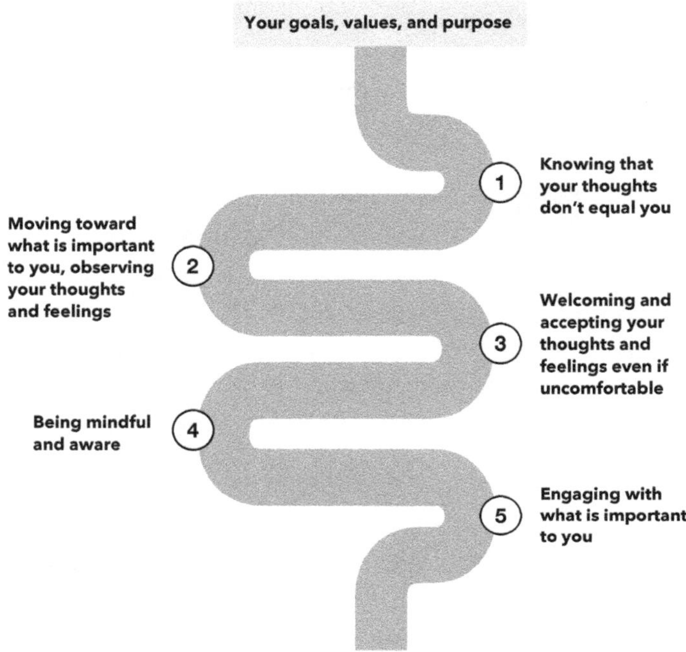

Source: Jacqueline Brassey, Nick van Dam, and Arjen van Witteloostuijn, 2017

We have developed an online assessment tool to help you identify which emotional flexibility skills you should focus on to further develop your authentic confidence.[16]

■ ■ ■

L&D professionals are always thinking about the resources people need to be productive and successful. They continually push professionals to be leaders within their organizations and look for the best tools to help people develop and grow. The neuroscience of anxiety and the steps to authentic confidence through emotional flexibility should be a core part of the L&D curriculum because they are vital for a successful and productive workforce. As our unpredictable world continues to cause higher stress levels, these tools will be even more critical for individuals to thrive, both in their personal and professional lives. ■

[1] The US Army War College first introduced the concept of VUCA in the early 1990s to describe the multilateral nature of global threats.

[2] For more information on the effects of stress, see "Three out of five employees are highly stressed, according to ComPsych survey," *ComPsych*, October 30, 2017, compsych.com; and "Depression," Anxiety and Depression Association of America, accessed May 31, 2018, adaa.org.

[3] Sally C. Davies, "Chief medical officer's summary," in Nisha Mehta, ed., *Annual report of the chief medical officer 2013,* Public mental health priorities: Investing in the evidence [online], London, Department of Health, pp. 11-9, assets.publishing.service.gov.uk; and Julian Foster, "Mental health problems are very common in the workplace—so why don't we talk about it more?," Computershare SalaryExtras, November 25, 2015, blog.computershare-salaryextras.com.

[4] *Global burden of mental disorders and the need for a comprehensive, coordinated response from health and social sectors at the country level,* World Health Organization, December 1, 2011, apps.who.int.

[5] *Quantifying and cultivating confidence: Summary of Tupperware research with Georgetown University,* TupperwareBrands, January 2017, cbpp.georgetown.edu.

[6] Assistant Professor Jacqueline Brassey (Universiteit Tilburg), Professor Nick van Dam (Nyenrode Business Universiteit), and Professor Arjen van Witteloostuijn (Vrije Universiteit) are currently conducting research on more than 650 respondents. The full findings will be published in their new book in the third quarter of 2018.

[7] Elizabeth Karle and Catherine Pittman, *Rewire Your Anxious Brain: How to Use the Neuroscience of Fear to End Anxiety, Panic, & Worry,* Oakland, CA: New Harbinger Publications, Inc., 2015.

[8] For ease, we use the terms "prefrontal cortex" and "cortex" as synonyms.

[9] We recognize that the brain and its functioning are much more complex than described here. But the aim of this article is to explore some important basics around the neuroscience of confidence to help explain what happens and how building emotional-flexibility skills can help curb these processes.

[10] James A. Carr, "I'll take the low road: The evolutionary underpinnings of visually triggered fear," *Frontiers in Neuroscience,* 2015, Volume 4, Number 414, doi.org/10.3389/fnins.2015.00414; and Srinivasan S. Pillay, *Life Unlocked: 7 Revolutionary Lessons to Overcome Fear,* New York: Rodale Books, 2011.

[11] Joseph E. LeDoux, "Emotion circuits in the brain," *Annual Review of Neuroscience,* March 2000, Volume 23, pp. 155-84, doi.org/10.1146/annurev.neuro.23.1.155.

[12] Kristen K. Ellard et al., "Neural correlates of emotion acceptance vs worry or suppression in generalized anxiety disorder," *Social Cognitive and Affective Neuroscience,* June 2017, Volume 12, Number 6, pp. 1009-21, doi.org/10.1093/scan/nsx025.

[13] We recognize that reality is complex and that individual experiences may vary along the axes; the categories are not exhaustive.

[14] For more information, see contextualscience.org.

[15] Ronald Heifetz and Marty Linsky, *Leadership on the Line: Staying Alive through the Dangers of Leading,* Boston, MA: Harvard Business Review Press, 2002.

[16] The free test, "Authentic Professional Confidence," is available at reachingyourpotential.org.

CHAPTER

08/

CURATION:

Moving beyond content management

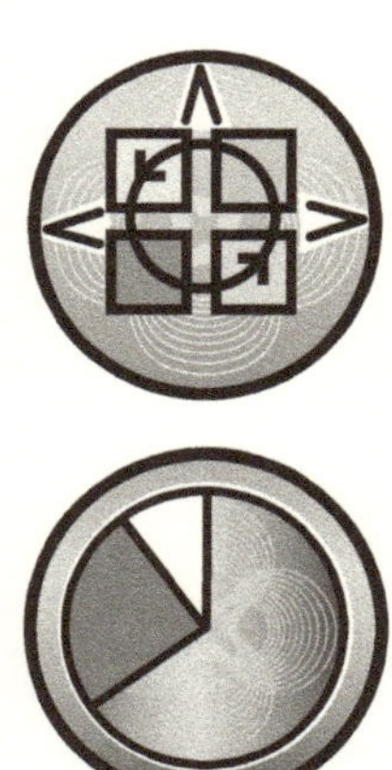

AUTHORS
Sarah Gisser
Gina Webster
Cathy Wright

With all the content out there, curation is critical in connecting learners with the right solutions at the right time.

Curation is the art and science of getting the right content to the right people, at the right time, to meet a specific learning objective or need. Just as a museum curator intentionally chooses a specific assortment of paintings or objects from a museum's vast collection, so too there need to be context, theme, and purpose behind the choices a learning or knowledge curator makes when selecting assets. Curation is more than just selecting items from a variety of sources and sharing them with an intended audience. The curator needs to know the audience and its needs, to actively source and create content based on audience context, and to distribute that content to users at the right time. Playlists, for example, abound in consumer media—curated collections of music or podcasts—but they must be actively promoted so users can find them when they're interested.

Imagine you are a management consultant or another professional driven by client demands. It's the end of the work week, and you've just been assigned to a new team that has an important client meeting on Monday. You don't have much time to get up to speed on the industry, the client, and the business challenges. What do you do? If you're like many people, you would research the client by taking a buckshot approach—conducting online searches and emailing experts and colleagues in the hope that some of your efforts will pay off in useful information. However, in a curated scenario, you'd automatically receive a package of relevant content, compiled by both internal and external subject-matter experts, pertaining to the specific industry, client, and topics under consideration. This package would allow you to quickly home in on exactly what you need, so you can spend most of your time considering the client's situation more deeply and developing hypotheses and ideas about how to solve the client's problem rather than trying to define it. You'd be able to work quickly and efficiently and come to the meeting prepared for a rich, informed discussion with the client.

While the high cost of building content and enabling systems used to make curation difficult to scale, technology now makes it easier to create, discover, compile, and share relevant collections of content. Moreover, metrics make it easy to evaluate impact. The key is to build a comprehensive curation system with clear priorities, skilled curators, high-quality content, repeatable processes, and a strong technology backbone.

Three forces are making content curation more essential

In the learning industry, the concept of curation is not new. We've been finding, evaluating, choosing, transforming, and disseminating select pieces of content for some time. But several factors are making the process more important than ever and creating an urgent need to rethink the who, how, what, and why of curation.

The enormous amount of content available

In today's information-rich world, it has become harder for learners to quickly find the most relevant content when they need it. Free information and tutorials exist on nearly every topic, with search engines and content platforms such as LinkedIn Learning and Lynda.com making it easier than ever to browse or do targeted searches. Advances in software continue to lower the barriers to creating and editing material and assets, and user-generated content has become the norm for many social and professional interactions. The growth encompasses both new content types and more content overall, as libraries swell with not only documents but also video, visualizations, data, and so forth. As a result, learning-and-development (L&D) professionals find themselves hard-pressed to sift through the content.

The impact of information overload on individuals

The proliferation of content is as much a challenge for the individual as for the L&D function. While technology has provided faster access to more content, learners' capacity to process information hasn't kept pace. In his 2004 book *The Paradox of Choice,*[1] Barry Schwartz argues that shoppers with a broader range of choices had a harder time deciding than shoppers who were asked to choose from a narrower range of products. Learners are similarly fatigued by information overload. They can only take in so much, and when increased input is not met with a similar increase in ability to process, people become scattered, overwhelmed, and, paradoxically, less productive. Learners today can access an explosion of content any time of day or night. The challenge facing L&D professionals is to help learners cut through the clutter and access the content they need, when they need it. For most people—including highly educated professionals—less is more.

The demand for easy access to personalized content

A one-size-fits-all approach to learning does not work. Modern learners require (and expect) easily accessible, personalized content—whether it's short, just-in-time performance support for a single purpose, or more structured, sequenced content that teaches a broader set of learning objectives. As learning-technology expert Elliott Masie wrote in 2015, "As employees have ever more choices at

While technology has provided faster access to more content, learners' capacity to process information hasn't kept pace.

home—including the timing, format, and packaging of content—it may result in a great demand for 'personalization' and time-shifting of scheduled learning activities at the workplace."[2] Three years later, that time is upon us.

Building a systemic capability for content curation

Good curation helps learners sift through the noise and focus quickly on the content that is best suited to their immediate needs, thereby increasing the impact of learning. Envisioning the ideal user experience is easy, but implementing that experience requires seamless integration across people (curators and consumers), content, technology, and processes. We suggest L&D functions focus on five elements: clear priorities; accountable and skilled curators; access to high-quality content; deliberate, repeatable processes; and fit-for-purpose technology.

Clear priorities

L&D professionals typically must serve a broad spectrum of learners, from entry-level employees to senior executives (and everyone in between). These learners need support in developing leadership, professional, and technical skills as well as insights relevant to the organization's domain and the individual's role and function. All of these needs vary in depth; some learners need a basic introduction, while others need deeper insights or more advanced capabilities.

How many use cases result from these multiple dimensions? And which are most important to the organization? The full scope of needs and priorities is often left unsaid. In the absence of clear priorities, L&D professionals tackle the most urgent (or loudest) demands that make it to the front of a long queue.

A better approach is to start by defining desired outcomes. For example, is the objective to reduce duplicative efforts, increase efficiency, align employees around a new strategy, or build new skills? Once objectives are clear, use cases can be prioritized by their impact on those objectives, and tackled accordingly. Great curation is about effectively filtering out the noise and amplifying the content that matters most. (For more on learning-needs analysis, see chapter 4.)

Capability checklist:

- We have clear learning objectives, tied to measurable outcomes.
- We know who our target learners are.
- We have prioritized the topics and capabilities to promote with curated content.
- Priorities are well understood and agreed upon across the organization.
- Priorities are periodically revisited to meet evolving organizational needs and improve results.

Accountable and skilled curators

Few learning organizations have designated curators. Instead, curation is undertaken by people across a variety of roles based on their availability, their interest in the topic, the nature of the project, and other factors. Instructional designers might curate learner resources for a new program, for example, and knowledge managers might curate content to help colleagues get up to speed on key trends or market dynamics. In essence, everyone is a curator, which often means that no one is truly responsible for curation. In addition, curation is often delegated to people with no real subject-matter expertise, which can lead to subpar results.

Good curation depends on a clear definition of the curator's role and the skills required, as well as designated subject-matter experts on given topics and priorities. While curation can be delegated across many roles and parts of the organization, there should be a standard approach and a clear understanding of who is accountable for curating which topics. A central governing body—for example, a learning function or a virtual community—can lead this. (For a discussion of L&D organizational structure, see chapter 1.) The end user can play an important role in curation as well. By providing ratings, comments, and shares, end users supply curators and other learners with feedback on which content and channels resonate most.

Ideally, curators play three distinct roles. First, they act as domain experts who understand the topic(s) they curate and keep in close contact with important content sources, expert communities, and trends. Second, they act as social networkers to source diverse sets of content and expertise and weave them together to tell an inspiring story. And third, they take on a content-marketing role, using digital tools to optimize content and metadata, amplify reach across multiple channels, and analyze learner data to improve outcomes. Since curators are often subject-matter experts, they may need to be trained in the art of digital dissemination. Tools that automate workflows, enable multichannel publishing, and offer user-behavior dashboards can certainly help curators learn while promoting a standard curation approach across the organization.

Capability checklist:

- Leaders champion curation by investing in the system and rewarding and recognizing successes.
- We have responsible and accountable curation owners, including a central governing body and designated curators across the organization.
- We have sufficient resources in place to support curation activity.
- Curators have the subject-matter expertise and skills needed to bridge content expertise and learning outcomes.
- We have effective mechanisms in place to evaluate curation outcomes, and to incentivize and reward those who curate and disseminate (not just create).

Access to high-quality content

Content can be housed in a growing number of asset-management systems and repositories "owned" by different groups. Content repositories can include centralized learning systems, knowledge libraries, business-unit or functional-group intranet sites and newsletters, channels for collaboration and knowledge sharing (for example, Slack, Trello, email groups), file-sharing systems (for example, Box, Sharepoint), and even hard drives on individual laptops. As technology becomes cheaper and easier to adopt, more "shadow systems" (for example, intranet sites for departments or groups within a company) are deployed by different parts of the organization for their specific purposes. But these repositories tend to be siloed. Acting as distinct entities, they often don't communicate with one another or share a common architecture, taxonomy, or metadata. Trying to source or search content in these systems is time consuming and confusing, and curators and learners often find duplicative and conflicting content—or don't find what they need at all. In the end, people spend more time trying to navigate and reconcile the overwhelming mess than learning from the content that exists.

Of course, many people research external content sources as well. Increasingly, learners can find excellent learning material at low or no cost through a simple internet search. By including external content in their selections, curators can spend less time on creating content and more on reaching the learner. With a well-curated content management system, small organizations can offer learning curricula to rival those of large organizations.

To be effective, curators must have access to a stream of high-quality internal and external content with rich metadata, easily discoverable by searching a shared classification schema. We suggest that curators focus the majority of their efforts on selecting and organizing content rather than searching for it or reconciling inconsistencies.

Capability checklist:

- Curators build collections using an array of digital asset types, from both internal and external sources.
- Curators track trends, sourcing content on emerging thinking about critical topics.
- Content is organized and maintained using a common classification schema (for example, by topic, by proficiency level) and consistent metadata to aid discovery and management of content.
- Content is organized and published in ways that support priorities.
- Curators use feedback loops to understand consumption patterns and user experience and to manage content.

Deliberate, repeatable curation processes

While access to high-quality content is a core component of good curation, it's not true that "if you build it, they will come." Learners are deluged with content from multiple sources. Yet many organizations have not outlined clear processes or best practices for curation beyond trying to capture content, leaving curators to figure out how to reach learners on their own—often reinventing the wheel or making rookie mistakes.

To get the right content to the right learner at the right time, curators must take an end-to-end view. Curators should routinely conduct user research to understand the gaps between what learners need and what they get. They must actively manage content, not only by bringing new insights to learners but also by archiving outdated content. They should also rigorously evaluate the impact of their dissemination methods so they know which channels and tactics (push versus pull) work best for specific learner groups, topics, and objectives.

Capability checklist:

- Curators deeply understand learner needs and behaviors.
- We have effective processes for identifying, organizing, managing, publishing, and evaluating curated content.
- Curators follow established standards around different content types and channels.
- Curators know how to make curated content available to learners at the time of need and in the flow of their work (push versus pull).
- Processes are well understood, and followed, by curators across the company.
- Curators can connect as a community to share best practices and resolve issues.
- We have mechanisms to identify, prioritize, and implement workflow and process improvements.

Fit-for-purpose technology

Learners and learning professionals alike are turning to technology to help them find, package, and share curated resources. The market has responded with a broad arsenal of easy-to-use new tools and apps that enable users to quickly create videos and other content and package assets into dynamic, customized learning solutions. Learning-experience platforms are emerging to complement learning-management systems, streamlining (or automating) curation while offering a more engaging, personalized user experience (see sidebar, "Content curation in action"). Unfortunately, the promise of technology to help us wrangle the flow of information hasn't completely solved the problem; as Steven Rosenbaum explains in *Curate This,*[3] the robots are also drowning in content: "Digital overload is swamping the current recommendation engines, making the sharp knife of human editorial a better filter than the blunt instrument of algorithmic recommendation." In other words, while machines might help with tasks such as identifying broad trends within an industry, they're not ready to replace humans in tasks that involve nuance.

Technology is most effective when it enables or promotes a particular component of the curation system. For example, technologies that promote easier access to and discovery of content, digitize manual processes and workflows, and provide insight into user behavior and feedback can be extremely valuable. The most exciting technological advances are in the areas of asset management; knowledge graphs that can create relational connections across topics; and big-data technologies such as semantic search, natural language processing, and automated, virtual agents to enable one-to-one connections between learners and content. However, deploying these technologies is often easier said than done, as organizations wrestle with legacy systems and fragmentation. (For more on improving L&D's use of technology by optimizing the function's partnership with IT, see chapter 3.)

In the end, a fit-for-purpose application that delivers on a specific use case can be very effective, even if it cannot anticipate your learners' every need. By all means test and learn these new technologies and adopt them if they prove themselves to meet users' needs—but remember that great curation can often be accomplished by better leveraging the applications that your learners are already using.

Capability checklist:

- Our technology infrastructure facilitates our curation priorities.
- We have a user research panel composed of curators and learners who test and evaluate ideas before we make large investments.
- We actively test (and adopt) new technologies to digitize our workflows and improve the user experience through personalization, search, asset management, curator workflows, user feedback, behavioral tracking, and other means.

Content curation in action

After years of experimentation, a global financial services company was no closer to cracking the code on curation than when it started. Although learning-and-development (L&D) leaders had tried to take advantage of existing content repositories, incorporate curated content into learning journeys, and use social tools and wikis to disseminate great content, they still felt unable to curate and share content at the scale and pace their business required.

It wasn't until they turned their curation paradigm on its head that they started to make progress. "Just like in the other parts of our business, our L&D team realized we needed to offer a platform and facilitate [curation] transactions, instead of delivering the service ourselves," a global L&D leader at the company said. Instead of driving or managing curation centrally, "our priority is enabling curation and sharing by anyone in the company."

When the company looked beyond L&D, it found a number of highly skilled curators among its more than 50,000 employees. These "grassroots" curators were already adept at sharing cutting-edge insights with their colleagues and keeping them abreast of emerging technologies, market dynamics, and more.

"The best content, particularly in knowledge-driven parts of our business, like AI and robotics, was coming from subject-matter experts," the learning leader observed.

The organization set out to give these natural curators a larger stage and help them share even more effectively by, among other things, developing a new learning-experience platform and taking a user-centric approach. The L&D function also worked closely with "superusers" to create a technology platform, as well as processes and guidelines, that make it easier for curators to publish and easier for learners to navigate content.

In the true spirit of empowerment, when the platform launches, access won't be restricted to superusers. Anyone in the company will be able to curate content and set up a channel to share with others. "We worked with our superusers early on, but we embrace anyone who is interested in curating," the L&D leader said.

Company leaders recognize that this open approach carries potential risks; for example, multiple curators are likely to cover similar topics in their individual channels. They also expect to see content with less-than-optimal quality or content that doesn't reflect effective learning design, and they anticipate some challenges in defining and refining the taxonomy that streamlines content management and navigation for learners.

To mitigate these risks, they have built a powerful tool into the platform: user feedback. The platform relies on robust feedback loops—ratings, comments, view counts—so learners can share their opinions on the content they consume. L&D will monitor this feedback and share insights with the curators on what's working and what's not. Over time, poorly rated content will be removed, and the best curators will be rewarded. "We might even add [curation] as a formal part of their role and free up their time to share more," said the learning leader. In effect, curators will be accountable to learners for delivering high-quality, value-added content.

Despite the promise of the new platform, the company recognizes that it still has a long way to go on its curation journey. "We still feel we're at the beginning of our curation journey," the learning leader concluded. "Our role in L&D is changing. The learner will decide what's best."

Where to begin

It might be a bit cliché, but the first step in improving curation is to recognize that you have a problem. Learning leaders should first assess how well their organization is getting the right content to the right learner at the right time. Leaders can then identify where their capabilities are strong and where there are gaps. Estimating the impact of closing gaps, along with the relative ease or difficulty in doing so, helps prioritize where to invest first. And of course, the objective(s) must be clear. Some companies might focus on reducing the time employees spend looking for knowledge, while others might focus on providing content that teaches new skills or improves employee performance in existing skills. Still others might aim to increase the use of learning content, reduce costs by eliminating shadow systems, or improve content quality by consolidating, centralizing, and standardizing assets.

Once it's clear where to focus and how to measure impact, learning leaders can launch a change program to improve those

> Learning leaders should first assess how well their organization is getting the right content to the right learner at the right time. Leaders can then identify where their capabilities are strong and where there are gaps.

capabilities. Such a program can be designed as a special initiative or built out as a permanent center of excellence, depending on the perceived need for continuous improvement and accountability. With better curation, organizations can reduce the effort needed to find, learn, and apply new knowledge, thereby elevating the development of their employees. ■

1 Barry Schwartz, *The Paradox of Choice: Why More is Less,* New York: HarperCollins, 2004.

2 *Elliott Masie's Learning TRENDS,* "Badges for learners, on the job learning LAB, CES wrap up," post by Elliott Masie, January 12, 2015, trends.masie.com.

3 Steven Rosenbaum, *Curate This: The Hands-On, How-To Guide to Content Curation:* Magnify Media, 2014.

CHAPTER

09/

HOW TO IMPROVE EMPLOYEE ENGAGEMENT WITH DIGITAL LEARNING

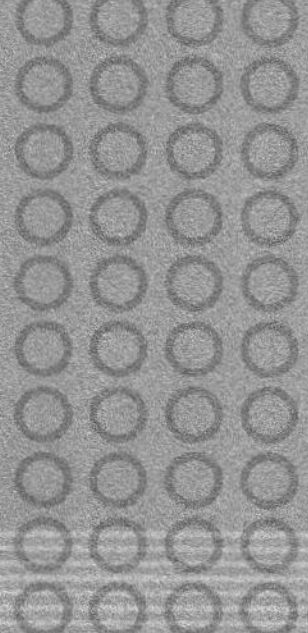

AUTHORS
Stephanie Gabriels
Maeve Lucey

To encourage better adoption and use of digital-learning material, L&D functions must focus on three key elements of behavior change–motivation, abilities, and triggers–and personalize learners' journeys.

Over the next 15 years, up to 375 million people will need to be upskilled or reskilled because their jobs will become automated.[1] The entire workforce will be reimagined—and learning-and-development (L&D) functions across industries will be tasked with training workers for the new reality. Digital learning will be a critical solution given its potential to develop employees when, where, and how they want.

Many companies already have extensive suites of digital-learning material available; research by the Association for Talent Development found that 45 percent of formal learning hours in 2016 were technology-based, up from 36 percent in 2009.[2] There are tremendous opportunities for organizations of all sizes to take advantage of the power of digital-learning solutions to develop their workforce at the speed of business.

Despite increasing financial and resource investments in digital learning by companies of all sizes, engaging learners remains a challenge. According to a recent LinkedIn survey, in fact, the number-one challenge in talent development is "getting employees to make time for learning"—more so than limited budgets, demonstrating return on investment (ROI), and the size of the

L&D team.[3] The same survey found that 58 percent of employees prefer to learn at their own pace, and 49 percent prefer to learn at the point of need. Digital learning is uniquely situated to meet these needs, but it currently falls short for a variety of reasons, including poor design of some digital-learning solutions, generic or outdated content, hefty time commitments, lack of clear expectations or incentives, and a generally lukewarm impression of digital learning largely driven by experience among employees who have participated in compliance e-learning solutions.

L&D efforts to combat these obstacles and engage employees in digital learning have mostly focused on improving the courseware by, for example, breaking up courses into shorter segments or investing in snazzy learning-management-system (LMS) interfaces. Learning designers have also adopted strategies from other digital media—such as gamification—with mixed results depending on the quality of and investment into digital-learning design.

But borrowed strategies are not sufficient to effect real change in learner engagement. L&D professionals must seek to understand learner behavior and how to influence it through personalized, easily accessible platforms that help employees form digital-learning habits. By applying a popular behavior-change model to the context of digital learners in corporate settings, L&D professionals can better engage learners and serve their organizations.

E-learning, then and now

When e-learning emerged in the 1990s, many companies viewed it as a cost-cutting measure and used it largely for compliance and other required training. Because learners had to complete these courses to maintain a professional license or as a requirement of their jobs, participation was mandatory—and engagement was assumed. And because these groups of learners had a shared, narrowly defined learning need, the courses could be designed for large groups of people with little customization of the content from one learner to another.

Today, organizational learning has shifted its focus away from formal, mandatory courses—causing a dramatic drop in learner participation—to a more learner-centered environment. At the same time, digital-learning formats and channels are increasingly sophisticated and diversified, creating a potentially overwhelming number of options and competing priorities for learners.

To design platforms that spark learner engagement and form digital-learning habits, L&D professionals must follow the lead of disruptive product designers by applying the principles of psychology to understand employee behavior. A key component of this effort is to build a library of carefully curated and categorized content from both internal and external sources. (For details on this process, see chapter 8.) L&D professionals must also implement digital applications that can build personalized packages of content and predict future learning needs based on a robust set of data about each individual learner.

The role of behavior in digital-learning engagement

Behavioral psychology examines why humans behave the way they do. In recent years, researchers in this burgeoning field have demonstrated that a clear understanding of motivations and stimuli can help us modify negative or destructive behaviors—at both the personal and the institutional levels. Private- and public-sector organizations alike have established behavior units to achieve this goal.

Behavioral psychologist BJ Fogg, the founder of Stanford University's Behavior Design Lab and author of *Persuasive Technology: Using Computers to Change What We Think and Do,* developed a new way of thinking about behavior called the Fogg Behavior Model. According to the model, engagement in certain behaviors depends on three things: motivation, ability, and a trigger (or cue). If one of these elements is misaligned, the desired behavior does not occur. To engage employees in learning, then, L&D professionals must understand the motivations, abilities, and triggers underlying their learners' behavior. They can use this understanding to design digital-learning solutions that help learners build desired behaviors into habits.

Understanding learner motivation

According to Fogg, "when motivation is high, you can get people to do hard things."[4] Chapter 5 of this book describes how to boost intrinsic motivation by helping employees build lifelong-learning mind-sets. However, even when learners have such deep-seated motivation, L&D must design external motivators to help overcome the myriad situations and cognitive biases of learners (discussed below).

To better understand the motivations behind learners' decisions and actions, L&D professionals should conduct a thorough analysis of usage data on platforms and courseware as well as data collected via interviews and surveys. For example, the data might show that disengaged learners don't see the point of engaging in a certain program that is designed for long-term benefit rather than short-term performance support. The collection of data can be synthesized through the creation of empathy maps, which help L&D professionals better understand their learners' perspective. (For more on empathy maps, see chapter 13.)

Understanding learner ability

Enhancing people's abilities by making tasks simpler is where product designers see the most return on their investment. In our experience, however, increasing simplicity (that is, ability) is one of L&D's biggest barriers to increasing digital engagement. As Fogg puts it, "Simplicity is a function of your scarcest resource at that moment. Think about time as a resource; if you don't have 10 minutes to spend, and the target behavior requires 10 minutes, then it's not simple."[5]

Indeed, a critical barrier for many learners—beyond time—is that formal digital learning is not part of their daily routine. Learners are generally not in the habit of seeking out answers in digital courseware—or they may not know where to look for what they need. Furthermore, people's perceptions of themselves may deter them from seeking out formal learning on a digital platform (see sidebar, "Overcoming the cognitive biases that impede learning"). For example, they may feel they have all the knowledge they need to do their current job.

Given that neither of these barriers involves content, L&D budgets might be better spent on providing greater access to its often large catalog of existing offerings than on creating new offerings. The L&D team can advocate for learning systems that prioritize the user experience, make efficient use of time, and integrate easily into existing employee habits. L&D will need to work closely with IT to develop a shared language and clear purpose in order to design a great user experience. (For more on the relationship between L&D and IT, see chapter 3.)

Building triggers

Well-designed, persistent triggers can help turn a one-off behavior into a habit. In the learning context, triggers tend to involve strategic communications—for example, using software plug-ins to insert hyperlinks to relevant courseware into an employee's workflow or into the signature lines of relevant automated emails, as well as promoting applicable courseware through regular processes such as quarterly manager meetings. Triggers can be especially useful in helping learners overcome their own cognitive biases by nudging them in directions they might not have chosen otherwise. (See sidebar, "Overcoming the cognitive biases that impede learning.")

L&D budgets might be better spent on providing greater access to its often large catalog of existing offerings than on creating new offerings.

Creating learning triggers is currently a manual process, but we envision a future in which nudges will be automated—for example, employees starting a new project might automatically receive an email with a list of relevant courses or content. To implement automated nudging, however, L&D functions will have to incorporate a much greater degree of personalization in their digital-learning platforms.

Building habits

Before trying to influence employee behavior, L&D professionals need to consider some fundamental questions: What do they need their audience to do? What habits does the audience need to form? What habits can L&D build from? What *is* working, and how can L&D do more of it? Most of us want our audiences to seek out learning on our central technology platform, for example. How realistic is that expectation?

Overcoming the cognitive biases that impede learning

Cognitive biases are common, systematic errors in rational thought that can prevent people from learning (Exhibit 9A). Learning-and-development professionals can persuade learners to go against their own (often unconscious) biases by using a variety of communication techniques as triggers.

Course titles, descriptions, and communications must set clear expectations of time commitment and effort. They must also answer the question, "So what?" L&D must ensure they are in line with learners' expectations by being explicit about not only what they'll learn but also what they will tangibly gain or lose from the time invested. For example, a course description might include: "This 30-minute course will save you an hour every time you enter a new employee into the people-management system."

Exhibit 9A: **Learning-and-development functions can overcome cognitive biases with strategic, persuasive communications.**

Cognitive bias	How to overcome it
Framing effect: People are influenced by presentation.	Pay attention to how learners perceive L&D communications; present learning programs as important opportunities for learners to invest in themselves rather than as requirements.
Social deviance: People hesitate to deviate from social norms.	Leverage FOMO (fear of missing out) by highlighting course popularity with learners' colleagues and individuals in similar job descriptions.
Loss aversion: People are more motivated to act by fear of losing something than by hope of gaining something.	Design communications that emphasize not only benefits of courses for participants but also potential losses for nonparticipants. Make course completion and credit time bound; remind learners of expiration date to motivate them to return and finish.
Overconfidence: People often overestimate their abilities, decreasing motivation to learn more.	Be very specific about learning outcomes to help participants recognize gaps in knowledge and ability.
Endowed progress effect: People are more motivated to complete something if they've started already and can see progress.	Drive continued engagement by defining groups of courseware and showing progress toward overall program goals. Include a required or popular module at the beginning of a course so most people will finish, see how much they've completed, and be motivated to continue.
Anchoring effect: People use one piece of information to make decisions.	Rather than cite multiple reasons why learners should take a course, cite single most powerful reason for a given audience.

Learner data—courseware usage, surveys, and so forth—will help L&D professionals answer those questions, set realistic goals, and help employees build habits. Introducing a new tool or process during an in-person learning session can be an effective way to build learner habits. To do this, L&D should set an expectation that learners will use the tool after the program ends, teach learners how to use the tool, and finally, ask learners to commit to using it for a set period of time—weeks or months. This kind of commitment, especially when made alongside a cohort of peers, plays upon people's inclination to stick to social norms and increases that their use of the tool will turn into a habit.

The vanguard of L&D: Personalized, predictive digital learning

In our experience, employees are heavily biased against formal learning platforms that offer what they see as generic content. Such a perception can immediately sink motivation, even in the presence of persuasive communications and a flashy interface. In this era of hyperconnectivity and personalization, digital courseware must motivate learners by providing a highly personalized experience that adapts as learners move through the modules.

Few L&D functions have mastered personalized digital learning, but those at the vanguard are developing learning platforms that draw on individualized data about each learner to create customized learning experiences. These easy-to-use platforms, often referred to as learning-experience systems, are accessible from any device (including mobile) and can be built on top of learning-management systems. They collect data on each user's role, tenure, certifications, and relevant experience; they might also examine user opinions, preferences, and interests.

Using advanced analytics, the platform then crunches the data to predict individual learners' needs—the skills required to advance along an established career trajectory, for example—and then presents each learner with a customized, curated set of content and courseware. Courses may be chosen for an individual in a certain role because she shares characteristics with others who have given the courses a high rating, for example.

Even those beyond the vanguard have many opportunities for increased personalization. For example, the industry's will soon be equipped to enable learners to assess their own skills and create a plan for building them. Based on that information, the platform could then recommend learning opportunities. This future is not far off—and it will up the game in terms of digital-learning engagement.

■ ■ ■

In today's fast-paced workplace, few employees prioritize learning enough to make time for it in their busy schedules. Increasing engagement in digital learning must be a high priority for L&D professionals. To that end, L&D must look beyond the digital-learning approaches to which it is accustomed and use insights from behavioral psychology to build learning strategies and customizable platforms for the workforce of the future. By taking a habit-forming and personalized approach to learning engagement, L&D can set up learners, and businesses, for a successful future. ■

The authors would like to thank Tonya Corley and Matthew Joseph for their contributions to this chapter.

1 For more, see "What the future of work will mean for jobs, skills, and wages," McKinsey Global Institute, November 2017, on McKinsey.com.

2 *2017 state of the industry,* ATD Research, December 2017, td.org.

3 *2018 workforce learning report: The rise and responsibility of talent development in the new labor market,* LinkedIn Learning, 2018, learning.linkedin.com.

4 "3 core motivators, each with two sides," BJ Fogg's Behavior Model, accessed May 31, 2018, behaviormodel.org.

5 "Ability–make behavior simpler to do," BJ Fogg's Behavior Model, accessed May 31, 2018, behaviormodel.org.

CHAPTER

10/

CHANGING MIND-SETS AND BEHAVIORS:

Our role in personal and organizational change

AUTHORS
Terrence Hackett
John Sangimino
Nick van Dam

Organizational change is more likely to succeed when companies put proper focus on the ways people adapt, learn, and evolve.

As learning professionals, we are responsible for creating and implementing strategies and programs for growth and development. The research and technology available to us today enable more sophisticated approaches than ever before, yet we still find many instances when our learning solutions underdeliver relative to our desired impact. Even the most optimistic estimates suggest that these solutions translate into real behavior change in the workplace just 34 percent of the time.[1] As disruptive new business models, changing customer demands, and external factors continue to force significant, constant change requiring new knowledge and skills, learning professionals have to understand how to close that gap.

To start, we must focus on how individuals can adapt and evolve through mind-set and behavior change. Changing mind-sets is crucial for developing people over the long term; for employees to grow, develop, and obtain important new skills, they need a mind-set that allows them to become the best version of themselves. Carol Dweck, a leading researcher on this topic and the author of *Mindset: The New Psychology of Success,* calls the belief in one's ability to constantly improve and build new skills a growth mind-set. People with a fixed mind-set, by contrast, believe that their qualities are largely carved in stone and determined by birth—that their intelligence, personality, and creativity are all fixed and cannot be developed. This mind-set is extremely limiting, but it can be changed.[2] In organizations, we encounter both mind-sets and various behaviors we seek to change for better learning and development (L&D) outcomes, and ultimately better business outcomes.

A model for changing mind-sets and behavior

To address mind-set change, we turn to a framework McKinsey has written about and used for many years, known as the "influence model." The influence model lays out four actions that can drive mind-set and behavior change and is based on an extensive review of academic research, as applied through practical experience.

The influence model recommends four actions to bring about change: fostering understanding and conviction, reinforcing changes through formal mechanisms, developing talent and skills, and role modeling (Exhibit 10A). All four must function in concert to achieve sustained change. These levers are rooted in human nature—from how we react to and perceive change to our unconscious behaviors. Incorporating these four actions into L&D design can help with change and learning adoption.

Exhibit 10A: **The influence model addresses four different areas necessary for change.**

Fostering understanding and conviction

People understand what's being asked of them and that it makes sense. Knowing the "why" behind the change helps support its adoption.

Reinforcing mechanisms

People view the structures, processes and systems with which they interact as supporting the changes they are being asked to make.

"**I will** change my mind-set and behavior **if . . .**"

Developing talent and skills

People can develop the skills needed and are given the opportunities necessary to behave in the expected new way.

Role modeling

People see and are influenced by leaders, colleagues, and staff all behaving the same way. People tend to mimic those around them, both consciously and unconsciously.

Challenges in incorporating the influence model often are rooted in time and resource constraints. When organizations are reacting quickly to marketplace shifts or other external factors, learning professionals can often feel rushed to get a program underway and fail to use the model when structuring it. But making small changes and incorporating elements of these four actions can add up to a larger systemic effect.

Just as organizational change is challenging, personal change can be equally difficult. The good news is that our brains are up to the challenge. Insights from neuroscience reveal that throughout our lives, our brains remain amazingly "plastic"—making us capable of learning and adopting a positive approach to change. Neuroscience also provides strong evidence that techniques like mindfulness can help us stay calm in the midst of the volatility, uncertainty, complexity, and ambiguity that can seem so ever-present in our lives. By seeking and maintaining the proper mind-set, we can control our thinking, reduce stress, and stay focused and positive, which is an important part of learning and behavior change.

Here, we explore the influence model in more detail to understand the strong interplay that should exist between the design of individual learning experiences and the broader framework for change. In doing so, organizations can truly realize the potential of learning programs and strategies.

Fostering understanding and conviction

Clear communication is crucial—people need to know the "why" behind the change. Before asking colleagues to make a change in their mind-set or behavior, leaders need to provide them with a purpose for the change, why it's important, and expected outcomes—essentially, a change story. This helps people understand the change and believe in its purpose, which makes them empowered to act. Research shows that a transformation is 5.8 times more likely to be successful at organizations where CEOs communicate a compelling change story.[3] It's easy to assume that the rationale is clear to everyone, or to assume that "growth" and "skills development" alone serves as a change story. But to persuade people to change something as foundational as a mind-set or behavior, they need more to go on.

Reinforcing with formal mechanisms

Sustained behavior change requires regular reinforcement. In a professional environment, formal mechanisms—processes, structures, and systems—must align with the behavior or mind-set change and reinforce its importance. Reinforcement can come in different forms, including rewards or incentives; feedback and performance reviews; or process changes. For example, as part of a project management training for junior employees we might encourage them to adopt certain behaviors to improve their project management. If they're not evaluated on these behaviors during a performance review, there is little incentive to change.

Reinforcing through gamification and rewards

Game designers have known for a long time how to engage, challenge, and reward people. Much has been written about the link between game design and learning; for instance, James Paul Gee, author of *What Video Games Have to Teach Us about Learning and Literacy,* spelled out 36 learning principles that good game design follows.[4] This has led to the rise of gamification, particularly in the L&D space, as designers apply game-like principles to learning programs—rich context, options for multiple skill levels, immediate feedback (in a video game, a "ding!" signals a successful move), and a reward system. Games, then, can serve as a way to reinforce the importance of the behavior and mind-set change we ask of our professionals.

In one example, a learning team was tasked with changing how an automotive client's national salesforce talked about the characteristics of the client's new car line. To do so, the team created a series of online games. The games were short and relatively simple, and they caught on quickly. Data collected showed that people were playing the games well into the night. Through interviews, we learned that the games were successful because they were fun, fueled a sense of healthy competition, and helped the sales force adjust their talking points about the cars' features before heading to the showroom floor the next morning. The games helped reinforce the change their employer wanted them to adopt.

Rewards can shape behavior and change, but organizations have to be mindful of what motivates people. One of the findings we've seen over time is that small, unexpected gestures can have a disproportionate effect. Games, badges, and other ways people can share their knowledge and demonstrate their expertise can be very motivating. While money is often used as a reinforcement mechanism to support change, it's the most expensive way to motivate people, and thus more difficult to secure than small rewards. Small gestures provide motivating impact without the challenges that come with monetary compensation.

Being mindful of what motivates each individual

Remember that what motivates one person may not motivate another. While it's important to tell a broad story of change, we also need to let people tell their own stories.

Motivation is particularly important in designing learning. Two of the most significant factors in learner motivation are autonomy and connectivity. In their book *Changing Employee Behavior,* authors Nik Kinley and Shlomo Ben-Hur write that autonomy—the sense of being in control and having choice—is the "single most important ingredient for feeling intrinsically motivated to do something." In the learning field, we may shy away from offering choices to learners because variation creates complexity. Individualized options might be costly and hard to deliver, whether in a classroom or digitally. However, choices are highly motivating for learners because they offer a way to personalize the experience.

At a recent program for a large cohort of learners at McKinsey, choice was a key factor in the design for a hands-on solution. The approach, called "The Art of the Possible," presented ten unique learning stations within a large physical space. Learners could choose their own path through the space, visiting stations that interested them and spending as much or as little time there as they liked. The learners were motivated by the autonomy—instead of spending time in areas they'd already mastered, they could determine their own path based on what would give them the most value. In a post-session survey, participants praised the variety of formats, the interactive nature of the stations, and the option to spend their time as they wished.

Another influencing factor for motivating learners is connection—or, as Kinley and Ben-Hur call it, "relatedness."[5] As they describe it, people need to feel a sense of connection to what they are doing and see the purpose in it. They need to connect with a goal personally, understand how to achieve it, and relate to it on a very practical level. Along the same lines, we have consistently found that people are highly motivated by connections with other individuals who share their journey or experience.

While digital solutions help scale learning programs and reach people when it's convenient for them, the connectivity offered by live programs is essential and highly motivating. Many organizations tend to have people spread out all over the world, each with demanding jobs. Coming together physically for several days gives people a chance to rejuvenate, strengthens connections, and helps reinforce a "one-goal" culture. Live programs can help change mind-sets in a variety of important ways. They create time and space away from the pressures of the workday for people to reflect. They offer opportunities to learn

We have consistently found that people are highly motivated by connections with other individuals who share their journey or experience.

and draw inspiration from others. They also give us time to connect, share stories, and build relationships—tapping into the core reality that humans are social creatures and have an intrinsic need to be around other humans. Our need for connection and relatedness never ends.

Build a supportive environment

Change requires support, consistency, and proper incentives. There must be harmony between the structures, processes, and systems of an organization and the experience of learners in the classroom, or important lessons may fall flat. A supportive environment, especially in a fast-paced business world, is a priority for many business leaders. Laszlo Bock, former head of people operations for Google and current CEO of Humu, says that he aspires to a "high-freedom environment" where people feel empowered and can learn and grow. "One of the things that make great teams work is a sense of psychological safety, that people feel comfortable raising their voice," he says.[6]

The task of building a supportive environment is too often overlooked. As a result, an organization often sends mixed messages about change. It's as if you ran a collaborative training session for your employees but failed to set up the workspace in a way that fosters collaboration; the environment we create must match the message. Fortunately, many creative opportunities exist to help us provide a supportive environment for learners.

Developing talent and skills

Learning professionals spend much of their time understanding how people develop talent and skills and designing programs to help them do so. When it comes to behavior and mind-set change, learning professionals must ensure that people are equipped with the right skills and talent to make that change. When designing learning programs that support change, the L&D function should focus on learner needs and mind-sets.

Learn about your learners to guide change

As learning professionals, we've had plenty of conversations with business leaders that involve the statement, "We need a training program for this topic." In the rush to deliver, we quickly assemble a classroom session to address the need, but despite our best intentions it can fall short of the objective. In our haste to create it, we may have ignored clues from our learners—about their needs and mind-sets—that are crucial to understanding how we can provide the skills training they need to help them change their mind-sets and behaviors. In our role, we must be relentlessly curious about our learners. Equipping the learner with the skills and talent they need to change is often about designing programs that are feasible given their constraints.

In one example, an L&D function launched a program to assist a group of learners on the topic of entrepreneurship and client development. The learners knew the importance of entrepreneurship and applying an entrepreneurial approach to develop new clients more effectively, but they were lacking a structure, roadmap, best practices, and time to practice the necessary entrepreneurial skills. Early diagnostic information showed that there was a knowledge gap for the learners. But as the L&D team gleaned more information from the interviews, they understood that the learners actually had the skills and some of the knowledge; the learning barriers that emerged were lack of time, not having an overall structure that fit their schedule, and the need for ongoing, helpful guidance. The learners wanted more—but they didn't know how to articulate their specific needs or what would work for them.

Using various inputs, the L&D team identified the core objectives of the learning program and what the learners should focus on to adopt more entrepreneurial behaviors and mind-sets: developing a strategy to contact the right clients with a compelling message; conducting successful first meetings; building awareness of risks and opportunities; communicating new, innovative solutions more strategically; and best practices for writing proposals, including pricing models and writing techniques. Knowing that time and lack of structure were an issue, the L&D team designed a program that would address those.

The solution embedded the topic of entrepreneurship into their daily work over a period of 14 weeks, making it suitable for learners without having to devote extra time to the program. As part of day-to-day client service, the learning program offered short, digital, mobile-friendly tips and advice on relevant topics, plus access to coaching from a senior colleague. They had a clear structure for adopting an entrepreneurial mind-set and behaviors, and checkpoints throughout the program. The combination of work, coaching, and small chunks of mobile-accessible digital content proved successful; numerous survey results showed that learners were changing the way they prepared for meetings; adopted broader, long-term perspectives; and were truly excited about the program and the opportunities it provided.

The key thing L&D professionals must focus on as they help learners develop talent and skills is that the solutions must be tailored to learners to be successful. There's great potential for mind-set and behavior change when the path to those skills is clear and the solution is easy to adopt.

Role modeling

Before people can begin changing their own mind-sets, they need to see change in their leaders and colleagues. People take their cues from influencers around them, and they need to see change in action.

For example, people in many organizations struggle with burnout. They don't take time off, and their work-life balance is unhealthy. Communication about balance and well-being may not do the trick; employees may feel like they've heard the message repeatedly but it differs from the actual expectations or the company culture. To change this thinking, the organization can take a top-down approach and leaders can role model the change they want to see. A quick story about their own vacation or an encouraging email before a long holiday weekend can help demonstrate the behavior that the organization wishes to see in others.

L&D professionals can use this concept in learning solutions to bring behavior and mind-set change to life for learners.

Live and digital role modeling

Live simulations provide a prime opportunity to see expertise in action and for leaders to role model specific actions and behaviors that we want learners to adopt. In L&D, we use role modeling simulations in a wide variety of contexts –for example, helping team leaders work with team members with different backgrounds and areas of expertise, or practicing dialogue skills such as getting to know a new client or conducting a difficult conversation. All of these require practice. It can be uncomfortable to try, as people don't always want to be seen as lacking a given skill—but a safe environment allows learners to see others displaying the goal behavior they want to change, get input from a more experienced colleague, and practice the behavior without fear of failure. As people open themselves up to constructive feedback, they can grow and apply what they've learned on the job. (For a more in-depth look at feedback in organizations, see chapter 15.)

Opening the door to feedback and being comfortable with failure requires resilience, which is one of the key characteristics differentiating a growth mind-set from a fixed mind-set. Carol Dweck posits that people with a growth mind-set are continually seeking opportunities to practice, learn, and receive guidance on what they can do better. They may fail or receive a negative result in a situation, but their resilience allows them to bounce back and use the experience to direct their next steps and future attempts. Those with a fixed mind-set, she writes, lack the resilience and confidence to see a setback as a learning opportunity. Instead, they see it as confirmation of their failings.[7]

Role modeling is a powerful way to build resilience in people, but given busy schedules and the cost of running live programs, what other options exist? Digital role modeling offers one creative solution. One L&D team created a customized program that allowed learners to observe two versions of a client situation: a "good" scene and a "better" scene. In between, they weighed in on how well the consultant handled the situation and compared their thoughts with those of senior experts. This form of digital role modeling is a valuable complement to live practice sessions, and one that is highly accessible—digital scenarios are available on learners' phones and can serve as quick reminders or mini-practice sessions.

Shlomo Ben-Hur and Nik Kinley also reference role modeling in *Changing Employee Behavior*, noting that psychological capital is a key to behavior change. "Whether you call it determination, perseverance, or sheer stubbornness, the inner strength and steel to keep going and not quit is a key component of psychological capital," they write.[8] Changing behavior almost always involves setbacks of some sort, so being able to move on from them is critical. While much of the research on this topic has focused on children who have overcome difficulties, Ben-Hur and Kinley note that an increasing body of work demonstrates that resilience is just as important in the workplace.[9]

One L&D team created a customized program that allowed learners to observe two versions of a client situation: a "good" scene and a "better" scene. In between, they weighed in on how well the consultant handled the situation and compared their thoughts with those of senior experts.

Simulations can also help identify and diagnose mind-sets to provide learning professionals with the information they need to guide their learners. When transitioning to a new role, for example, there are a number of mind-set shifts involved. On a client service team, associates or managers own the complex problem of a given client study. Associate partners or more senior level team members need to adopt a broader role, working to understand the client on a more holistic level and taking a broader perspective on the client's business. To ease the transition, L&D teams can construct immersive role plays that allow learners to work on these new skills. It's also important to include feedback sessions from peers and experienced partners, who can help the learning team focus deliberately on behavioral clues that indicate the learner is not in the proper mind-set. Beyond the confines of these multiday programs, small working teams and coaches remain in virtual contact to support learners as they make this important transition into their new role. (For an in-depth look at immersive learning, refer to chapter 14.)

■ ■ ■

Changing mind-sets and behaviors can be a challenge. For L&D professionals tasked with making their programs more effective, prioritizing these four actions—fostering understanding and conviction, reinforcing through formal mechanisms, developing talent and skills, and role modeling—can help. Often the need for a quick training or various activities prevent learning professionals from incorporating these actions into solutions. Doing so, however, can spur lasting behavior and mind-set change that benefits both the individuals and the organization. ■

1 Monica Belcourt and Alan M. Saks, "An investigation of training activities and transfer of training in organizations," *Human Resource Management*, November 2006, Volume 45, Number 4, pp. 629–48.

2 Carol S. Dweck, *Mindset: The New Psychology of Success*, New York, NY: Ballantine Books, 2006.

3 "The power of people transformations: McKinsey Global Survey results," February 2017, McKinsey.com.

4 James Paul Gee, *What Video Games Have to Teach Us About Learning and Literacy,* New York, NY: St. Martin's Press, 2003.

5 Shlomo Ben-Hur and Nik Kinley, *Changing Employee Behavior: A Practical Guide for Managers*, Houndmills, Basingstoke, Hampshire: Palgrave Macmillan, 2015.

6 Dan Bigman, "Former Google people chief Laszlo Bock on the future of leadership," *Chief Executive*, March 12, 2018, chiefexecutive.net.

7 Dweck, *Mindset: The New Psychology of Success.*

8 Ben-Hur and Kinley, *Changing Employee Behavior.*

9 Ben-Hur and Kinley, *Changing Employee Behavior.*

CHAPTER

11/

MARKETING THE IDEA OF LIFELONG LEARNING

AUTHORS
Sara Diniz
Allison Stevenson

Cut through the clutter and encourage colleagues to take advantage of learning opportunities with a product marketing approach.

Disruption pervades today's business world. Emerging digital approaches, including artificial intelligence and advanced analytics, are changing the way we work and connecting us globally in unprecedented ways. The most innovative organizations are meeting these disruptions head-on by augmenting their learning-and-development (L&D) functions in targeted ways, using cognitive brain research, innovative technologies, and learner-focused design. Learning functions are scaling their teams and efforts, becoming more professional, and curating world-class content to fill the growing number of capability gaps. Many organizations provide learners with access to a thoughtfully planned catalog of thousands of digital-learning solutions.

Despite these investments, learner engagement remains a challenge. Learners often are unaware of the content available, the strategic imperative to use it, and—most importantly—how using it will benefit them personally. L&D professionals find that the impact from their efforts comes up short compared to the time and money invested in understanding learner needs, curating great content, and designing the best curricula.

Digital technologies can help L&D functions serve up opportunities for personalized learning journeys; immersive, on-demand resources; and even machine-learning-driven course suggestions. But are your learners visiting these digital-learning platforms? Are they aware of the many digital solutions you've tailored to meet their learning needs and prepare them to confront the changing landscape? How can you get your learners to listen?

Why is it hard to get learners' attention?

Learner engagement is an issue for institutions across the board. In one recent study, for example, two-thirds of L&D professionals reported difficulty in engaging employees with learning opportunities.[1] Business leaders agree that information overload is one of the key obstacles they face in engaging learners. In a recent study from Bersin, Deloitte Consulting LLP, 68 percent of leaders agreed that the number-one factor preventing knowledge workers from thriving is an "overwhelming volume of information" that "makes it difficult to notice and keep track of useful information." In second place, with 34 percent of respondents, was "lack of effective tools (such as search)," making it "difficult to find the most useful information to use" (Exhibit 11A).[2]

Exhibit 11A: **Knowledge workers don't have the tools to cut through information clutter.**

What do you believe holds back knowledge workers in your organization?, %

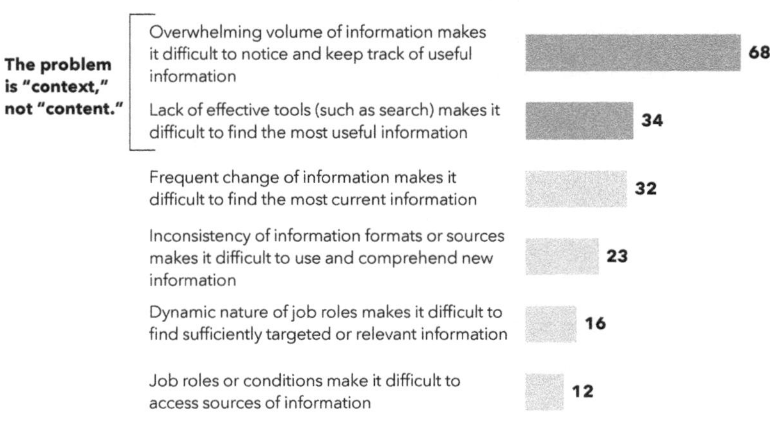

Source: Bersin, Deloitte Consulting LLP

The challenge, then, is to find a way to help learners navigate through the sea of information, capture their attention, and pique their interest in new approaches. The organizations that put the proper emphasis on reaching learners and getting them to actually learn will pull ahead in building the workforce of the future.

A new approach

You might have all the courses, tools, and technology required to support your learners' tactical needs, but you still need a strategy to engage learners. Even the best-equipped learning functions need marketing support. Your learners are already facing an increasingly challenging workload, so the mere existence of learning materials won't inspire them to do more.

Here we can borrow a page from companies that are at the forefront of marketing and cognitive science. Consumer product companies dedicate substantial budgets to product development, marketing, business development, and sales. This approach ensures that the products are high quality and meet consumers' needs—and also that consumers can quickly identify that these beneficial products exist and easily access them. L&D departments should take a close look at better integrating their course and material (or "product") development with marketing and communications efforts.

Consumer product companies dedicate substantial budgets to product development, marketing, business development, and sales.

Udemy, an online learning and teaching marketplace, uses a marketing-based framework to promote its online courses much like product companies approach the launch of a new consumer product (Exhibit 11B).

Using a marketing-based framework can help structure your thinking and focus your efforts on the strategic communications that are necessary to build learning mind-sets. Working through a set of organized elements fosters thoughtful analysis and planning, which in turns supports successful execution. Communicating to a large audience of learners is not straightforward, but applying a framework and answering the following questions will help.

- *How are you communicating?* Your learners lead busy lives, so messages about learning can feel intrusive and annoying. Don't make it worse by using corporate speak or corporate objectives that they have to deconstruct. Simplify your message and convey a clear benefit to the learner.

Exhibit 11B: **A four-pronged marketing approach can encourage learning adoption.**

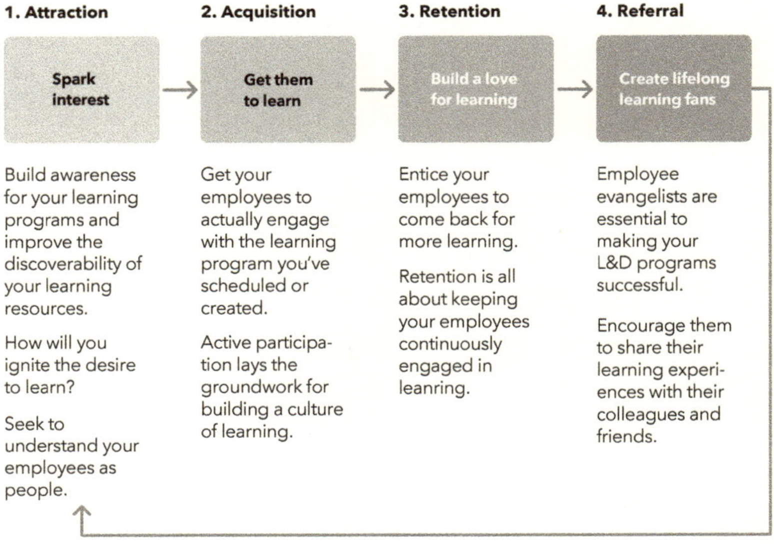

Source: Yvonne Chen, "Four marketing steps to ignite workplace learning," Udemy, March 2017, business.udemy.com

- *Who are your learners?* Understand your learners inside and out. It's not enough to understand organizational roles; we need to understand what learners need, how to address their challenges, and what inspires them to action.

- *How are you reaching learners?* Strong branding and messaging can help you build a distinctive learning program. Learners are more likely to notice and remember your communications if you use consistent nomenclature, relevant language, and distinctive visuals (such as colors, fonts, and logos). Also, take advantage of all the communication channels accessible to your learners to reach them when they are most open to your message.

A product-marketing strategy for learning

Learning engagement and adoption is a sizable challenge, but it is not insurmountable. There are a few core strategies learning professionals should consider as they design and implement a product-marketing-based approach to engage learners.

Set a clear vision early

Define how learning will help the organization advance, and how learning ties into the big picture for the future of the company. At the heart of every vision is a specific and purposeful "why." Articulating and refining a vision statement gives everyone the same clear focus and direction, which should guide individuals on each new learning journey.

Everyone must buy into the organization's shared vision, especially executive stakeholders and the L&D function, and it should be easy for learners to understand. A unified vision transcends all levels of the organization, focusing on one common goal. If the vision is too complicated, it will inevitably complicate the strategy and execution—and eventually undermine the goal of creating a robust learning environment and changing learners' mind-sets.

The vision must be unique and reflect the organization's DNA. It must be relevant and echo the language and values of the organization. Keep messaging simple, actionable, and direct. The vision is where you introduce the learning function as a trusted and strategic partner to each individual learner. Explain in simple terms why learners should be interested in using your learning content and demonstrate the clear benefits of doing so.

Get to know who your learners really are

Skip the superficial details. Getting to know your learners well gives you insights into how to influence their behavior and inspire them to learn. This task can be challenging and time consuming, but it pays off in better results. The findings from formal and informal research, surveys, focus groups, or learner-needs diagnostics uncover key themes and insights that translate into an actionable communication engagement plan. The approach you'll take depends on the complexity of the research results. Here are some tools to help you gather information about learners' wants and needs.

- *Learning-needs assessment:* an interview-based assessment focused on understanding the key wants and desires of a representative sampling of learners

- *Change-impact diagnostic:* both an interview-based and observational study to understand what impact the learners expect or desire

- *Focus group:* small, representative sample groups organized to discuss key questions and topics in an informal atmosphere to identify a common set of needs and insights

- *Stakeholder interviews:* targeted interviews to document the opinions, thoughts, and assertions of influential individuals throughout the organization

A typical time frame for studying learner needs is four to 12 weeks, depending on the size and complexity of the organization. It's important to develop the timeline with your organization's resources and priorities in mind. When you have completed the analysis and defined learners' wants and needs, you will have a solid, fact-based foundation on which to build your communication strategy.

Execute well, starting with a brand

Having a clear vision and a strong understanding of your learners' wants and needs will help clarify your approach to execution. The execution itself, though, usually involves a bit of grit and gusto.

Start by building a brand—one that is both relevant and visually appealing. Brands build memory structures that help link L&D opportunities, courses, and messages to distinctive, consistent icons and images, making your communications immediately recognizable and easier to process. This construction also helps build trust with learners; they know where the message is coming from.

Once you have your brand, you are ready to initiate your product launch. This moment is an opportunity to create a sense of intrigue and leave your learners wanting to know more. Learners have gotten used to the same old patterns of communication, so step outside the box and give them a reason to learn more. Teasers, games, and incentives are a great way to get learners excited about doing something big rather than just checking the box for mandatory training. Empower and incentivize learners to ask for more.

Once you have sparked your learners' curiosity, they will be open to hearing more from the learning function. Now you can focus communications on their learning journeys and opportunities, keeping the language centered on the target vision. The message, brand, actions, and communication channels must be part of a coherent strategy to resonate with learners in a meaningful, sustained way.

Brands build memory structures that help link L&D opportunities, courses, and messages to distinctive, consistent icons and images.

The communication plan should be a living, breathing plan that evolves with your learners over time. Your work in understanding and defining your learners' wants and needs will help you create a clear strategy for targeting learners with personalized messages. If you can reach learners on a more personal level, they are more likely to react or respond. As you build your communication plan, remember to:

- Clearly define your desired outcomes and how learning solutions will help you achieve them.
- Highlight how your learning solutions align with the organization's strategic priorities.
- Use a WIIFM (what's in it for me) messaging framework to inspire action.

Increase your reach through ongoing efforts that keep learning programs top of mind for learners. Employ multiple communications vehicles, such as email marketing, intranet articles, branding and signage in common spaces, and the messaging within the learning-management system. You can also involve people to serve as strategic influencers (for instance, line managers) to advocate and role model new norms. Invite your learners to rate and review your offerings, and serve as learning evangelists.[3] As leadership and change expert John Kotter put it, "Being relentless is key. This means role modeling with as many mechanisms as possible, as often as possible and involving as many people as possible."[4]

At every communication touch point, be sure that your messaging follows these principles:

- Reinforce the overall vision.
- Communicate simply, sharing the "why" and reinforcing with "how."
- Include a clear call to action to drive engagement.

Finally, to understand whether your communication engagement strategy is working, you need to articulate how you will measure effectiveness. Your options will vary based on your stakeholders' priorities and the technology, tools, and resources that are available to you. The simplest way to get started is to access existing data in your organization, such as end-of-program surveys, organizational health surveys, or LMS data on program registration and engagement. Leverage early findings to identify both successes and opportunities for improvement, then increase the sophistication of your communication engagement and measurement organically over time to meet the needs of your organization.

■ ■ ■

Using brand marketing strategies and tactics can help you cut through the clutter and capture learners' attention, which in turn creates a culture of learning that feels exciting to them. Don't give up, and don't succumb to the belief that most efforts to instill change are doomed to fail. You can build it, and if you properly market and communicate, they *will* come. ■

1 Dani Johnson and Todd Tauber, "The real challenge with learner engagement: L&D has a marketing problem," Bersin, Deloitte Consulting LLP, January 2015, bersin.com.

2 Bersin, Deloitte Consulting LLP.

3 Byron Sharp, *How Brands Grow: What Marketers Don't Know,* Oxford, UK: Oxford University Press, 2010.

4 John P. Kotter, *Accelerate: Building Strategic Agility for a Faster-Moving World,* Brighton, MA: Harvard Business Review Press, 2014.

CHAPTER

12/

HARNESSING ANALYTICS TO SHAPE THE LEARNING-AND-DEVELOPMENT AGENDA

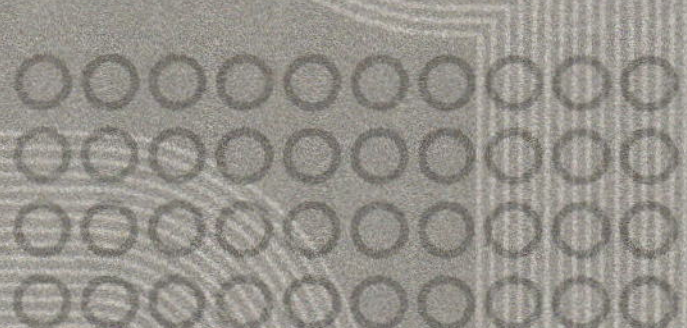

AUTHORS
Gina Fine
Gene Kuo
Maeve Lucey
Lois Schaub

Measurement and analytics have the power to dramatically increase the impact of learning and development across an organization.

More than ever, analytics is informing business decisions across industries and disciplines. Learning and development (L&D) is fairly new to analytics, relative to other business functions, but L&D professionals are finding that today's learning methods and programs offer a vast amount of data with the potential for rich analysis and insights.

Learning analytics is the practice of gathering, analyzing, and visualizing data to better understand, measure, and improve the impact of L&D programming, while strengthening an organization's overarching talent strategies.

At its core, learning analytics serves three primary purposes:

- Enabling better measurement and assessment of L&D performance, thus informing data-driven strategies to strengthen learning
- Augmenting L&D as a source of explanatory and/or predictive insight about employees (for example, as part of a talent-management strategy)
- Directly improving the engagement, effectiveness, and efficiency of L&D through adaptive and/or more personalized learning solutions

We're seeing more organizations pursue learning analytics in pursuit of these goals, and the field is rapidly gaining traction, attention, and investment. L&D organizations and leaders are introducing new methodologies, programs, technologies, and tools to meet the following organization-wide goals:

- *To improve talent-management practices:* Companies are beginning to invest in new L&D analytics platforms and technologies to capture patterns and trends related to talent. For example, new tools like the Experience API (xAPI) can capture how, when, and where top-performing employees are engaging in learning experiences. Acquiring this type of data in great breadth and depth, L&D professionals can uncover patterns in their learning behavior, which can be used to then predict other high performers while recognizing when and how to be more proactive about others.

- *To draw connections and understand business impact:* Some larger companies with great stores of data are taking a data-layering approach that ties highly granular learning-experience data to business performance metrics. By applying analytics to learning, companies can better tie their L&D function to business metrics.

- *To deliver personalized learning:* Access to large stores of data helps companies create new and personalized learning solutions based on patterns they see from employees. In one example, a financial services company used an automated platform to push tailored knowledge and learning microbursts to each call-center employee based on his or her demonstrated real-world behaviors (for example, a mishandling of a particular kind of customer issue on a call) and identified needs.

Access to large stores of data helps companies create new and personalized learning solutions based on patterns they see from employees.

Obstacles to building a learning-analytics capability

Despite the promise of learning analytics, and the ramp-up in investment and innovation we've already seen in the corporate and education sectors, a number of barriers have made it difficult for companies to make major strides.

It's a new discipline that's still taking shape

Learning analytics does not yet have fully established protocols, solutions, and technology. There is no standardized road map, so implementation takes more time and resources than some organizations are willing to invest. Many organizations lack the data architecture to harness learning analytics, making it difficult to accurately measure and mine for insights. Powerful data protocols that do exist—such as xAPI—are still in the early part of their adoption curves, as companies wrestle with what data they should even be capturing and how xAPI can best work alongside (or perhaps even replace) older, legacy learning-management systems (LMSs).

Because the discipline is still emerging, the body of proven business cases outside of educational contexts is small. This dearth of evidence makes it difficult for learning professionals to justify the investment in learning analytics, which involves various components—the right technology, capabilities, and data collection and architecture for analysis and insights, as well as corresponding investments in talent—including dedicated data scientists, data engineers, and "translators" who can turn raw model outputs into meaningful insights and recommendations.

Privacy, confidentiality, and context concerns

Learning traditionally takes place in a risk-free environment where learners feel protected from the consequences of their mistakes. Many solutions, such as simulations, are designed to let people fail, which can be a powerful learning experience. As organizations increasingly use learning data to inform their talent-management strategies, learning can start to feel more evaluative. This evolution must be addressed in a meaningful way to ensure that learners still get the most from their experiences and feel free to go through the process authentically.

Likewise, even though tailored, personalized learning is well intended, the use of certain kinds of data about an individual—such as past job performance—can be seen as invasive. Yet it is exactly this type of data that can supercharge personalization and spark broader improvement in learning programs. L&D professionals need to articulate the value of data use and ensure enough anonymity that learners feel comfortable.

Legacy mind-sets and a lack of communication strategy

Many learning professionals tend to use outdated approaches to data capture and measurement, such as administering lengthy surveys at the completion of a course. Today, new forms of learning—for example, microdigital learning, social learning, and performance-support solutions—require new data-collection methods and standards. Adopting these new methods requires a shift in mind-set. (For more on changing mind-sets, see chapter 10.)

A lack of communication strategy is often an obstacle preventing buy-in across the organization. It's important that learning teams create a communication plan to discuss these changes in data capture, solutions, and mind-sets. The communications should be clear and understandable across the organization to support investment in learning analytics as well as the use of existing data across teams and functions. Using the right language can help L&D coordinate with the overall talent-management system and learn from their data sources; for example, understanding whether learning solutions have had a measurable impact on a learner's performance review. An organization-wide communication strategy isn't always a top priority for learning departments, but it's important to open the door to a company-wide dialogue on learning analytics.

Crucial elements for success: A playbook for learning analytics

L&D leaders can strategically mitigate these obstacles by following seven crucial steps to ensure alignment and investment across the organization and maximize the value of learning analytics.

Establish a plan for measuring impact, including a vision and focus areas

Learning professionals need to align their work with business objectives. To that end, L&D departments must articulate a clear vision and goals and identify what's necessary to achieve the vision—focus areas, people and process updates, and technology needs. These elements serve as a foundation and strategic plan for the learning-analytics function (Exhibit 12A).

Exhibit 12A: **L&D functions should set a clear vision for learning analytics and what they need to achieve it.**

Example vision: Learning analytics will help determine L&D priorities and identify talent and skill gaps that the organization needs to advance its mission

Focus areas:

Measuring impact	**Integrating with people analytics**	**Personalizing learning**
Use data beyond traditional surveys.	Gain access to more data and link learning outcomes with "people outcomes" including development, advancement, and satisfaction.	Provide various approaches and adaptable programs for learners to tailor their experience.

People and process updates:

Develop a communication strategy.	Integrate learning analytics into existing processes (needs analysis, solution design, resource allocation).	Build learning analytics talent and skills.

Necessary technology:

Employ easy-to-use survey and assessment platforms.	Invest in modern reporting and data visualization tools, including new learning technology specifications such as xAPI.	

Develop a measurement strategy and identify data needs

Learning teams need to articulate their desired outcomes before they can decide what to measure and how. Corporate learning isn't as linear as it once was, and changes in digital, social, and informal learning are providing new avenues for data collection and changing the types of metrics L&D professionals can and need to track.

To meet these new demands, L&D professionals need to work closely with design and development teams to build measurement structures that facilitate the collection of comprehensive, accurate data. There are many data sources to connect—the LMS, people systems, survey systems, and other digital platforms. Without proper planning and partnerships with IT for a data warehouse, resources can be wasted on corralling data rather than analyzing it. And analyses must be tailored to what's important to the organization so that the L&D function can produce reports that business leaders will actually read and see real bottom-line impact.

A governing measurement framework can help an organization define what to measure, where to focus, and how to communicate performance. The model in Exhibit 12B illustrates the simple but important relationships among five key measurement elements: engagement, experience, impact, coverage, and cost.

Experience: Measuring the learning experience typically focuses on evaluating quality of faculty, environments, interfaces, and materials.

Engagement: We can no longer just assume that learners will engage with L&D programs, so learning engagement must be the starting point. Engagement is closely linked with experience, as even engaged learners need to have a positive experience to maximize the value of learning. Measuring the learning experience typically focuses on evaluating quality of faculty, environments, interfaces, and materials.

Exhibit 12B: **Learning-and-development functions should develop a framework for measuring performance.**

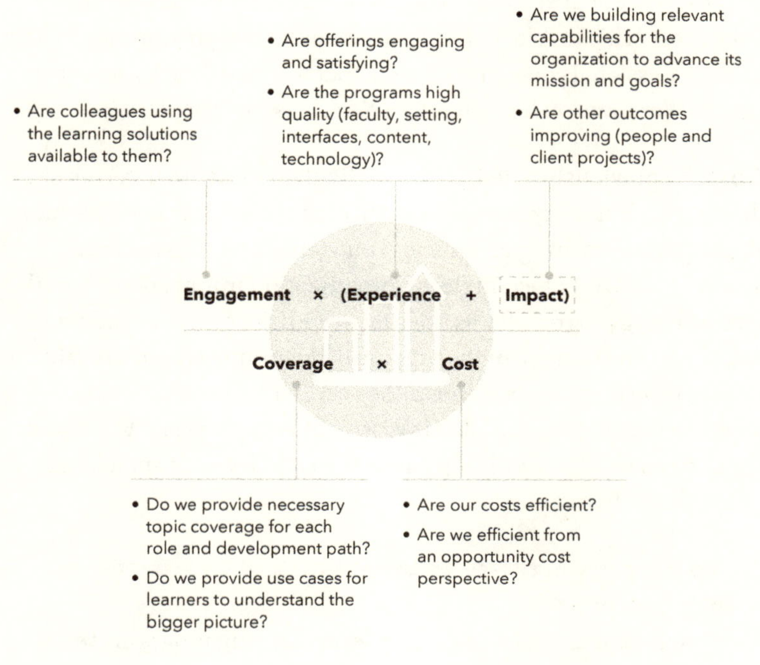

Impact: Traditionally, impact has been the most controversial dimension of learning measurement. Rather than trying to quantify return on investment (ROI)—which can present a challenge because so many variables are in play—L&D should measure impact in terms of strategic alignment with the business, whether the right capabilities are being built, and whether learning is supporting the organization in matters such as employee satisfaction, engagement, and retention. Each of these impact areas should be assessed using a mix of traditional metrics and advanced analytical approaches. The L&D industry knows that it needs to link learning to hard-data business outcomes such as sales performance. To find those links, L&D must work with business functions across the organization.

Coverage: The coverage element of the framework helps ensure that the L&D function provides learning programs that are not only effective but also inspiring—and that cover topics that are perceived to be most critical. A learning-needs analysis can provide data to help L&D professionals design programs that respond directly to learner needs. (For more on learning-needs analysis, see chapter 4.)

Cost: As previously noted, ROI is difficult to measure in terms of direct cost, but analytics and measurement can offer insights into the impact of learning on business outcomes and thus serve as a proxy for ROI. For example, an organization might spend heavily on a learning program for its sales team with the goal of improving sales. The L&D team can then quantify the improvement to evaluate whether the program was worth the cost. This type of question—whether the scale of the L&D investment is appropriate to achieve the desired results—will help gauge the right levels of spend and quantify the ROI.

Move from program- or course-centric views to learner-centric journeys

As more organizations design long-term learning programs that span delivery methods, themes, and content, it can become challenging to tie outcomes to one specific program, course, or training module. It's no longer sufficient to tie data to individual programs and courses with a survey; learning analysts can get more value from the data by shifting to a learner-centric view. A learner-centric, journey-based view looks at outcomes and activity through the lens of multiple learning modalities and experiences—in-person and digital; formal and informal; individual or group learning—to understand how they work together for the learner. This "journey view" can provide transformative insights to improve programs and processes for today's learners. For example, we can identify different behavioral segments or stages in the journey, which can inform how we market our offerings and at what stage learners benefit the most from different programs. The journey view also allows us to see how much of what we define as "core learning" to a particular group of employees is actually being consumed, and what the consumption patterns look like. Such a view would also include course-agnostic data that provides insight into capability levels and needs for a group of learners over time, which in turn helps inform shifts in curricula strategy and identify areas for increased learning investment.

Learn from the education space

One New York–based organization, New Classrooms, took a learner-centric approach to analytics, using data to provide customized daily lessons for students. This solution was based on the knowledge that any given classroom includes students at multiple skill levels, and even the best teachers can't consistently differentiate lessons for 30 students. Students also come to class with different learning styles: some learn best online, while others need to work one-on-one with a teacher. New Classrooms uses a technology platform to diagnose and assess each student's current learning and then customize curricula, skill libraries, and lesson banks to provide exactly what each student needs. Lessons are followed by assessments that provide rich, actionable feedback.

Corporate L&D instructors are often in the same boat—learners across the organization have multiple skill levels and vastly different stores of knowledge, and assessing the gaps for every individual would be a huge undertaking. Learning analytics can provide identifiable patterns and actionable data that can be translated to personalized, learner-centric journeys. This offering makes L&D professionals' work more scalable and measurable, better equipping them to evaluate impact.

Find the right learning-analytics talent

The relative nascence of the learning-analytics field means that not many individuals combine a strong understanding of data science with meaningful experience applying analytics to L&D. Organizations already invested in the field of people or talent analytics can apply its expertise to L&D to help bridge gaps and find insights specific to the learning enterprise. And this adoption will expand the talent pool of L&D analysts, given that the field has surfaced as a core discipline in educational and corporate landscapes; for instance, some universities are now offering graduate-level programs in learning analytics. In the meantime, companies looking to recruit learning analysts from these current smaller talent pools will need to entice prospective hires with attractive opportunities.

Set the foundation by linking learning data to performance data

In addition to developing processes for data identification and collection, learning professionals need to establish a rich data architecture that permits the ongoing flow and linkage of data among the learning function, talent, and business outcomes.

Learning analytics should play a role in an integrated data-capture approach that includes HR, so all functions benefit from the acquired insights. This rich data can be examined from a variety of perspectives—including HR and recruiting—to assess competency, knowledge, expertise, employee satisfaction, and more. Linking the data provides a tangible, credible demonstration of the impact of learning and helps answer questions such as: Is learning helping to retain high performers? Is it supporting a quantifiable improvement in a stated development goal or need?

Learning data must be connected to other business performance measures, such as sales revenue, customer satisfaction, safety, and operational efficiency. By obtaining the performance metrics that are most important to leadership and tying those metrics to the learning behaviors of individuals or groups, L&D can gain credibility as an impact driver rather than a cost center.

Experiment with low-fidelity tailored learning

For L&D organizations with limited resources, the best approach to personalized, analytics-driven learning is to start small. The following steps offer an easy path to implementation:

- Provide options for learners to “test out” of certain content if they have existing knowledge or abilities.
- Survey learners about their learning preferences, strengths, and development needs prior to an instructor-led program, then selectively share survey results with faculty and coaches.

- Leverage simple demographic data to offer personalized learning recommendations (for example, "Others in your role and tenure have taken the following electives . . .").

Experiments such as these can establish a proof of concept and generate momentum, setting the stage for additional step-change innovations.

■ ■ ■

The corporate appetite for data and analytics will continue to grow, helping learning analytics evolve into a well-established element of the L&D function. This change will lead to more standard processes and approaches for many of the challenges learning-analytics teams face today, including addressing privacy and context concerns; developing communication and mind-set shift strategies; collecting and warehousing data from multiple sources; and building the right analytics capabilities to transform learning. As L&D leaders use data and metrics to quantify results and improve programs and processes, they can do more for their organizations and their learners. ■

CHAPTER

13/

REINVIGORATING BLENDED LEARNING

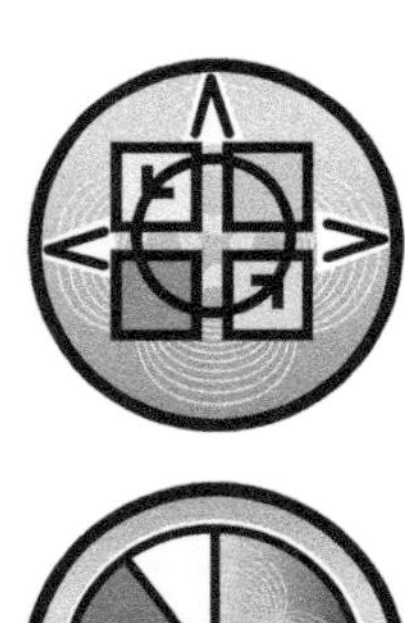

AUTHORS
Mary Andrade
Stephanie Gabriels

Blended learning doesn't always = digital learning + in-person sessions. A whole world of possibilities and approaches exists to deliver great business outcomes.

Shortly after the inception of e-learning two decades ago, "blended learning" emerged as a practicality—a way to reduce in-person class time and, therefore, time and resources. When blended-learning programs were first conceived, they simply combined in-person learning with e-learning. Since then, these programs have evolved to encompass myriad digital-learning delivery methods, such as virtual classrooms, simulation games, and social media.

But the most sophisticated and effective blended-learning programs go a step further. In what might be considered blended learning 3.0, completely new learning designs involve innovative delivery methods, formats, and instructional strategies, such as discovery learning, apprenticeships, flipped classrooms, coaching, on-the-job assignments, and virtual classrooms. However, few learning-and-development (L&D) organizations have matured their programs to this level of blended learning.

The urgency of evolution is clear. Today, most L&D professionals who design blended programs focus on learning-delivery methods—the *where* of learning—instead of on instructional strategies—the *how* of learning. This is because in today's learning programs, delivery methods are often selected based on content type and what platforms are easily available. Informational content is placed into digital modules and delivered through a learning-management system (LMS), for example, while soft skills are reserved for in-person modules. (For more, see sidebar, "The best platform for your strategy.")

Furthermore, blended programs are frequently created by L&D professionals who take a knife, instead of a scalpel, to cut modules from in-person programs to "convert" them to a digital form. And the approach to creating the digital courseware is either overly rapid or in isolation from the larger program. This process continues over time; more and more modules are cut and converted. What frequently happens is the original thread or connective tissue of the in-person program is lost. The context showing how the topics relate to one another fades. Learners are not engaged and click through digital courseware as quickly as possible. The opportunity for learners to construct their own meaning and connect it to their day-to-day work disappears. Learning retention is poor, and resources are wasted.

So then, how do we make blended learning better? Rather than just being a set of blended delivery methods, blended learning should be a thoughtful mix of instructional strategies developed to connect learning to day-to-day work and achieve the best possible learning outcomes. These strategies should then affect design decisions about the means of delivery—not the other way around. With this focus, learning can become part of employees' weekly routines, and learning outcomes can be measured in terms of business-impact metrics.

Blended learning should be a thoughtful mix of instructional strategies developed to connect learning to day-to-day work and achieve the best possible learning outcomes.

For organizations to progress toward blended learning 3.0 and create these optimal learning outcomes, L&D professionals must shatter their existing mind-sets about blended learning, opening themselves to new possibilities focused on outcomes and learner needs. They can start by sharply defining the business problem their learning program is meant to solve, then iterating on the program's design and development. Organizations that succeed will observe a significant increase in learning transfer as a result of their learning programs.

Creating a custom approach: A case example

Similar to successful in-person programs, the best blended-learning programs are full redesigns or designed from scratch. One midsize US company, for example, implemented a blended-learning program with the goal of increasing data-based decision making within particular functions. Over a six-month period, the course content was meant to impart new skills to a few select team members to help them employ a specific, effective methodology for defining a business problem, setting business-impact measures, and evaluating results through the completion of a distinct project that, by design, was part of their day-to-day work.

This learning team had its learners' needs in sharp focus, addressing business context and potential barriers to success head-on. For example, learners had diverse educational backgrounds—some with high school diplomas and others with master's degrees. The learners' previous experiences with the content also varied; for some it was completely new, while for others the course was a formal demonstration of existing proficiency. Learners' work roles and geographic locations varied as well. All of these factors created a situation where the content was challenging to some learners and the team suspected the coursework would be more rigorous than what many learners would anticipate—requiring good study habits, enduring motivation, and sustained attention.

To meet these needs, the company's learning team chose to blend four instructional strategies:

- *Action learning.* Essentially formalizing learning by doing, action learning asks learners to solve real problems or complete a real project while reflecting on the process along the way.

- *Coaching.* Of course, coaching pairs more experienced individuals with learners to help them achieve their goals—which goes hand in hand with action learning. A coaching strategy can also enable personalization by pairing up learners with coaches who have specific expertise.

- *Personalization.* When learning can be customized to address individual needs, interests, or aspirations, it is personalized. Action learning, for example, allows personalization by enabling learners to craft the topic and scope of their real project in partnership with their mentors and managers.

- *Spacing.* A term meaning the repetition of concepts over time, spacing increases retention in the long term by mitigating the forgetting curve. Increasing the time between repetitions can, to a point, decrease the total number of repetitions needed.

The program design addressed learners' needs in three key ways. First, the team configured each cohort by asking managers to recommend one or two people from their own team. As a result, learners felt excited, recognized, and rewarded for good work when they were invited to the program. Second, the program started with an in-person session; after a half day together, learners felt connected and understood the program's expectations and requirements, as well as key concepts needed for successful completion. In-person sessions occurred two more times, at the midpoint of the program and for project presentations at the end. Third, learners felt personally supported because they were assigned to and then guided by a mentor during one-on-one meetings, and they reviewed assignments with mentors who provided personalized instruction in small groups. The program allowed for further personalization, as the learners themselves crafted the topic and scope of their project in partnership with their mentors and managers. Learners were evaluated on the quality of their project's end result; they would not get credit for all the time invested if their projects did not meet certain standards.

Predictably, the time commitment on the part of the learners was not an easy sell to the company's leadership team. This type of program is indeed difficult to implement, but because the project work directly affected participants' day-to-day jobs, measurable business outcomes were baked in—even if calculating an exact return on investment (ROI) was a complex exercise. Still, it did not take many cohorts before positive reviews began to spread and leaders saw the business impact. Soon, managers were excited about sending their team members through the program.

Because mentors played such a prominent role, the company's program was high touch but low tech. Program materials were organized by cohort and module, and shared on a simple but well-designed collaboration platform, instead of through the LMS. Web-conferencing technology enabled small groups to review and discuss homework across various offices. And because individuals who completed the program went on to be mentors of future cohorts, the program was sustainable and scalable.

How your organization can get to next-level blended learning

Companies that wish to reinvigorate their blended-learning programs must start by challenging their existing approaches. They may find they are bogged down in outdated ideas of what blended learning should be. For example, not every approach needs to include live classroom events. It's possible to combine any number of face-to-face, self-paced, and live e-learning methods as long as they are in harmony with your program's mix of instructional strategies, and the learning experiences are anchored by a cohesive framework. Indeed, choosing the right instructional strategies to meet your company's goals should always influence decisions about how the instruction is delivered, rather than the other way around.

In our experience, selecting the methods to craft a custom approach involves five key steps: adopt a new mind-set, define the problem the approach is meant to solve and empathize with learners, develop the right framework, select instructional strategies to blend, and prototype and test the approach.

Step 1: Adopt a new mind-set

Despite the fact that much has changed in the world of learning since we started blending learning methods, the vast majority of learning professionals are settling on basic formulas that lack customization. This reality is surprising, given significant investments in learning platforms, sophisticated developments in the design of digital courseware, and the evolution of learning-evaluation strategies in general.

So before learning professionals can get excited about the possibilities of blended learning, they must work to change their mind-sets. To adopt a new mind-set, start by questioning what is influencing your choices in your blended-learning design: break free from your budget spreadsheets and develop an agnostic view of your technology infrastructure. Unmoor yourself from your legacy content and preferred programs. Identify what aspects of the program have the biggest impact, then test and perfect those key elements to improve the program on multiple dimensions. Channel your expertise to determine what works, and objectively jettison what doesn't.

It is always challenging to innovate within business constraints; too often, L&D teams endure obstacles that prevent them from being creative. But as the case example shows, technology investment is not always necessary; much of the content employed already existed and was repurposed. And any increase in development time was justified through measurable business impact.

Step 2: Define the performance problem and empathize with your learners

Performance-based design requires the learning-design team to understand what behaviors need to change and how to measure that change. This approach results in a better understanding of how learners typically spend their time, which, in turn, allows you to link the learning to their work.

Focusing on performance requires you to communicate your vision or end goal so that your team and stakeholders begin with the end in mind. A learning-needs analysis is a critical step in learning design—and one that is frequently cut when teams face time and budget constraints. We don't always have enough lead time to employ the rigor we would like. However, there is always time to gather even a small sample of learners and business stakeholders to interview at the start. (For more on learning-needs analysis, see chapter 4.)

Methodologies such as empathy maps also encourage learning professionals to better understand their learners and gain perspective on performance. These maps can provide insightful answers to the most important questions, such as: What are the barriers to program implementation? What are common mistakes? What are the incentives for learners to change their behavior? For example, you might uncover that a junior team member never had the opportunity to witness a particular leadership behavior, making it quite difficult for the individual to demonstrate that behavior. This insight might lead you to incorporate video scenarios into that program.

Step 3: Create a framework aligned to learners' day-to-day tasks

We see learning professionals make two key mistakes when planning learning programs. First, learning professionals design blended programs around how the performance objectives are grouped rather than aligning them with a process or milestone. After completing a needs analysis, it can be tempting to use the categorization and hierarchy of performance objectives as the framework for the program. However, this holistic view is not evident to the learners, so the categories are not meaningful to them. In fact, the categories may add confusion when learners try to apply what they are learning to their day-to-day activities. For example, one media company looking to create a blended onboarding journey organized the program by the following categories: product knowledge, systems, skills, and supporting functions. The learners struggled to make important connections, such as accurately identifying the products in the systems or matching the best product to customer needs. A more learner-friendly approach might have been to create a framework focused on exploration (how to discover background facts), preparation (what to know and do before meeting with a client), and delivery (how to conduct effective calls and submit orders). This architecture would have helped learners seamlessly connect what they learned with their jobs and know what to expect at each stage of the learning program.

Second, learning professionals often design blended-learning programs based on delivery method—the type of content drives when and how it's delivered. This approach is problematic because in this scenario, the knowledge objectives are often addressed in digital modules while the skill-building objectives are addressed during in-person sessions. This arrangement frequently results in a scattered or disjointed experience for the learner. By explicitly linking the program to learners' day-to-day work, however, you'll increase learning effectiveness.

Step 4: Select instructional strategies to blend

In our experience, some of the most effective blended-learning strategies are used the least. Many L&D professionals don't consider using action learning, for example, perhaps because they are simply unaware that it's an option. But it can be a great addition to your evolved approach. Action-learning projects can be completed by teams or individuals, with small groups of learners reflecting on key takeaways. This strategy creates and sustains engagement because assignments can build upon one another and have meaningful outcomes. For skills that directly fit within the context of learners' day-to-day work, action learning enables you to curate content and deliver it "just-in-time," allowing learning professionals to dictate the sequence and pace of the real-world work. (For more on content curation, see chapter 8.) When the learned skills directly affect a learner's job performance, action learning can greatly facilitate the measurement of program outcomes via business impact. In organizations where people feel they are too busy for learning programs, action learning should be a go-to strategy.

Of course, action learning would not be as effective without coaches and mentors, which can create implementation challenges. Delivery specialists must recruit enough coaches to support a cohort of learners, after all. These challenges may be overcome by simultaneously rolling out programs to specific groups to create a critical mass of coaches who are likely to be more engaged if they see they are part of a larger initiative that will benefit their group, and the company, long term.

Other instructional strategies such as spacing, scenario-based activities, simulations, and games reflect the very nature of blended learning yet still require thoughtful consideration in the design. It's the combination of these strategies in a well-designed blended program that gives blended programs the potential to be more effective than in-person learning events.

Step 5: Prototype and test

At this point, one or two designs become front-runners. Before choosing one option over the other, create a focus group with the learners you engaged during the needs-assessment stage and get their input. Don't hesitate to show them even primitive prototypes; test aspects of your design that are most innovative or that you're most unsure about. You can create PowerPoint versions of your program's platform and even do a trial run of in-person or video-conference sessions. You can have people talk through how they would approach an assignment and see what questions or

The best platform for your strategy

Often, learning professionals must choose a platform based on the technologies available within their organizations. Their options may not have key features to support a blended program, such as an easy way to release content in a precise time frame, or they may not have a social platform to incorporate.

Although learning management systems (LMSs) are the go-to platform for most companies, these systems are not well designed for hosting blended programs. The user interface of most LMSs displays courseware and events in nested lists. A blended-learning user interface, however, is designed to group and display a number of courses and events so they are not overwhelming and do not require more than three clicks to launch. Some blended-learning platforms use features such as accordions and tiles; accordions allow you to label groups of courses in a compelling way, and tiles can include images. More customizable platforms can incorporate graphics within the interface, which can further frame the organization of the content and aid learner understanding. For example, you might feature a flowchart of a process that includes clickable areas in which you could navigate to different modules. Blended-learning platforms can take many forms, including platforms created for massive open online courses (MOOCs) and small private online courses (SPOCs).

MOOCs are a form of blended learning, and in our experience both MOOC and SPOC platforms include features that are important for the administration of blended-learning programs. MOOC platforms have well-designed user interfaces and organize content and assignments within a certain framing architecture. Content can be scheduled in advance and released over time. These platforms have ways of displaying and grouping large numbers of assets without overwhelming users. Another helpful feature is the ability to upload homework assignments, even videos.

However, an internal wiki or popular collaboration site can also work well for organizations without the resources to invest in a platform. Whatever the platform, the most important feature is the ability to organize what the learner needs to do and when, in a way that is clearly linked to the framing architecture.

challenges they anticipate. The process of gathering learner input early helps you identify what aspects of your design are most engaging and conducive to learning. Then you can amplify those aspects and simplify, or even discard, others.

We've found that habitually checking in with your focus group along the way will help you continue to streamline the design and development of your blended-learning program. It is a constant battle to figure out what to include and what to leave out. Stakeholders almost always push to add more information than what's possible within the time frame, but focus groups will provide great direction as to what you should cut and what you should keep. As you get closer to a fully fleshed-out design, consider running a pilot before scaling up.

■ ■ ■

By letting go of what blended-learning programs used to be, learning professionals can carry blended learning into a bright future. This framework leads to continual learning and improvement based not on what's expected and convenient but on how to best engage learners and bridge the gap between formal learning and day-to-day work. Learning professionals who succeed in implementing blended learning 3.0 can help their companies retain talent and better compete in a rapidly changing world. ■

CHAPTER

14/

PROVEN STRATEGIES TO INTEGRATE IMMERSIVE LEARNING INTO YOUR ORGANIZATION

AUTHORS
Nick Pappas
Ron Rabin
John Sangimino

From skill building to addressing values and mind-sets, immersive learning should be a part of every organization's learning strategy.

> *"For the things we must learn before we can do them, we learn by doing them."*
>
> –Aristotle

Immersing learners in authentic experiences—having them learn by doing through realistic practice—is not a new approach, and some industries have been employing it for years. Recent advances in the sophistication and affordability of simulation technologies, including virtual reality (VR), have made it possible for learning professionals to construct the kinds of intricate, visually complex experiences that used to be limited to high-stakes learning environments, such as pilot and astronaut training, medical education, and military war games.

At their core, immersive-learning solutions blend authentic context and interactive elements to create the necessary conditions for learning. This type of learning environment offers obvious advantages over lectures, webinars, and digital tutorials. The popularity of video games, for example, demonstrates just how highly engaging and motivating immersive experiences can be. Games don't begin with an announcement of learning objectives and end with quizzes or smile sheets; they plunge players into a challenging situation, provide rich and frequent feedback, reward progress, and give players a sense of mastery and accomplishment over tough challenges. The same is true of immersive learning for professionals.

This approach is arguably of greatest value to those who have the least amount of real-world experience in a topic. Many professionals have used immersive simulations for a broad range of capability-building activities—and to great effect. There is great power in constructing a complex, multidimensional environment and inviting people to navigate ambiguous terrain, take chances, and learn firsthand from their experiences.

> *"All knowledge of reality starts from experience and ends in it."*
> –Albert Einstein

Advanced learners can benefit from immersive learning too, especially experiences that address learning gaps, challenge areas, or existing behaviors that require adjustment (see sidebar "Immersive learning in action"). Immersive learning is also a low-risk way to influence mind-sets, which is particularly valuable for advanced learners. When situated in a rich context in which they make decisions, advanced learners can experience the effects of those decisions and examine causal relationships—an opportune time to reflect on their values and mind-sets.

The solution outlined in the sidebar is effective in part because it was based on David Kolb's Experiential Learning Model (ELM),[1] which comprises four key elements:

- Concrete experience—making decisions and taking actions in an authentic context

- Observation and reflection of experience—contemplating outcomes, including cause and effect and the impact of choices made and not made

- Formation of abstract concepts based on reflection—drawing conclusions and modifying associations, expectations, and mind-sets

- Testing of new concepts—applying refined thinking and mental models to new situations

Immersive learning in action

In one example of immersive learning, a company designed an experience specifically for its leadership. The company had struggled with price competition; often undercut, it had reduced its fees, which triggered price wars in the industry. Learning-needs analysis revealed that leaders had the underlying mind-set that providing superior services at competitive prices would increase profits. This mind-set was flawed because it emphasized price instead of customer value, leading to suboptimal decision making. The existing mind-set of "I must price aggressively so customers purchase our services" needed to change to "I need to quantify the total value of our services so customers view them as strategic investments."

The learning simulation allowed leaders to practice forming customer strategies, making pricing decisions, and competing on profit. They experienced firsthand the systemic impact of flawed thinking and saw how different mind-sets can lead to better decision making and ultimately better business results. In the 18 months following this immersive-learning program, the company achieved significant improvement in its key financial metrics. While numerous initiatives contributed to this result, many leaders cited the simulation as the key turning point in their thinking.

Whether used in a group setting (as in the sidebar) or individually (such as in an online serious game), ELM provides a useful framework for engaging learners and helping them construct meaning and develop skills.

Despite the potential power of immersive-learning experiences, learning-and-development (L&D) teams often fall short in developing solutions that both engage learners and achieve the intended degree of impact.

> *"Education in the 20th century is like being taken to the world's greatest restaurant and being fed the menu."*
>
> –Murray Gell-Mann

Barriers to immersive learning in organizations

As with any new technology, methodology, or framework, immersive learning can be met with some resistance and challenges when first introduced to an organization. Our experience and research show that the major barriers center on a few key themes:

A new approach in the corporate setting

As jobs increasingly prioritize cognitive capacity over physical capability, organizations have gradually moved away from "learning by doing." Although centuries old, immersive learning can still feel very new to some companies. The approach is used more often in settings where the cost of failure is high, as in aircraft pilot or medical training, than in corporate settings. But stakes can still be high even in corporate settings—for example, the success or failure of business-client relationships can make or break an organization.

New and unproven programs such as immersive learning still raise questions, particularly the what-ifs: What if the program fails? What if the return on investment (ROI) isn't there? What if we can't get all stakeholders behind the idea or the investment?

Increased complexity, development time, and resources

Immersive learning presents a unique set of challenges. Since context-rich simulations are inherently complex, they place higher demands on everyone from subject-matter experts (SMEs) and instructional designers to learners. The key to an effective immersive experience is to offer cognitive realism, which means incorporating sufficient fidelity into the cognitive tasks that learners are being asked to master.[2] In other words, we want our learning experiences to look and feel authentic (with all the benefits VR and other simulated experiences can provide). Designers must make important choices about the degree of fidelity required in both context and interactivity to achieve the learning outcomes. This decision making adds to the complexity, development time, and required resources. The creation of the experience requires the participation of multiple stakeholders, as well as ongoing testing, to validate balance points, represent complex dynamics, and calibrate models.

Budget and cost relative to other methods

While the cost of immersive technologies (for example, simulation-development software) is decreasing as more options become available, budget is still a top concern for immersive-learning designers. Creating a truly authentic context and interactivity can result in more investment than methods such as webinars or e-learning and sometimes feels prohibitive.

Addressing challenges and implementing a road map

To create effective immersive-learning solutions, companies should follow a three-step process to address the aforementioned challenges. Issues can arise at each stage of the process, and failure to plan for them could result in wasted investment. With careful planning, however, most barriers can be avoided or managed.

1. Develop a strong communications plan

Throughout the development process, L&D leaders must manage the expectations of stakeholders and budget owners and educate them on the development process. You can mitigate the concerns that come with unfamiliar territory by creating an effective communications and development plan that includes the following elements:

Results of a learning-needs analysis. A learning-needs analysis is a critical first step in developing learning solutions. (For more on learning-needs analysis, see chapter 4.) At this stage, you will have determined your needs gap and identified an immersive-learning solution to address that need in a meaningful way. The learning-needs analysis will help you make a strong case for immersive learning by demonstrating the need, defining the desired outcomes, and providing a clear link to how immersive learning can meet those outcomes—and why the solution is so well suited to this particular need.

The learning-needs analysis will help you make a strong case for immersive learning by demonstrating the need.

If the learning-needs analysis shows that your learners need simple or rudimentary knowledge and skills, immersive learning is likely overkill. Your communications efforts should focus on the areas that immersive learning is uniquely suited to address: changing mind-sets, behavior, knowledge, and values through solutions in which learners make decisions, take action, experience effects, and reflect deeply on the connections (see sidebar "Immersive learning for operations excellence in a shifting marketplace").

Anticipated outcomes. Describe the outcomes you hope to achieve, along with a broad outline of the solution type (for example, an online, single-player simulation or an in-person group immersion in a physical, model environment).

Cost. Provide a summary of costs, including how they compare with those of other methods, and a breakdown of cost figures for multiple options. This level of transparency is important when getting stakeholders on board with a new concept.

In addition to developing an initial communication plan, you should be prepared to communicate throughout the process and involve stakeholders, or their designated proxies, in testing. This groundwork will help build support and excitement and create additional avenues for innovation early in the process.

Immersive learning for operations excellence in a shifting marketplace

Markus Hammer

Disruptive technologies and dynamic markets are continually reshaping the way things are made, procured, and dispatched, putting nearly constant pressure on operations teams. Tasked with balancing price, quality, and speed, operations leaders must ensure that their employees have the knowledge and capabilities to maintain consistent production in the face of change.

Immersive learning can address these challenges and accelerate capability building by providing learners with unique, hands-on experiences. In a realistic learning-factory setting, employees have the opportunity to solve problems and learn processes in a risk-free environment, allowing them to make decisions, use new tools, and build knowledge without fear of error.[1] Successful model factory exercises typically begin with theory sessions on concepts and approaches, followed by immediate application on the shop floor. Participants spend 50 to 70 percent of their time on the floor, and this hands-on experience can be transformational. Workers who participate in every step of a process see physical changes in production, repeat best practices, and gain a deeper understanding of the entire process.

McKinsey research on the impact of immersive-learning sessions such as model factories and "factory-in-a-box" setups found this method to be much more effective than other approaches.[2] Indeed, we found that recall rates for participants are seven times higher than with traditional lectures and discussions. These types of solutions not only create a "muscle-memory" effect but also enable important mind-set shifts. Being able to think and act in a risk-free setting can inspire employees to be more comfortable with change, push for improvements, and articulate their decision-making process.

One high-tech equipment manufacturer, for example, used a model factory to instill a lean approach in its workforce. More than 500 employees participated; the majority reported a significant improvement in their ability to support the company's ongoing transformation efforts. Thanks to the program's success, the manufacturer has accelerated the rollout of its lean approach and identified additional improvement ideas. Further, the company is in the process of building its own experiential-learning curriculum.

For operations leaders who need to address marketplace and industry shifts without sacrificing volume, speed, price, and quality in their manufacturing, model factories offer a powerful approach.

1 At the Fifth Conference on Learning Factories in 2015, researchers proposed that the term "learning factory" is to be used "for systems that address both parts of the term—elements of learning or teaching as well as a production environment. Learning factories provide a reality-based production setting as a learning environment. This means processes and technologies inside the learning factory are based on real industrial sites." For more information, see Eberhard Abele et al., "Learning factories for research, education, and training," *Procedia CIRP,* 2015, Volume 32, pp. 1–6, doi.org/10.1016/j.procir.2015.02.187.

2 Claus Benkert and Nick van Dam, "Experiential learning: What's missing in most change programs," August 2015, McKinsey.com.

2. Ensure organizational readiness and plan for changes

If your organization has never developed an immersive-learning solution, you likely will need to overcommunicate with senior stakeholders and SMEs throughout the process. You should also allow additional time for development and testing, and earmark additional budget for opportunities that emerge along the way. In addition, the core team must be organized in such a way that it can focus on the most valuable elements of a design, develop product versions quickly, receive feedback, and iterate accordingly.

The biggest challenge for the core team is the fear of presenting unpolished work to senior team members and SMEs. However, waiting too long to share your work can result in a solution that doesn't provide authentic context or enough interactivity, requiring more time and budget modifications. Ultimately, the best way to stay on track is to set expectations with reviewers, clearly define roles and tasks, and schedule frequent touch points.

Communicating broadly is critical—not only with senior leadership and SMEs but also with technology teams. Several points should be considered: Is the solution compatible with your LMS? If not, is that reasonable? Does it satisfy IT security requirements? Bring the appropriate people on board early in the process to ensure that you can deliver the solution in the target environment. Similarly, faculty should be adequately prepared for this new type of experience, from the dynamic nature of a simulation to shaping debrief conversations in real time. New technology may require guidance from support personnel who play a key role in bringing the experience together. Clear expectations, good communication, guidance, and time are essential to setting up critical roles for success.

Stakeholders will pay close attention to cost and budget. We recommend that you keep plenty of budget in reserve, because with ongoing feedback and testing—at least three user tests, a beta, and a pilot—modifications will undoubtedly be needed. What's more, ideas are sure to emerge during the development process. For example, designers may identify a need for additional or different functionality than anticipated during the initial design phase. Good planning will help avert the need to request additional budget.

3. Incorporate familiar learning approaches

In a risk-averse environment, a blended approach can open the door to more immersive exploration. (See chapter 13 for more on blended learning and how learning professionals with different specialties can work together to customize learning.) Take a one-day program on the banking industry that relies heavily on presentations. Traditionally, participants spend most of their time viewing the presentation, so interaction is minimal. A blended approach might include a microsimulation on a more complex or ambiguous topic that takes place before participants engage with the resident expert. For example, the topic might be the short- and long-term benefits of implementing a variety of digital strategies at financial institutions. The participants could practice forecasting, making decisions, and exploring the potential impact of those decisions. This adaptation would supplement the presentation, providing an in-depth experience that encourages engagement.

Keep an eye on objectives and multiple dimensions of immersive learning

Context is key in immersive learning. Most projects can't completely replicate real-world environments, but that level of fidelity isn't always necessary to achieve learning outcomes. For each outcome, determine how authentic the visual, auditory, gustatory, olfactory, and tactile elements of the experience must be, and the interactivity required, to achieve the learning outcomes (see sidebar "Harmonizing the learning experience").

The degree to which context fidelity must be replicated depends largely on how much real-world experience target audiences have with similar elements. For example, if participants must make a decision based on whether they perceive a burning smell, it is reasonable to assume that most adults already have a real-life experience as reference, so the smell need not be replicated as part of the experience. However, if the type or nuance of the smell is critical to decision-making and the distinctions required are unfamiliar to most audience members, then you will likely have to reproduce them.

Interaction is a two-way street. Regarding fidelity, designers must determine both the degree to which participants can act on the environment and the degree to which the environment responds to actions performed.

For example, if a retail company wants its district managers to plan and manage activities more effectively, one simulation might require managers to decide which stores to visit, the sequence of those visits, and the activities they will prioritize when they get there. The experience of driving from one location to another doesn't need to be replicated; instead, the simulation can reproduce interactions with local employees. Can this interaction occur online, or must it be done live, with the help of an actor? And if it's done live, how will the participants' choices and actions affect the model that underlies the learning design? From whether the local employees' facial expressions change to how the district managers' choices affect the business, designers must determine the level of interaction fidelity that will achieve the desired learning outcomes.

Reporting and analytics

Immersive-learning experiences create rich opportunities to generate and capture data on participant performance. Avoid the temptation to track and capture everything; focus instead on the key individual and collective data that will provide insights on where people perform well, where they struggle, and where to focus L&D efforts in the future.

The following questions should serve as a guide for elements to include in reporting and analytics:

- What key decisions and actions will participants perform in the experience?
- At what level of granularity can you capture data on performance—and at what level should you?

Harmonizing the learning experience

Immersive-learning solutions must blend both authentic context and interaction elements to create a robust learning environment. Most design choices involve either increasing or decreasing the fidelity of a context or interaction element in the experience. Ongoing testing ensures that any incremental design changes support the target learning outcomes.

One US-based global company realized that its worldwide business units were making decisions independently rather than in an organized, interconnected fashion. The results adversely affected the company's overall performance. An immersive-learning simulation helped unit leaders experience the effects of their decisions over time and practice identifying and executing ways to work together. The original design called for leaders to direct operations in a fictional country, making decisions that required the same kind of thinking that they used in their real jobs. Testing showed that while both the context and the degree of interactivity were realistic, the learning outcomes weren't being achieved.

Designers then modified the interaction dimension (by requiring leaders to make predictions on how their decisions would affect other parts of the organization) and the context dimension (by showing the effects of those decisions).

This combination of modifications increased participants' focus and engagement, heightening the immersion and creating the necessary conditions for impactful learning.

- Which results of the experience will be most interesting to senior leaders—for example, to inform strategic decisions about future L&D investment?
- Which results of the experience will be of most interest to designers—for instance, to inform future updates to the solution?
- Is compliance reporting necessary, and how will it be managed?

To measure overall impact and ROI, evaluate effectiveness in levels one through four of the Kirkpatrick model: reaction, learning, behavior, and results. Stakeholders and designers should align in the project-planning stage on how each of these will be measured, and modify as necessary throughout development to ensure accurate and useful reporting.

Implement a feedback process to inform updates to the program, immersive-learning projects with other teams, and planning and development processes. Throughout development, you will perform numerous tests, each with its own objectives—but no matter how thorough the testing and how helpful the feedback, you will undoubtedly gain many more insights once real learners start to go through the program and you can observe their performance, receive feedback, and review analytics.

If you feel rushed at the end of the development phase and have concerns about how the solution will be received, consider a soft launch, which will give you additional feedback that can help you make improvements before the official release.

■ ■ ■

Immersive learning is not a new trend in the L&D industry; it's one of the oldest, most proven learning methods. From ancient times, when hunter-gatherers learned survival skills from their elders, to today, when professionals learn through apprenticeships, learning by doing has always been authentic, intensive, and effective.

Still, simulations are not a silver bullet. They add cost and complexity, so you should only apply them to problems that require the feedback loop and level of fidelity that immersive learning provides. By using the approaches outlined here, you can ensure that the immersive-learning solutions you design will create value for participants—and your organization.

Although designing an immersive experience is more complex than other kinds of learning and can be fraught with challenges, a thoughtful, thorough approach can enable learners to achieve outcomes that few other methods can match—and *that* is well worth your efforts. ■

1 David A. Kolb, *Experiential Learning: Experience as the Source of Learning and Development,* Englewood Cliffs, NJ: Prentice Hall, 1984.

2 Janice Herrington, Ron Oliver, and Thomas Reeves, "Immersive learning technologies: Realism and online authentic learning," *Journal of Computing in Higher Education,* September 2007, Volume 19, Number 1, pp. 80-99, doi.org/10.1007/BF03033421.

CHAPTER

15/

MAXIMIZING THE IMPACT OF FEEDBACK FOR LEARNING AND BEHAVIOR CHANGE

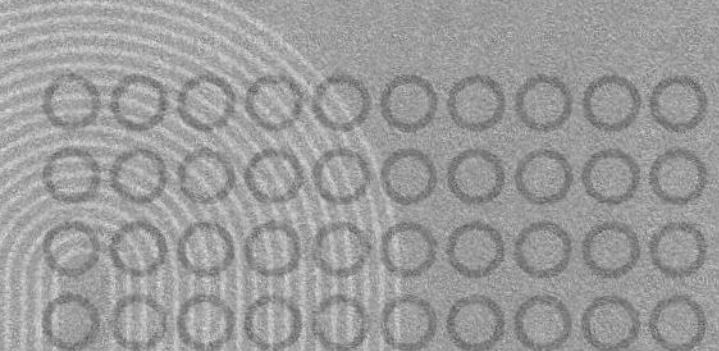

AUTHORS
Jacqueline Brassey
Brodie Riordan

Context, emotions, and individual differences play an important role in the feedback experience for individuals and organizations.

Feedback is an excellent tool for learning, growth, and development. In fact, it's critical—without effective feedback, professionals and organizations are limited to their own perceptions. Still, most people are deeply uncomfortable both giving and receiving feedback.

Emotions and context play a significant role on both sides of the feedback exchange—we fear that we'll be evaluated, judged, and found wanting. Ongoing research by Jacqueline Brassey, Nick van Dam, and Arjen van Witteloostuijn shows that providing feedback is one of the top three situations people avoid when they lack con-fidence. But effective feedback can be invaluable in helping us gauge our strengths, identify areas for growth and improvement, and understand the impact of our behavior.

We can help individuals and companies realize the potential of effective feedback by reframing it as a tool for learning and behavior change, applying best practices, and incorporating research on emotion, confidence, and the mental processes involved.

Where we find feedback in organizations

Feedback comes at us constantly from a diverse array of sources. Most people associate the term with formal experiences. But in fact, most feedback is self-generated and is based on our observations, judgments, experiences, and environments. Most of the feedback we receive from others may not even register as feedback. For instance, someone told you a meeting date wouldn't work, so you proposed an alternative; this is a feedback exchange, though it's rarely taken as such.

When people think of feedback in organizations they think about annual performance reviews, which can be daunting. If feedback flowed more freely all year long, the annual sit-down review would feel much less so. There would be no surprises, no major issues that have been festering for months. Instead, the conversation could be an opportunity to reflect on the past year—both challenges and successes—and look forward to the possibilities of the coming year.

Obstacles that prevent feedback from fostering learning and growth

Changing human habits and behaviors isn't as simple as implementing new organizational processes. Even with new processes in place, many managers and employees still struggle with giving and receiving feedback, for the reasons we outline below.[1]

Failing to consider emotions

Feedback can be a high-emotion experience for all involved, and a failure to understand the potential speed and strength of this emotional reaction can stand in the way of a meaningful, effective exchange. Giving, receiving, or even anticipating criticism can trigger a threat response in our brain. Our brains are hardwired to respond in a similar way to all threats, whether it's a grizzly bear on an afternoon hike or a critical review of our performance. Any threat can activate the amygdala—the emotional hub of the brain—which triggers reactions in the sympathetic nervous system. These reactions range from discomfort (sweating, stuttering, nervous feeling) to a complete takeover of the rational part of our brain (amygdala hijack), thereby interfering with our ability to think logically and remain calm. We might disconnect from the situation altogether via a fight, flight, or freeze response.

We are also only privy to the behavior we observe in others and biased by our own blind spots. Feedback providers and recipients alike make mistaken assumptions about each other's intentions, which can lead to misunderstandings and an unproductive dialogue. Being aware of this tendency helps us to refrain from judgment and focus on understanding the individual.

Looking back without looking forward

The point of feedback is to influence future behavior and learning, yet we often focus it entirely on the past. When getting feedback on something that happened yesterday or last week, people are more likely to reject or disregard the feedback and focus on justifying the behavior. This delayed feedback results in a missed opportunity to learn from past experience.

Focusing on the person, rather than the behavior

Feedback that focuses on the person—one's character, abilities, or personality—is difficult to act on and likely to elicit a defensive reaction. Moreover, praise that focuses on people's abilities, as opposed to their behaviors or efforts, reduces their resilience in the face of future failures.[2]

Making broad generalizations

When feedback is specific and evidence-based, recipients are better able to understand what they did and why it matters. Evidence-based

> **Feedback can be a high-emotion experience for all involved, and a failure to understand the potential speed and strength of this emotional reaction can stand in the way of a meaningful, effective exchange.**

feedback that incorporates observable behaviors is also harder to refute than opinions or generalizations. The greater the specificity, the easier it is to target exactly what behavior needs to change and in what way.

Emphasizing formal feedback over ongoing delivery

Many organizations turn feedback into an event, and feedback events can be intimidating—the prospect of an annual performance review often fills both managers and employees with dread. Yet feedback is also a fundamental part of how we engage with one another in everyday interactions. Examples of formal feedback include annual performance reviews and other meetings where the intent is to have a sit-down and share criticism. Informal feedback is the day-to-day feedback that we may not even notice. This kind of feedback happens in real time, focuses on something specific, and often results in an immediate shift in behavior. Organizations that disproportionately favor formal feedback miss out on significant opportunities for learning and growth that are better enabled through informal, timely feedback.

All of these feedback pain points—and plenty of others—can be managed. In our research and practice, we've identified two strategies that can help people feel more comfortable with giving, receiving, and seeking out feedback—and with engaging in feedback more frequently: understand what happens in the brain when giving or receiving feedback; and classify feedback into four component parts so that it is easier to both deliver and accept: source, message, recipient, and context.

Understanding the neuroscience of feedback: The fear system

Anxiety and other emotional reactions can impair our performance, ability to learn, and well-being. (For more on the neuroscience of fear and anxiety, see chapter 7.) Receiving feedback, or even anticipating it, can often provoke these reactions, especially in our brain's cortex. Once the emotions kick in, our ability to listen objectively and respond strategically declines. For example, a feedback recipient hears that she is not meeting expectations in her role. This feedback might get her thinking: will she face a pay cut, diminished career opportunities, or even job loss? Then the worries escalate: will she be able to pay her mortgage? Will friends and colleagues lose respect for her? Will she be able to provide for her family?

The first step toward better feedback exchanges is to recognize how quickly emotions come into play. Cognition takes time to catch up with emotion, and we must allow immediate emotional reactions to pass before we can understand the feedback we receive. Only after feedback is mindfully processed can learning, growth, and development occur.

Providing feedback can also be intimidating. As emotions take over, the feedback provider's ability to think decreases—especially when giving upward feedback to an older or more senior colleague. When anxiety makes it difficult for the feedback provider to give clear, constructive feedback, the likelihood of any real learning or behavior change is diminished.

Decades of research have illuminated the key characteristics of effective feedback. Below, we highlight how to apply that research to the four elements that make up any feedback exchange in a way that should make giving and receiving feedback a little less daunting.

The four elements of any feedback exchange

All feedback exchanges—whether formal or informal—consist of four elements: the source (the "giver"), the recipient, the actual message, and the context in which it is given.[3] Jane Brodie Gregory and Paul E. Levy outlined a four-part model of the feedback process in their book, *Using Feedback in Organizational Consulting*. We seek to build on their model by adding a fifth element, emotion (Exhibit 15A). Each of the elements has an impact on the extent to which the feedback is heard, accepted, valued, and put to use, and each element presents a risk that negative emotions will undermine the value of feedback. By considering these elements and their implications, we can improve exchanges and maximize the value of feedback.

Exhibit 15A: **There are five elements in any feedback exchange.**

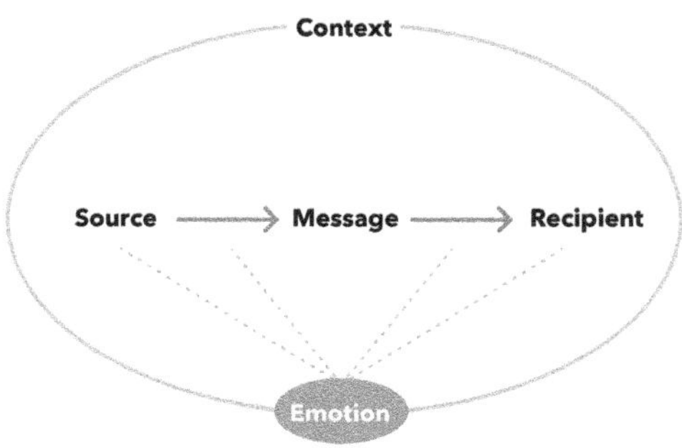

Source: Adapted from Jane Brodie Gregory and Paul E. Levy, *Using Feedback in Organizational Consulting*, Washington, DC: American Psychological Association, 2015

The feedback source

Direct, personal feedback is more complex than feedback we give ourselves or that comes from an object such as a computer or scale. Feedback providers bring past experiences to the exchange, along with their own attitudes and emotions—all of which have an impact on the context in which they provide feedback, the message they convey, and how the recipient interprets it. Research has consistently shown that a feedback recipient's perceptions of the source's credibility and trustworthiness can make or break a feedback exchange.[4]

When a feedback recipient feels anxious or threatened by either the feedback source or the anticipated content of the message, this threat response can trigger an amygdala hijack that sends the individual into fight, flight, or freeze mode.[5] Additionally, the strong wave of negative emotion can get in the way of truly hearing and mindfully processing the feedback and handling the situation in a constructive way. Managers and learning professionals need to remember the significance of the source in a feedback exchange.

The feedback message

Whether positive or negative, the feedback message must be specific, timely, behavior-focused, and forward-looking. When negative feedback is delivered poorly, recipients can experience an amygdala hijack that leads them to reject the feedback and miss an opportunity to learn and grow.

Earlier in the chapter, we outlined some of the issues that can interfere with the feedback experience. Actively counteracting those issues can help feedback providers craft an effective message. Some ways to do this include:

Look forward. Rather than leaving the recipient feeling criticized and unsure of how to act, make it clear what the person should do next time the situation arises.

Focus on behavior. Avoid broad statements like, "You are a bad manager because you yelled at a colleague" and focus instead on behavior: "You did not demonstrate respect to your direct report when you yelled at her." Feedback that focuses on behavior is less likely to threaten the employee's self-image or self-esteem.[6]

Focus on specifics. Vague or general feedback tends to make people defensive, leaving the real issue and the required actions unclear. Sloan Weitzel's "situation-behavior-impact" (SBI) model offers a useful framework: pinpoint the situation in which the behavior occurred, identify the behavior, and describe its impact.[7] For instance, "In this morning's team meeting when you yelled at a colleague for coming in late, you upset him and created an uncomfortable environment for the rest of the team."

The feedback recipient

How someone perceives and reacts to feedback—their feedback orientation—is influenced by many factors, including past experiences, personality, current mood, expectations, and individual differences.[8]

Individuals with a strong feedback orientation are more likely to value, accept, use, and seek out feedback, whereas those with a weaker orientation are more likely to react defensively and avoid or ignore feedback. Because feedback orientation is heavily influenced by past experiences, it can also be shaped and strengthened over time. As people get more comfortable with, and find value in, the feedback they receive, their feedback orientation grows stronger.

Strong self-awareness makes it easier to handle challenging feedback, and emotional flexibility helps people approach conversations with authentic, calm confidence. (For more on authentic confidence, see chapter 7.) Simple tools to support an effective feedback conversation include reframing the situation ("How can I look at this in a different way?"), managing one's inner voice in an effective way ("I am not my thoughts" or "What is happening for me at this moment?"), developing a growth mind-set, and being clear about one's purpose and values.

One way to boost learning while developing an individual's feedback orientation is to provide process feedback—feedback given while the individual is working on a task—rather than outcome feedback, which is given once a project has been completed.[9] Outcome feedback comes too late for the employee to change course or boost performance, while process feedback gives employees the opportunity to make immediate changes based on real-time feedback. People are more likely to accept, use, and seek additional feedback when it is delivered in process.[10]

Context

Context—including timing and physical setting—has a significant impact on how feedback is perceived and received. In Gregory

One way to boost learning while developing an individual's feedback orientation is to provide process feedback–feedback given while the individual is working on a task.

and Levy's model, context permeates every aspect of the feedback exchange.[11] It affects how the feedback source behaves, the type of feedback messages that are provided, and the thoughts, feelings, and actions of the feedback recipient.

Feedback is most useful when it is provided as soon as possible after an event, rather than at a formal feedback event like an annual review.[12] When feedback is delayed, the feedback loses its value as a tool for learning. It may be too late to take action, and the feedback recipient may not even fully recall the situation.

The only time feedback should be delayed is when the setting is not conducive to a feedback exchange. Feedback is best delivered in private. Public feedback is more likely to make people feel self-conscious, experience ego threats, and worry about their reputation and relationships. People are also less likely to seek feedback in the presence of others, which has important implications for learning. Managers, peers, or learning professionals should create private settings where individuals can seek feedback.[13]

Make feedback part of the culture

The degree to which organizations promote and support learning, growth, risk-taking, and communication has important implications for feedback behavior at all levels of the organization. A learning culture, where leaders, managers, and organizational practices support L&D, fosters openness to feedback.[14] When employees feel comfortable asking one another for feedback, sharing perspectives, and discussing the feedback they receive, the organizational culture becomes a place of learning, collaboration, and meaningful behavior change.

Every organization has a culture around feedback behavior—typically referred to in research as the feedback environment.[15] In a weak environment, employees receive infrequent feedback, feedback has a negative connotation, people are not held accountable to act on feedback, and individuals avoid seeking feedback. A strong feedback environment, with productive and ongoing feedback and accountability, can strengthen an employee's feedback orientation. Similarly, a critical mass of employees with strong feedback orientations can elevate the organization's environment.[16]

■ ■ ■

Feedback is an important part of empowering an organization's talent and improving processes and practices. Helping people understand what's happening in their minds and arming them with a few essential best practices can make a dramatic difference in behavior and attitudes toward feedback. Creating a strong feedback environment and culture—one that promotes frequent, effective feedback—lays the foundation for continuous learning, growth, and improvement across the business. ■

1 These are our top five concerns. Although backed by science, our choices are non-evidence-based.

2 Carol S. Dweck, *Mindset: The New Psychology of Success,* New York, NY: Ballantine Books, 2007.

3 Jane Brodie Gregory and Paul E. Levy, *Using Feedback in Organizational Consulting,* Washington, DC: American Psychological Association, 2015.

4 Cynthia D. Fisher, Daniel R. Ilgen, and M. Susan Taylor, "Consequences of individual feedback on behavior in organizations," *Journal of Applied Psychology,* August 1979, Volume 64, Number 4, pp. 349-71, doi.org/10.1037/0021-9010.64.4.349.

5 Diane Musho Hamilton, "Calming your brain during conflict," *Harvard Business Review,* December 22, 2015, hbr.org.

6 Jane B. Gregory and Allison L. O'Malley, "Don't be such a downer: Using positive psychology to enhance the value of negative feedback," *The Psychologist Manager,* October 2011, Volume 14, Number 4, pp. 247-64, doi.org/10.1080/10887156.2011.62 1776.

7 Sloan R. Weitzel, *Feedback That Works: How to Build and Deliver Your Message,* Greensboro, NC: Center for Creative Leadership Press, 2000.

8 Paul E. Levy and Beth A. Linderbaum, "The development and validation of the Feedback Orientation Scale (FOS)," *Journal of Management,* June 2010, Volume 36, Number 6, pp. 1372-405, doi.org/10.1177/0149206310373145; and Manuel London and James W. Smither, "Empowered self-development and continuous learning," *Human Resource Management,* March 1999, Volume 38, Number 1, pp. 3-15, doi. org/10.1002/(SICI)1099-050X(199921)38:1<3::AID-HRM2>3.0.CO;2-M.

9 P. Christopher Earley, Cynthia Lee, Terri R. Lituchy, and Gregory B. Northcraft, "Impact of process and outcome feedback on the relation of goal setting to task performance," *Academy of Management Journal,* March 1990, Volume 33, Number 1, pp. 87-105, doi. org/10.5465/256353.

10 Jane Brodie Gregory, Paul E. Levy, and Megan Medvedeff, "How attributes of the feedback message affect subsequent feedback seeking: The interactive effects of feedback sign and type," *Psychologica Belgica,* June 2008, Volume 48, Number 2-3, pp. 109-25, doi.org/10.5334/pb-48-2-3-109.

11 Gregory and O'Malley, "Don't be such a downer."

[12] Fisher, Ilgen, and Taylor, "Consequences of individual feedback."

[13]Susan J. Ashford and Gregory B. Northcraft, "Conveying more (or less) than we realize: The role of impression management in feedback seeking," *Organizational Behavior and Human Decision Processes,* December 1992, Volume 53, Number 3, pp. 310-34, doi.org/10.1016/0749-5978(92)90068-I; and Michelle D. Albright and Paul E. Levy, "The effects of source credibility and performance rating discrepancy on reactions to multiple raters," *Journal of Applied Social Psychology,* April 1995, Volume 25, Issue 7, pp. 577-600, doi.org/10.1111/j.1559-1816.1995.tb01600.x.

[14]Francisco G. Barbeite, Todd J. Maurer, and Debora R. D. Mitchell, "Predictors of attitudes toward a 360-degree feedback system and involvement in post-feedback management development activity," *Journal of Occupational and Organizational Psychology,* December 2010, Volume 75, Number 1, pp. 87-107; and London and Smither, "Empowered self-development and continuous learning."

[15]London and Smither, "Empowered self-development and continuous learning"; and Paul E. Levy, Andrea F. Snell, and Lisa Steelman, "The feedback environment scale: Construct definition, measurement, and validation," *Educational and Psychological Measurement,* February 2004, Volume 64, Number 1, pp. 165-84, doi.org/10.1177/0013164403258440.

[16]Manuel London and James M. Smither, "Feedback orientation, feedback culture, and the longitudinal performance management process," *Human Resource Management Review,* Spring 2002, Volume 12, Number 1, pp. 81-100, doi.org/10.1016/S1053-4822(01)00043-2.

CHAPTER

16/

DEVELOPING AN ORGANIZATIONAL COACHING STRATEGY AND CULTURE

AUTHORS
Maria Eugenia Arias
Brodie Riordan
Allison Thom

Organizations that value coaching and foster a company-wide coaching approach see benefits such as higher performance, increased productivity, and cost savings.

In a world of ever-increasing demands, accelerating pace, and digital disruption, professionals and organizations face tremendous expectations for performance. Ongoing improvement and learning are essential. Trends in the learning-and-development (L&D) landscape—including the shift of development responsibilities to individuals, demands for new ways of learning, and increasing pressure to engage employees and customers—are pushing us to make fundamental changes. Developing a coaching culture will help you address these trends by providing agile, self-directed, and personalized approaches to employee learning and development.

Coaching in organizations has grown rapidly from remedial interventions for underperforming executives to development opportunities for individuals and teams with potential.[1] The scope of the term "coaching" has also expanded beyond traditional external professional coaching to include "manager as coach" and peer coaching within organizations.[2] Coaching has become an important component of performance-management processes, with many organizations expecting managers (and peers) to replace traditional formal reviews with ongoing coaching to promote meaningful growth, development, and behavior change.

Coaching differs from mentoring in three ways. First, coaching is typically nondirective—the coach acts as more of a guide, helping employees think through challenges and come to their own conclusions, while a mentor is more likely to offer concrete advice based on their own experiences. Second, coaching is outcome-oriented, typically focusing on problem solving or developing specific skills or capabilities, whereas mentoring is more open-ended and informal. Third, a coaching relationship has a defined scope and time span (for example, three to 12 months) while mentoring relationships can last indefinitely. It is also important to distinguish between coaching and feedback. Chapter 15 explores feedback as a tool and its role in learning and development. These two topics may complement one another but are often confused as one and the same. One way to differentiate the two is to view feedback as a "push" of information to the other person, where one shares their input and observations. Coaching, on the other hand, relies on asking thoughtful questions, engaging with others in a nondirective way, and helping employees think through challenges and come to their own conclusions. Feedback is also inherently backward-looking, whereas coaching conversations look toward the future. (We discuss how to ensure feedback influences future behavior and learning in chapter 15.) There is some interplay between the two; feedback can serve as a data point in a coaching conversation (for example, a coaching discussion might focus on working through feedback from others and deciding how to act on it), and some of the best feedback exchanges incorporate elements of coaching (for example, a manager asking how an employee would do something differently next time). Though they're related, it's important to consider coaching and feedback as very different tools.

Why a coaching culture matters

A coaching culture is one in which when leaders and employees infuse coaching into everyday interactions—how they approach performance, learning, and interpersonal interactions.[3]

Research has shown that organizations with a strong coaching culture enjoy a number of enviable business outcomes, such as higher engagement and accelerated development among employees, higher levels of performance and productivity, revenue growth and greater market share, and increased customer satisfaction.[4] Coaching helps organizations address mounting pressure to build relevant skills and capabilities and creates a better work environment by promoting generative dialogue and allowing people to be more authentic in the workplace.

Shifting demographics in the workplace are creating new opportunities for coaching. Millennials are joining the workforce in large numbers, and they expect frequent coaching and feedback. In fact, a recent survey showed that millennials want feedback 50 percent more often than other employees, but only 46 percent agreed that their managers delivered on those expectations. What's more, they value support for their personal development from managers more than managerial direction. These new demands are pushing organizations to focus on building a culture of coaching and training managers to coach.[5]

Challenges to creating a coaching culture

As with any culture change, building a coaching culture can bring challenges. But you can overcome those challenges with strategic planning and coordinated efforts.

Disconnected coaching practices

One common pitfall is a failure to take a holistic, systemic approach to coaching. Coaching practices are piecemeal and disconnected in many organizations, resulting in duplicated efforts, missed opportunities to harness the power of multiple forms of coaching, excessive spending, and inconsistent experiences for both coaches and learners. We recommend that you look at the coaching ecosystem as a whole. Take a centralized, consistent approach to messaging and practices at all levels of the company, from C-level executive coaching to coaching-skills programs for employees.

Time and cost

A successful coaching culture requires additional resources. We know that investing time in a coaching conversation has a higher impact than simply providing an answer, but professionals face competing priorities and may not always have time for coaching conversations.

Similarly, the work required to embed coaching in processes, strategies, and approaches can be costly. But with leadership buy-in and a holistic approach, a coaching program can actually help the organization achieve strategic time allocation and cost savings.

Cultural notions of coaching

The word "coaching" has a negative connotation in many organizations, typically resulting from misuse of both the term and the practice—people often say "coaching" when they mean feedback loops, and coaching is sometimes used as a last-ditch effort to improve an employee's performance before letting that person go. If either of these examples rings true for your organization, you may need to invest in a company-wide communications campaign to underscore the role of coaching in helping employees solve problems and take ownership, unleashing leaders' potential, and sparking meaningful, outcome-focused dialogue across the organization.

Changing mind-sets

To truly embrace a coaching culture, leaders and employees need to believe that everyone in the organization has the potential to change and develop. In other words, they need to cultivate growth mind-sets. (For more on changing mind-sets and developing a lifelong-learning mind-set, see chapters 10 and 5, respectively.) Leaders need a clear and consistent change story to share with employees—what's changing, why the change is important, and what the goals are.

Conflicting processes and practices

Existing organizational programs or processes sometimes undermine a coaching culture. For instance, if your performance-management process rewards competition over collaboration and discourages risk taking, managers and employees will not adopt the mind-sets they need to coach and be coached. Organizations that don't value the feedback process are also less likely to have a successful coaching culture, as are organizations that don't foster learning and innovation.[6] As you assess your coaching culture, examine organizational processes and programs to surface any practices that have the potential to undermine your efforts.

Creating a coaching culture

A coaching culture encompasses coaching at all levels. At the top, leaders and managers incorporate coaching in everyday interactions. Learning programs help employees at all levels build coaching skills. And the company makes use not only of external professional coaches but also of certified coaches within the organization. Below we outline a strategic model for creating a deliberate coaching culture (Exhibit 16A).

Assess

Before you can develop a strategy for creating a coaching culture, you need to understand where your organization stands now. The assessment stage helps you uncover current processes or practices that could undermine a coaching culture, enabling you to make changes to increase your chances of success. It also helps you define your priorities and identify which areas will have the biggest impact, which is useful in securing resources if you're faced with time and budget constraints.

Exhibit 16A: **Apply this five-part model to develop a coaching culture.**

Assess	Perform a gap analysis to assess current and desired state of coaching culture–where we are and where we want to be, and why and when.
Develop	Develop a comprehensive, organization-spanning coaching strategy (may include manager coaching skill development, use of external coaches, internal coaching resources, employee upskilling, etc).
Implement	Implement coaching strategy (may include stakeholder buy-in, incremental roll-out, detailed timeline, connections to other organizational groups and processes, etc).
Evaluate	Evaluate strategy impact and culture development with key metrics (level and quality of coaching activity).
Connect	Connect coaching strategy and culture impact to broader outcomes (eg, retention, performance, development, engagement).

Input for this assessment process can come from a variety of sources, including organization-wide employee satisfaction surveys, HR system data, interviews with stakeholders, and anecdotal information. Procurement or contracting staff can provide details about external professional coaching activity—who you are working with (individuals, firms), how much they are charging per engagement, the scope of their work within the organization, etc. This type of analysis, an example of which is shown in Exhibit 16B, allows you to compare where you are now with where you want to be.

Exhibit 16B: **Organizations can use an example structure like the one below to determine gaps between current practice and coaching aspirations.**

(1) Type of coaching	(2) Current state	(3) Desired state
Leaders and managers coaching employees	Inconsistent	Add as a core capability in performance-review process–hold managers and leaders accountable; add to upward feedback survey.
Use of external professional coaches	No tracking of vendor use, procurement not centralized	Create centralized management in partnership with procurement to reign in spending, establish criteria for selecting vendors, get a "big picture" understanding of most urgent coaching needs.
Coaching by HR business partners	A few who have attained certifications on their own, but not organized	Leverage our HR business partners who are coaches and create a more centralized way of matching them with coaching needs; get more HR people certified over the longer term.
Coaching-skills capability building	Currently do not offer	Create a training program and support tools.
Peer coaching	Not currently emphasizing	Establish as part of a new performance-management process and include in peer feedback training.
Mentoring	Currently have a formal mentoring program, but it needs to be updated	Update program, re-launch in Q3, scale to more business units.

Develop

After identifying the biggest gaps and opportunity areas for your coaching culture, develop a comprehensive, organization-wide strategy that encompasses all the aspects of coaching to be targeted—such as developing managers' coaching skills, external coaches, internal coaching resources, and employee upskilling. This strategy should incorporate critical execution details, including specific goals and objectives for each activity, key stakeholders and owners, dates and milestones, contingencies, and metrics for gauging success. Boost your chances of success by creating a team to lead the strategy rollout and scheduling regular progress updates.

The most successful coaching cultures and programs are based on a company's unique needs and data and go beyond traditional notions of executive coaching (see sidebar, "How top companies get the most out of coaching programs").

Some ideas for nontraditional coaching including the following: coaching "office hours" in which employees sign up for an hour-long session with a professional coach on a designated day of the week,

How top companies get the most out of coaching programs

At Facebook, every employee is assigned an executive coach for one-on-one coaching. The company spends the largest part of its learning-and-development budget on coaches, providing a completely personalized approach to developing effective managers.[1] Google's Guru program trains a select group of coaches in the GROW model, covering topics ranging from career development to parenting, and provides feedback as they learn to coach. Guru coaching is highly rated on value for time spent and impact on the organization in speed of onboarding, increased self-confidence, and improved executive presence.[2]

[1] Richard Feloni, "Facebook's lead HR consultant explains how the company radically changed the way it trains managers," *Business Insider*, April 2016, businessinsider.com.

[2] *Growing at Google*, International Coach Federation, 2016, coachfederation.org.

or using an on-demand approach with apps that can connect an employee to a coach for a particular project or need. Organizations are also increasingly investing in developing internal coaching capacity by, for instance, training and certifying HR managers or other staff to coach leaders and employees in a more cost-effective manner.[7]

A successful program depends on a strong understanding of the company's needs at both an organizational and individual level (Exhibit 16C).

Exhibit 16C: **Consider eight points when developing your coaching strategy.**

- ☐ **1. Managers as coaches:** How we define coaching in our organization, what role managers play, their current skill levels compared with where we want them to be
- ☐ **2. Expectations for employees:** Empowering employees to seek out coaching; educating employees on the value of, and their role in, coaching (eg, don't expect someone to just give you the answer)
- ☐ **3. The role of HR in coaching:** Defining the role of HR (business partners and/or centers of excellence) in aspects of program management, helping people find coaching resources, etc
- ☐ **4. Coaching "upskilling":** Learning and training for managers, employees, HR, and others to support the roles articulated above. What these will focus on, how audiences will be segmented, if training will be "built or bought"
- ☐ **5. Internal coaching resources:** Deciding whether or not to develop internal coaches, whether full time or as an additional part of someone's role (eg, HR managers); investing in training internal resources
- ☐ **6. The role of external coaches:** Establishing guidelines on who can have access to external professional coaches; outlining criteria for external coach selection, the role of procurement in requests for proposals and contracting
- ☐ **7. Processes and technology:** Outlining mechanisms for people to utilize programs (eg, training, external coaches), and how technology will be used to support or enhance coaching (eg, coach management, matching, virtual coaching sessions)
- ☐ **8. Getting visible leadership support:** Identifying the key stakeholders whose buy-in and support will be essential for the success of the coaching strategy. Enrolling leadership champions to visibly promote and role model coaching best practices

Implement

Coaching has an impact on other processes, including performance management, L&D, and succession planning. For instance, holding managers accountable for the team members they're coaching has implications for how managers are evaluated and rewarded; so your strategy will need to include input from staff members who are involved with performance management, compensation, and talent management. Colleagues in procurement or contracting may be closely involved in managing relationships with external professional coaches, making them essential to the success of changes to that process, and internal communications colleagues can be invaluable in helping you create messaging to roll out changes or announce new programs and opportunities. (For more on communications and change management, see chapter 11.) Include as many of these key partners in your strategy as possible, and engage with them frequently during implementation.

Evaluate

Clear goals and objectives are an important part of your strategy and implementation plan. Key metrics and sources of data tied to those goals help prove the value of coaching to the organization as a whole and continually improve your coaching programs. For instance, if your strategy calls for centralized management of external coaches, define your desired outcomes and how you will measure success. Outcomes could include cost savings, higher-quality coaches, a faster process for matching employees with coaches and kicking off the engagement, or an increase in key insights regarding coaching needs across the business. If your strategy includes implementing a coach-training program for managers, your key metrics could include the

Holding managers accountable for the team members they're coaching has implications for how managers are evaluated and rewarded.

number of managers participating in the program, their evaluations of the program (for example, Kirkpatrick), and longer-term improvements in areas such as employee feedback, ratings of manager coaching behavior, and results for managers' teams.

Connect

Connect your coaching-strategy plans with organizational priorities. For instance, let's say a leader named Judy works with a coach to help her build communication skills and a stronger presence. Not only does Judy's performance improve, she also gains clarity of direction—which can lead to dramatic change in her area of the company. With improved communication, people will have better rapport with Judy and a better understanding of what's going on, leading to increased efficiency, less downtime, and higher retention rates.

Coaching-related improvements such as higher performance and decreased downtime have a direct impact on the organization's bottom line. Analyses of executive coaching often reveal an astronomical, almost unbelievable return on investment (ROI)—one study found an average ROI of 300 to 700 percent.[8] When you consider the potential financial impact on an organization, even a $30,000 executive coaching engagement can have a dramatic effect. In developing a coaching strategy, consider the broader organizational impact that coaching can have by changing behavior at all levels of the organization.

■ ■ ■

The world of work will become increasingly agile, complex, unpredictable, and virtual. To remain competitive, leaders, managers, and employees of all levels must adopt a mind-set of continuous growth and development, and take ownership for the development of their own skills and capabilities. Organizational approaches to L&D and talent will have to shift as well, with less emphasis on traditional learning methodologies and more on personalized, on-demand solutions to fit the needs and work styles of employees. Coaching is uniquely positioned to meet these demands, and organizations that are deliberate and methodical in creating and scaling their practices will enjoy the benefits of a developed, self-aware, growth-oriented workforce as well as the cost savings and simplicity of centralized, consistent practice. Using the five-part model described in this chapter can help you address challenges and realize the potential of coaching. ■

1 For the sake of clarity, we refer to Riddle, Hoole, and Gullette's definition of coaching: "a helping relationship with a developmental focus played out in conversations that stimulate the person or group being coached to greater awareness, deeper and broader thought, and wiser decisions and actions." See Emily R. Hoole, Elizabeth C. D. Gullette, and Douglas D. Riddle, *The Center for Creative Leadership Handbook of Coaching in Organizations,* San Francisco, CA: Jossey-Bass, 2015, p. 49.

2 Jane Brodie Gregory and Paul E. Levy, "Employee coaching relationships: Enhancing construct clarity and measurement," *Coaching: An International Journal of Theory, Research and Practice,* August 2010, Volume 3, Number 2, pp. 109-23, doi.org/10.1080/17521882.2010.502901.

3 David Clutterbuck and David Megginson, *Making Coaching Work: Creating a Coaching Culture,* London, UK: CIPD Publishing, 2005; and *Building a coaching culture,* International Coach Federation and Human Capital Institute, 2014, coachfederation.org.

4 Ritu Agarwal, Corey M. Angst, and Massimo Magni, "The performance effects of coaching: A multilevel analysis using hierarchical linear modeling," *The International Journal of Human Resource Management,* 2009, Volume 20, Number 10, pp. 2110-34, doi.org/10.1080/09585190903178054.

5 Karie Willyerd, "Millennials want to be coached at work," *Harvard Business Review,* February 2015, hbr.org.

6 Manuel London and James M. Smither, "Feedback orientation, feedback culture, and the longitudinal performance management process," *Human Resource Management Review,* Spring 2002, Volume 12, Number 1, pp. 81-100, doi.org/10.1016/S1053-4822(01)00043-2.

7 Amy Lui Abel, Sherlin Nair, and Rebecca L. Ray, *Global executive coaching survey 2016: Developing leaders and leadership capabilities at all levels,* Conference Board, September 2016, conference-board.org.

8 Merrill C. Anderson, *Executive briefing: Case study on the return on investment of executive coaching,* MetrixGlobal, November 2001, gvasuccess.com.

CHAPTER

17/

FINDING THE RIGHT FACULTY:

Teaching excellence means classroom success

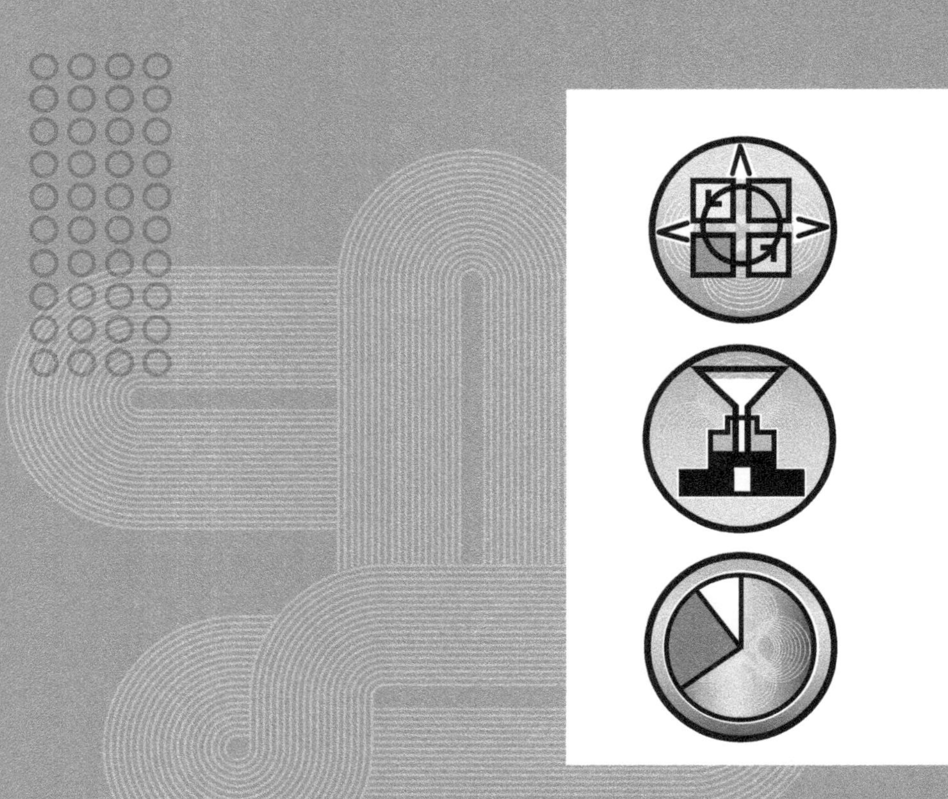

AUTHORS
Terrence Hackett
Janice Steffen

Learning-and-development professionals play a critical role in evaluating and training facilitators who can deliver the best possible outcomes.

Despite a tidal wave of digital change, the physical classroom still occupies an important place in corporate learning. Classrooms provide an ideal setting to build and maintain culture. They offer the opportunity for learners and leaders to spend valuable time sharing and reflecting on ideas with one another—an increasingly rare occurrence in our "always-on" digital world. And of all the factors that contribute to making a live classroom training successful, we believe the role of the facilitator is the most important.

Over the years, we have seen strong, highly skilled facilitators rescue a badly designed class. Sadly, we have also seen weak, poorly skilled facilitators render well-designed classes both ineffective and uninspiring. In many cases, faculty in corporate classrooms are not trained as facilitators; often they are subject-matter experts (SMEs) recruited for their content knowledge. While they may be interested in learning and professional development, they may not have the necessary mind-sets or skills to effectively run a classroom.

Even the most established and polished professionals—including senior executives—are not necessarily practiced in engaging a room of learners. Instead of sparking discussions that shed new light on complex topics, they often embark on long lectures, which research consistently shows to be ineffective. As a result, learning and development (L&D) are minimal. The considerable investment of both time and money is often wasted.

L&D professionals, particularly those who use SMEs from their own organizations as instructors, need to select and train facilitators carefully. What should they consider when choosing teachers? What specific skills do instructors need? How can L&D professionals ensure their faculty is ready to teach effective and engaging classes?

To help ensure that investments in live classroom training make a lasting impact on organizations, we have identified four mind-sets and five skills that are characteristic of great classroom facilitators. With these in mind, L&D professionals can evaluate prospective faculty members and help them shore up their skills before they step into the classroom.

Identifying effective facilitators

How does one assess a potential facilitator's mind-set? The four questions below offer guidelines for organizations that draw faculty from their own ranks. For those that hire outside faculty, these questions can serve as a starting point alongside other tools, such as an online questionnaire, to vet candidates before moving them further along in the hiring process.

Does the person believe learning can be transformative?

Great faculty believe that moments of insight and realization—"light bulb moments"—are always possible. These experiences can alter careers and even lives, and great faculty seek them out.

While even the best faculty may not always succeed in sparking transformation, they must step into the classroom believing transformation and growth are possible. Very little happens when a teacher merely stands in front of a class, mechanically reviewing content and asking a few cursory questions. Great facilitators demand far more: they embrace their roles and seek to make the classroom experience both inspiring and memorable.

Does the person have an "all-in" attitude?

A great facilitator brings energy and enthusiasm to the classroom and is capable of putting aside other work to be fully present for students. Learners know when a facilitator is "phoning it in." They also know when a facilitator is truly interested in what's happening in the classroom. Great facilitators let their learners know, through words and actions, that they are invested in creating a positive learning environment. The best faculty know their learners are investing valuable time to be there, and they respect and appreciate that dedication.

This mind-set reveals itself in many ways—from showing up to class on time to being well prepared and eliminating distractions to staying focused throughout the class. Great faculty spend time getting to know learners before class, during breaks, and at lunch. This reflects the committed and focused mentality that all great facilitators possess.

Is the person student-focused (and not self-focused)?

You want a facilitator who prioritizes the experiences of each student in the room over his or her own experience. For some people, teaching is a way of feeding their own egos by standing up in front of others and serving as conveyors of knowledge. When they do, they become the proverbial "sage on the stage" (and often not very "sage").

The best facilitators understand that they are in class to serve learners, and they are constantly learning themselves. Individual egos have no place in the classroom. The focus should always be on the learners.

Is the person comfortable wearing multiple hats?

Facilitators must be capable of juggling a variety of roles in preparing for and leading a class. Before launching a course, for example, facilitators need to coordinate with multiple teams to discuss site logistics, participant information, technology setup, and other important details. If the facilitator overlooks these steps, the class often suffers.

Once class is under way, facilitators function as timekeepers, making sure the content is covered according to schedule. Great facilitators also inspire learners, sometimes by following the energy of the class and even exploring topics beyond the scope of the faculty guide. Facilitators also have to maintain control over their classes by handling disruptions that could diminish the learning experience.

Will you know with absolute certainty that your faculty possess each of these important mind-sets? Perhaps not. But we have found that even a brief conversation with prospective faculty, coupled with other vetting methods, reveals a lot.

After assessing candidates to see if they possess these four important mind-sets, the next step is to ensure they have the necessary skills to excel in the classroom.

Five essential facilitation skills

Imagine the following scenario:

Inside a well-equipped corporate classroom, 15 learners sit eager for their session to begin. Ten minutes past the scheduled start time, the facilitator finally arrives. He's frazzled, and apologizes as he drops his overstuffed computer bag on a chair and frantically pages through the hefty faculty guide while also trying to get his laptop connected to the overhead projector. The learners wait. Some look down at their phones; others leave the room to get coffee. Eventually, the facilitator dives into the content. He talks fast and for extended stretches of time. He tells long stories about his experience on the topic at hand. He checks the clock, presses ahead, moving from topic to topic until everything is covered. Over the three hours, learners occasionally manage to ask a clarifying question or two. Otherwise, they speak very little. Some try to stay engaged, while others have clearly given up. When the class ends, it's a relief for everyone.

Unfortunately, this scenario might not be hard to imagine. In one form or another, we have all seen this type of facilitator in action. Facilitators often struggle in both obvious and subtle ways. But the point is that engaging, inspiring classes don't happen by accident.

They happen when faculty behavior and skills come together as detailed below, and L&D professionals should ensure that all facilitators demonstrate these skills.

Be prepared

Without exception, poor preparation by a facilitator seriously undermines a class. It's essential for a facilitator to know the content, the flow, the intent, and key steps in the activities as well as to understand the audience. Preparation is the price of admission as faculty. We have seen far too many facilitators stumble through a class simply because they thought they did not need to prepare. Winging it never yields positive results. First, it results in a waste of learners' valuable time. Second, it sends the broader message that faculty do not value the classroom experience or learners' time. This impression can turn learners off to future learning.

For a facilitator, preparation is empowering and builds confidence. A prepared facilitator has practiced everything from opening remarks to important stories and key transitions. Learners respond to this confidence and preparation by engaging more during class.

How much time should faculty spend preparing for class? One benchmark is to spend twice as much time preparing as it takes to teach. People often push back against this guideline, saying they are too busy to invest that much time. Certainly, when a facilitator repeats a class, the preparation time goes down. But each new class brings a fresh new group of learners, and great facilitators know that practice keeps them sharp and focused.

It's essential for a facilitator to know the content, the flow, the intent, and key steps in the activities as well as to understand the audience.

Good preparation also helps facilitators respond to any unexpected deviations from the lesson design, such as shortened class time, problems with technology, or a change in class energy level. When the unexpected happens, faculty must stay calm, go with the flow, and improvise, using the "Yes ... and" technique made famous by improv comedy troupes to explore promising new paths. Since great faculty are prepared and have created an open, honest, and trusting environment, they can take the risk of changing plans slightly.

We strongly recommend that you hold a train-the-trainer session before the class begins. Not only does this provide built-in prep time, it also gives co-facilitators time to strategize and coordinate.

Make it personal

Great facilitators make every class personal. There are numerous ways to accomplish this goal; here are three strategies that work especially well.

Set a positive tone

The facilitator sets the overall tone in the classroom. Creating an environment that is positive, safe, and inclusive is foundational to a successful class. Learners respond well to facilitators who demonstrate interest in them.

We have worked closely with many facilitators who are masterful in this area. It all starts with showing up early. Instead of burying their heads in their laptops or faculty guides, they stand at the front of the class and greet every learner who walks in the door. They shake hands, say hello, offer a smile, and ask a question or two. This engagement establishes a connection that they continue to nurture during class. They use names, listen attentively, and make sure that each person in the class is heard.

Watch for individual differences

Faculty can also provide a personal touch by recognizing individual differences. Even if all the learners in the class are from the same region or in the same job function, they all come to class with unique skills, ambitions, and goals. Great facilitators acknowledge these variances and use their listening and observation skills to account for them in class. One specific way faculty can personalize a class is through debriefing sessions that focus on how each learner can apply new knowledge and skills to his or her job.

Tell stories

Stories are uniquely effective at illuminating big, complex topics, and great facilitators tell great stories. We readily recall a great story because our brains give us access not just to the storyline but also to how we felt when we first heard it. Facilitators' stories in turn encourage others in the class to share, and the exchange of stories creates a marvelous setting where ideas and insights flow.

Strong storytellers share several key qualities: they prepare their stories meticulously before class; they tell brief stories—never more than a few minutes; they are clear about each story's key message; and they are descriptive. Incorporating these qualities takes practice (in other words, preparation), but over time it pays off.

Talk less–listen more

The best facilitators are great listeners. If learners feel that their facilitator is listening, they are more willing to talk—and learner engagement and comments are critical in helping the facilitator guide the progress of the class. Do the learners understand the material? Do you need to back up and review, or try a different approach?

We often see facilitators fall into the trap of monopolizing class time with their own thoughts and ideas rather than listening to what the learners have to say. This approach can be entertaining, but even if learners find it interesting, they don't always get the necessary takeaways.

We recommend that learners carry the conversation 70 percent of the time. An effective facilitator spends about 30 percent of class time guiding, probing, and revealing insights. It can be challenging for faculty with deep content expertise to step back in this way, but it is essential. When adult learners arrive at insights on their own, they feel invested enough to apply the insights to their daily work.

Ask questions

A facilitator's most important tool is a question. When a facilitator is curious, learners follow suit and start to ask questions too. Instead of answering every question, a facilitator might sometimes ask the rest of the class what they think. Great facilitators come to class prepared with a wide range of questions and use Socratic questioning to gauge whether learners understand a concept.

Experienced facilitators also check in with the class throughout discussions, asking "What questions do you have?" or "Why did you think that?" Such queries challenge learners, dig deeper into topics, and elevate the level of discussion in the classroom. Questions build energy in the classroom and help focus the discussion on the specific learning and performance objectives at hand. It's certainly appropriate at times for the facilitator to provide insight and reveal the "right answer" on a given subject. But it's often more powerful to probe and invite learners to share their perspectives.

Challenge your learners

A great facilitator seeks to challenge learners. As we have discussed, preparation, understanding individual differences, listening, and asking great questions all help.

We make this point because too often we see facilitators back off from truly challenging learners and instead allow them to take an easier path. In our experience, this approach always backfires. It's

Questions build energy in the classroom and help focus the discussion on the specific learning and performance objectives at hand.

true that pushing learners too far or hard can be bad. But in our experience, if a facilitator has done a good job of building trust and creating an environment for sharing and dialogue, learners will be willing to take risks. A great facilitator knows that failing in class can be a gift to a learner. Some ways facilitators can build trust are through a challenging role play or solving a difficult problem during team-building exercises.

Creating a faculty excellence program

L&D professionals understand better than anyone that high-performing organizations depend on employees who are constantly learning. Considering how many hours people spend in training, it is not hard to make the business case for ensuring that classroom faculty are truly qualified. Bolstering that case is the fact that facilitation skills are also extremely transferable to other areas. For example, the ability to engage and challenge others is also important when working with clients and leading teams. Capable team leaders are more likely to be chosen as facilitators, and faculty-training programs meant to hone facilitation skills will likely lead to better performance on the job—leading to a virtuous cycle of improvement.

At its core, a faculty-excellence program should include the following:

- *Master faculty.* Choose a group of master faculty from within the organization to teach the program. You can pair these individuals with external instructors, but it's important to show learners that the organization's own employees can be great facilitators.

- *Develop models and frameworks.* Materials that articulate core skills and behaviors for facilitation can become assets for training programs. You may have some of these already, but a highly qualified learning designer can help to develop a repeatable approach so you can scale your offerings. You can also develop 24/7 digital support for facilitators, including tools such as videos on how to conduct a tricky exercise or a sample list of Socratic questions.

- *Time to practice.* Build in at least a day for facilitators to practice key skills outside the classroom and receive feedback. Feedback from master faculty and peers helps build confidence alongside practice.

- *Consider certification.* We have found that certifying instructors is a powerful motivator. Not only do people take pride in getting certified, but it also helps ensure a level of quality and consistency among facilitators. Apprenticeship is often one element of a certification process.

- *Collect and track feedback.* Create a robust system for gathering and maintaining feedback on faculty. Invite your learners to provide input after each class through surveys or other tools, and make sure your L&D group stays up to speed on any red flags addressed by your faculty.

Companies often encourage their high-level executives to head up leadership-training programs. For learning programs delivered to external clients, you might consider using professional facilitators.

Keep in mind that it takes time to become a great facilitator. Practice matters. To improve at golf, you must keep playing rounds. To improve as a facilitator, you need to work at it, and you need to keep an open mind. Companies should consider implementing a program in which the best faculty observe those who are less experienced and provide feedback, as well as giving professionals the opportunity to teach on a regular basis.

■ ■ ■

New digital approaches to learning will certainly continue to be developed, but there will always be value in meeting face to face to connect and share our experiences and ideas. Therefore, there will always be a need for the highest-quality facilitators to bring these face-to-face classroom sessions to life.

As L&D professionals, we are all accountable for offering effective learning opportunities. However, the ultimate answer to "Are we getting it right?" will come from our learners. Are they energized and inspired? Do they have new ideas for making positive changes on the job? Have they gained new insights that will benefit their performance and that they can share with others on their teams?

If the answer to any, or all, of these questions is "yes," then we know that the facilitator in the classroom has brought the right mindset and the proper skills to be effective. The faculty's role has been, and will continue to be, the most important factor. It's up to us as L&D professionals to identify and train the best people to play this critical role. ■

CHAPTER

18/

THE LEARNING FACILITY OF THE FUTURE

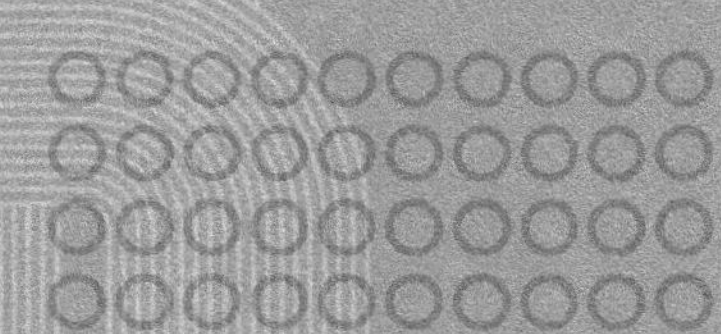

AUTHORS
Kim Blank
Janine Carboni
Gina Fine

Today's learning facilities, whether permanent or temporary, must do much more than the classrooms of the past. Best practices from leading learning-and-development functions around the world provide a blueprint for creating functional and inspiring spaces.

In the 1980s and '90s, it was common for larger companies to establish corporate universities, particularly in the United States. A dedicated physical space for learning demonstrated an organization's commitment to intellectual development and added to its prestige. While the golden age of huge, dedicated learning centers may be over, in-person learning is still going strong: a recent survey found that 49 percent of corporate learning hours in 2016 were spent in a traditional classroom and led by an in-person instructor.[1] The survey also found that smaller companies tend to spend more of their learning-and-development (L&D) budget on classroom learning than large corporations do[2]—but some large companies such as BASF, Deloitte, GE, and Visa have also made recent investments in existing or new dedicated learning facilities. Many other large firms conduct in-person learning at their own offices or in temporary spaces such as hotels or meeting facilities.

Regardless of where learning takes place, the learning environment is key to a successful experience. Educators and learning designers have seen firsthand how a physical space has an impact on everything from efficient use of time to influencing participant mind-sets. Indeed, a 2015 study by Brandon Hall Group found that improved classroom design supports better learning outcomes.[3] A well-designed learning environment can help you deliver on the promise of flipped classrooms and blended learning, facilitate new connections, and reinforce the organization's culture and mission. On the flip side, an ill-conceived physical space—with problems ranging from poorly functioning technology to inadequate room setups—can waste time and frustrate learners.

To identify best practices for creating successful corporate learning environments, we visited academic institutions, corporate learning facilities, and hotel and meeting centers. We also conducted interviews with technology and furniture manufacturers and surveyed our own teaching faculty and learners.

Our findings led us to the following important, but simple, principles:

- *Challenge your thinking about learning spaces.* We found that a great deal of learning at organizations occurs outside of the traditional classroom. Well-designed non-classroom spaces can facilitate connections and enhance well-being. And traditional classrooms shouldn't be the norm anymore. Within the classroom, consider moving away from round, U-shaped, and theater seating in favor of layouts that mimic the actual work environment.

- *Build flexible classrooms with ample resources for collaboration.* A clever room layout and movable furniture, combined with a range of low-tech collaboration materials such as whiteboards, are critically important for teams to work most effectively together.

- *Invest in IT infrastructure and technology solutions—and provide support for those solutions.* To succeed, you need a robust IT infrastructure that supports multiple technology offerings and meets evolving needs with on-site support and faculty training.

- *Reinforce company culture and provide an inspirational environment.* Learning facilities are an excellent opportunity to instill a sense of company pride, create a sense of community, and encourage a mind-set of curiosity and intellectualism through exhibits, personal touches, and displays

Following these principles will help you maximize the learning experience, provide opportunities for skill development and practice, strengthen your company culture, and ultimately build a stronger, more capable organization.

Best practices in facility design

Classrooms provide the most effective learning environment in many situations, not only for skill development and practice but also for connecting with peers and company leaders, conducting simulations, and providing time for reflection. In what has come to be known as a "high tech, high touch" approach to learning delivery, the characteristics of the physical space are mission critical.

According to our research, the most effective learning facilities are flexible, comfortable, and modern, with robust IT infrastructure and support. Not surprisingly, windows and light are key to keeping both learners and faculty energized and focused. Building your own learning facilities gives you the most control over these elements. But even if you use temporary spaces, such as hotel conference rooms, you can exert some control by selecting facilities with optimal furnishings, grounds, and recreational opportunities.

Build a mix of classroom and nonclassroom spaces

Our research found that one of the most important things you can do is to build a variety of spaces that serve different purposes. Traditional classrooms are a key element, but just as important are the complementary rooms and spaces around the classroom that facilitate collaboration and immersive learning. Best-in-class learning spaces are designed to encourage connections, foster introspection, and enable people to focus on positive lifestyle habits.

Nontraditional locations. Hotels and learning facilities can all feel the same, even if they're in another city or country. Learning sessions in unexpected or inspirational settings can change people's mind-sets and foster openness to learning. A training room at a mountain or oceanfront resort, for example, can put people in a very different mind-set than a windowless hotel ballroom. Learners can find inspiration in the natural surroundings and take walks during breaks. Assignments that include walking with others in the woods can have a much greater impact on relationships, self-reflection, and openness to change than sitting together in a room.

Casual meeting spaces. A primary purpose of in-person programs is to forge stronger relationships among colleagues, and facility design plays an important role in making that happen. In the course of our research we often heard that "meetings outside the meetings" were just as important to learning as classroom time. The best facilities have casual spaces with comfortable seating where project teams can discuss strategies and learners can network between classroom sessions. Ideally, these spaces have flexible seating with additional chairs nearby that can be brought in to expand the conversation. Consider outdoor meeting spaces as well, to offer a change of scenery. Stocked with mobile flip charts and baskets of office supplies, these areas can offer a literal breath of fresh air while participants remain on task.

Architecture students at the Massachusetts Institute of Technology worked with their school's food service provider, among others, to create the Steam Café, with the goal to "break through rigid business models, shyness and a complacent corporate food culture."[4] The Steam Café encourages serendipitous connections among students and faculty through the design of the space, the use of technology, and diverse food choices.[5] A bar/lounge can do double duty as a casual meeting space during the day and a locus for group activities in the evening. Coffee-break spaces or dedicated cafés are also natural spaces for people to come together and continue the conversation after a meeting.

Group-activity spaces. Thoughtfully designed spaces for group activities can also enhance the experience. Easily accessible recreational activities can lead to the unplanned moments that

A primary purpose of in-person programs is to forge stronger relationships among colleagues, and facility design plays an important role in making that happen.

are often the most salient and memorable parts of any program. Consider putting board games, musical instruments, a video-game console, or sporting equipment in strategic locations to encourage people who may not have a natural connection to engage in non-work-related activities together. We've also seen facilities provide food trucks, laser tag, karaoke nights, and morning yoga classes.

Immersive-learning spaces. Simulation labs, model factories, call centers, retail stores, and other immersive-learning spaces allow learners to build technical skills in realistic but risk-free environments. In the Window on the World (WOW) Room at IE University in Madrid, for example, experts from all over the world appear in hologram form to teach and interact with students. The WOW Room also features interactive robots, artificial intelligence, and simulations that immerse students in business crises, factory environments, and even diplomatic conflicts.[6]

Immersive experiences not only quickly build transferable skills, they also promote tighter, longer-lasting bonds among colleagues. Indeed, immersive experiences are often more effective than pure networking. For example, culinary students who work in a kitchen together are likely to form much closer relationships than those who simply attend the same training program.

Invest in IT infrastructure and support

In-person learning will always be a high-touch process, but technology plays a critical role in enhancing learning experiences. Of course, technology requires a strong IT support model. (For more on optimizing learning's partnership with IT, see chapter 3.)

Physical infrastructure. The most important technology investment you can make is in infrastructure. Hardware and software quickly become obsolete, but they all rely on basic infrastructure components such as networking (both wired and wireless), internet access, bandwidth, telecoms, and audio. When choosing advanced technologies, make sure you have a physical infrastructure that can reliably support them. Enabling corporate learners to use the company's proprietary networks and intranets on a remote site offers a seamless experience.

Accessible technology and training. Nothing brings an in-person learning experience to a grinding halt quite like an instructor struggling with technology. You can avoid that scenario by creating a seamless, easy-to-use technology platform that can support evolving technology choices over the long run. Because the technological savvy of instructors will vary, you also need to invest in training and support for facility faculty and staff. One well-respected business school created a full-time, dedicated technology response team to ensure a swift response to any technology-based classroom disruptions. This effort underscores both the frequency and the inevitability of problems with technology.

Best practices in classroom design

In designing traditional classrooms, best-in-class L&D functions seek to create welcoming learning environments that support faculty and learners alike. A 2016 study from Brandon Hall Group highlights how flexibility and comfort can enhance the in-person learning experience:

> "It is also worth examining the physical layouts of the classrooms and how they relate to new and future technologies. The classroom itself must be flexible and adaptive. A study by furniture company Herman Miller found that when classroom furniture is easily moved to allow for comfort and practicality, students' learning experience was heightened with increased seating comfort (32 percent), being able to clearly understand the professor (14 percent), and being able to view materials (17 percent). Besides students being better serviced by redesigned and malleable classrooms, educators also reported the benefits of increased lighting, better access to internet connections, improved ability to hear students and having more whiteboard space."[7]

Several of these lessons resonated with our interviewees, helping us create a simple but essential list of best practices for classroom design.

Design flexible classrooms

As classroom activities evolve from lectures to team exercises to participant-led discussions, the physical space should be able to adapt seamlessly. Many L&D professionals have been quick to adopt leading-edge classroom designs with no clear front of the room. Open classroom spaces with movable, comfortable furniture—including soft seating as well as traditional tables and chairs—can be configured in multiple ways, which facilitates collaboration and conversation. In simulations and action learning, a physical space that mirrors an actual work space helps learners retain and transfer what they're learning.

Modern flexible classrooms need plenty of power outlets, both to support participants' electronic devices and to facilitate changes in the room configuration. Ideally, movable walls or screens would allow you to change room sizes to accommodate everything from large lectures to multiteam collaborations to small breakout discussions (Exhibit 18A).

Exhibit 18A: **Classrooms with no clear front of the room can foster better learning and collaboration.**

Illustration by Vic Kulihin

Not only does a flexible space support an active and engaged learning environment, it also allows for frequent experimentation or redesign of programs.

Provide ample writing surfaces

Learners have grown accustomed to a baseline level of technology in classrooms, but our research found that participants and faculty still overwhelmingly value the opportunity to brainstorm, write out ideas, and collaborate in longhand. Therefore, low-tech writing surfaces—large whiteboards, flip charts and other portable surfaces, and even magnetic surfaces and tack boards—are critical classroom elements for collaboration and communication. One well-respected educational institution tested several physical writing surfaces. Somewhat counterintuitively, large-scale writable surfaces, such as chalk and blackboard, emerged as the most desired writing tools in classrooms.

Equip classrooms with a wide variety of technology solutions

Technology solutions with in-person learning applications include presentation technology, video capture, video conferencing/telepresence, audio conferencing, and collaboration tools. Choosing the most expensive, elaborate technologies throughout the entire facility does not ensure success. Focus your spending on solutions that will have the greatest impact—for example, most firms invest more heavily in high-end video-conferencing equipment for larger rooms, where more people will benefit from it, than for smaller spaces.

The solutions you choose may be somewhat aspirational. Many of the L&D professionals we interviewed said that learning facilities should be designed to support curriculum enhancement and expansion—not the other way around. For example, your current learning program might not incorporate video conferencing, but equipping your facility with conferencing capabilities opens up the possibility of hosting guest lecturers via video or using video-capture technology for real-time feedback. Similarly, some L&D organizations are considering investments in virtual reality, which may prove to be a game changer. As the cost of implementing virtual reality continues to drop, simulations once available only to the largest firms will become accessible to smaller organizations. By carefully surveying the options, you can simultaneously meet your learners' current needs and lay the groundwork for future opportunities.

Beyond learning: Creating an inspirational environment

In the age of globalization, in-person learning offers a rare opportunity to usher a large number of employees through a single shared space. Those spaces—whether temporary learning space or a permanent learning facility—can play a critical role in reinforcing an organization's culture and the company brand. To this end, L&D professionals can take a relatively basic space and infuse it with "soul."

The best facilities we visited do three things:

Instill a sense of company pride. Many organizations build exhibits about the company's values, history, and impact. At one of McKinsey's dedicated learning spaces, learners can peruse a collection of artifacts, including our founder's desk, and exhibits showcasing the firm's history. Mobile versions of such assets can also be used to make a temporary space feel more relevant and intimate. In permanent facilities, conference rooms can be named after people who have advanced human thought or cities that have played an important role in your organization's history.

Learners can peruse a collection of artifacts, including our founder's desk, and exhibits showcasing the firm's history.

Create a sense of community. Many of the best practices described in this chapter are aimed at improving collaboration opportunities. To connect that sense of community with the company's identity, offer a selection of branded items, such as welcome messages, sign-in boards, and so forth. Many people told us that personal touches—such as welcome packets or nightly pillow cards—can make the experience feel more personal and connected.

Encourage a mind-set of curiosity and intellectualism. Your employees may not be aware of the impact your organization is having on the industry and the world. Learning facilities are an excellent place to showcase news from around the company—prompting employees to make unexpected connections and pursue new experiences and activities.

Maximizing in-person learning without a dedicated facility

Many of the practices outlined here can be achieved without investing in a permanent learning facility. Some companies rent space off site, working with the proprietor and vendors to outfit the rented facility to meet their needs, or make investments in an external location. Others develop portable solutions—such as exhibits, simulation equipment, and portable classroom technology—that can be brought to a variety of locations. Temporary facilities must be carefully surveyed to ensure they offer the foundational IT infrastructure your curriculum requires. But with creativity and moderate investment, you can customize and personalize these spaces.

■ ■ ■

In-person training plays an integral role in supporting learning goals and in fostering a strong company culture. That's why it's essential to create effective in-person learning locations, whether permanent or temporary. While there is no one-size-fits-all solution, you can optimize the experience and create an inspirational environment by following the lead of best-in-class organizations in designing a facility. Indeed, the best facility design does more than provide for basic needs—it supports flexibility, streamlines the learning experience, encourages connections, and infuses the space with the company's own culture and values. ■

1 *2017 state of the industry,* ATD Research, December 2017, td.org.

2 *2018 workplace learning report,* LinkedIn Learning, learning.linkedin.com.

3 *Research summary: 2015 training study,* Brandon Hall Group, July 2015, brandonhall.com.

4 "Steam Café," Pilot Projects Design Collective, pilot-projects.org.

5 Scott Francisco, "MIT: Steam Café," *Learning Spaces,* edited by Diana G. Oblinger, EDUCAUSE, 2006.

6 "WOW Room takes IE's commitment to technology immersion in learning environments to the next level," IE Business School, October 20, 2016, ie.edu.

7 *Bringing the classroom into the 21st century,* Brandon Hall Group, August 2016, brandonhall.com.

CHAPTER

19/

MIGRATING LEARNING TO THE CLOUD

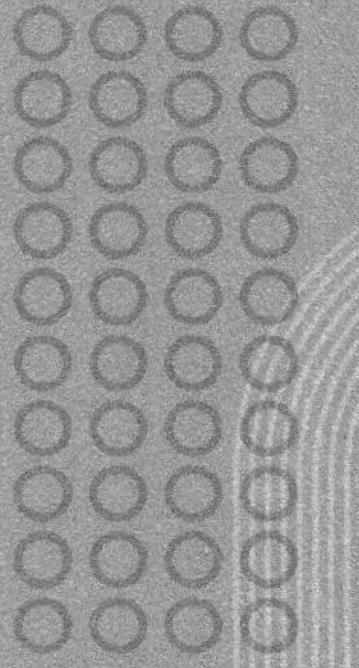

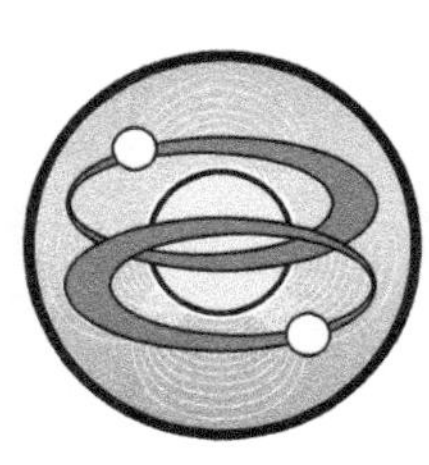

AUTHORS
Carissa Bell
Tonya Corley
Duncan Larkin

Learning-and-development functions can benefit greatly from a move to the cloud, but leaders must take the proper steps to ensure a smooth migration.

Cloud-based learning technology can play a key role in supporting learning-and-development (L&D) strategies, and L&D leaders are taking note. In the past few years, L&D leaders at many organizations have migrated content, legacy tools, and their entire learning-management systems (LMSs) from on-premises servers to the cloud.[1] This trend has been fueled by the key role that cloud-based learning-technology solutions can play in supporting the overall L&D strategy.

The cloud enables enhanced digital-learning solutions, facilitates the personalization of learning, and fosters on-demand learning solutions such as delivery on mobile devices. It offers several other strategic and operational benefits as well. For example, customizing and supporting on-premises infrastructure and solutions can be expensive. A move to the cloud frees up resources that can be reallocated to curriculum development, curation of digital-learning solutions, and updates of cloud-based technologies. Given the need in many organizations to track compliance, cloud-based learning solutions also optimize business processes through the use of technology (for example, evaluation, polling, and self-service enrolling in courses).

The application of cloud-based learning technologies can also increase the impact and effectiveness of L&D investments. In the past, companies often got stuck with an enterprise resource planning (ERP) vendor for many years because alternatives were unaffordable and too time consuming to implement. The cloud, on the other hand, offers access to "plug-and-play" solutions, allowing users to update their learning-technology infrastructure more rapidly to support innovation.

L&D's newfound embrace of the cloud has caused massive disruption in the industry—one that cannot be ignored if L&D organizations wish to remain relevant. To respond to this disruption and fully harness the benefits of the cloud, L&D leaders must adapt their IT approaches and plan accordingly. They should also be judicious when selecting their cloud platform, since offerings can vary significantly among vendors by working closely with the organization's IT professionals, L&D leaders can better understand what is required at each step of the process—from planning for a migration to managing the cloud vendor relationship after implementation. (For more on how L&D can forge a productive relationship with its IT department, see chapter 3.) The following road map can help you optimize your cloud migration.

Why L&D is moving to the cloud

To understand why the cloud has the potential to transform L&D, it is helpful to trace the evolution of learning architecture and focus on the specific benefits that the cloud has for the industry.

Customized, proprietary systems give way to the cloud

Historically, learning software and platforms were developed and maintained by individual organizations. Large, long-established companies once structured their L&D organizations using a traditional IT approach, which entailed on-premises, proprietary LMSs and other learning technology (such as learning-content-management systems and virtual classrooms) that hosted custom content. Before the advent of seamless communications and the exponential growth of the internet, digital learning was mostly a solitary, isolated affair that existed within the bounds of a company's firewall.

In other words, L&D software once belonged entirely to a single company. It was hosted on the company's dedicated, expensive L&D servers and was maintained by the company's costly team of full-time developers. Any residual bugs in the software or performance dips in the company's servers were the sole responsibility of the company. What's more, learning content was generated by the company's L&D team. If the company wanted to enhance its L&D offerings, it needed new content, new code, quality assurance, and end-to-end regression testing.

Enterprises owned it all—from the creation of an instructional video to the server that hosted this video to the software that led the user to the video in the first place. The company was solely responsible for tracking analytics and learner behavior, and for responding to learner questions, concerns, and frustrations.

In the early days of the cloud, many companies with substantial investments in legacy systems resisted it. They believed, in many cases correctly, that any large-scale transformation would be a complex and costly endeavor, requiring new business processes, cloud implementation teams, and the conversion of legacy data to the new platform. In addition, complexities during the cutover can hinder the change-management momentum required to sunset proprietary software and transition all learners successfully to the cloud.

Much of the L&D industry has finally embraced the cloud despite these hurdles, recognizing that it offers many benefits—including expanded content resources, reduced IT infrastructure costs, and lower risk. As a result, businesses don't have as many options to purchase non-cloud-based L&D software or create custom code that can be installed behind corporate firewalls, which limits the quality of the learning experience and makes a compelling case for migration. Some companies, however, are slow to make the transition or resist it altogether, citing worries about data security, an insufficient business case for the migration, and the complexities of decoupling learning systems from existing, on-premises people platforms.

Benefits of the cloud

Cloud-based learning technologies are generally based on one of the three following archetypes:

Content platforms. These repositories for digital-learning solutions house digital books (summaries), recording webinars, learning videos, online games and simulations, specific private online courses (SPOCs), asynchronous digital courses, and so on.

Learning-management systems. Enhanced content platforms provide learners with access to digital courses and in-person programs. An LMS also offers capabilities for administrative reporting and learner tracking that content platforms don't offer.

Learner-experience platforms (LXPs). LXPs are relatively new to the ecosystem of L&D digital offerings. Companies are finding that stand-alone LMSs don't sufficiently meet the rapidly changing needs of learners who, because of the threat to their jobs due to increased automation, find themselves needing to upskill and gain access to an ever-increasing variety of content across numerous platforms. LXPs such as EdCast and Valamis aggregate content for learners, simplifying content searches and offering contextualized, curated digital courses.

All three platforms offer the same strategic benefits:

Risk transfer. Cloud-based data is stored on servers owned by vendors—not by your organization. The cloud vendor manages all aspects of server performance, accessibility, overhauls, upgrades, and other maintenance.

Lower cost. Since cloud-based vendors own the learning system's hardware and software, they are responsible for supporting the infrastructure and architecture. Consequently, your organization's IT function doesn't have to maintain the system, create user accounts, fix bugs, or make updates.

Innovation potential. Traditionally, on-premises vendors have had limited funds for innovation. Cloud-based L&D companies invest heavily in innovation, because deploying cutting-edge solutions is one of their main selling points.

Integration. Most cloud vendors have invested in functionality to support cloud-to-cloud integration with their customers' existing systems.

Choosing the right cloud solution

Selecting the right L&D cloud vendor is one of the most important decisions that organizations will face and should be made with proper due diligence. Close collaboration with IT and procurement during the vendor selection process can ensure that L&D leaders are aware of best practices and common pitfalls.

Best practices

First, conduct in-depth stakeholder interviews, articulate the organization's needs, and prioritize them. When evaluating a cloud vendor, you should not only engage with the vendor's sales teams but also request access to the vendor's developers, architects, and software engineers to gain a full understanding of capability. Some cloud vendors prefer not to engage on technical issues until after the sale has been made, so make sure your engineers meet with the vendor's so that you don't invest in a solution that isn't technically viable.

Second, talk to other companies that have already implemented cloud solutions to learn about the pitfalls, the vendor selection process, and the drawbacks of specific vendors. Support during and after implementation is crucial, so gather insights about each vendor's help desk, staffing, workflow software, and ticket resolution and escalation to ensure that you'll have the guidance you need. You should also verify the vendor's support model and service-level agreements (SLAs) for issue resolution.

Last, organizations must recognize that when they select a vendor, they are entering into a longer-term relationship—so it is important to learn as much as possible about the vendor. Evaluating the vendor's leadership team, growth strategy, financial viability, road map, and points of differentiation can provide some assurance. Other areas to explore include the vendor's ownership structure (public versus private), the degree of collaboration among its internal departments, and whether its system can be customized, both on the front end (user interface) and on the back end (such as its data model, content, and architecture). Prospective vendors should be able to support the user experience on mobile devices and provide reporting metrics. One of the major benefits of a cloud vendor is automatic software updates, but organizations need to find out the product release schedule.

Pitfalls to avoid

Never make a "buy" decision without technical vetting from your company's IT organization. When evaluating candidates, don't assume that a cloud vendor will provide round-the-clock support or that users will be able to access the cloud seamlessly anywhere in the world. If your company has a global reach, make sure you understand the details of access and support in every office location around the world. Since many learners will use their smartphones or other mobile devices, you need to explicitly address how your website will perform on a low-bandwidth smartphone. Understanding how the vendor has designed its infrastructure will help your company alleviate any frustration with poor service levels and connectivity.

Prospective vendors should be able to support the user experience on mobile devices and provide reporting metrics.

Ensuring a smooth migration to the cloud

Once your L&D function has decided which software to purchase and selected a vendor, it's time to plan for a successful migration (see sidebar, "The ten phases of a successful cloud migration"). Remember that planning for your migration is just as important as actually implementing the solution. The following tips will help you make a smooth migration to the cloud:

- Build the business case by securing and aligning executive commitment to the migration.
- Carefully vet and assemble a team of high-caliber project managers who have completed cloud migrations.
- Establish a program management office to take responsibility for integrating project plans across all work streams of the implementation.
- Clearly delineate roles and responsibilities between L&D and IT. Clarify who will do what in each phase.
- Gain an understanding of all relevant data that supports the cloud system's requirements. Compare legacy data with cloud data inputs and learn what kind of data conversions will be required as well as the time and cost to complete the conversions.
- Work with all migration stakeholders to identify, redesign, and standardize core learning business processes.
- Inventory all legacy learning content that will migrate to the cloud (for example, Flash to HTML5 conversions).
- Assemble a dedicated team to train new users and administrators on the cloud-based learning system and manage company-wide communications about the implementation, its benefits, and what will change and what will not change post-implementation.
- Staff an operations team that can prepare your organization for each product release and interact with the vendor to report and resolve any bugs or issues.

- Gain a clear understanding of the following nuances of a migration:
  - — The cloud vendor's architecture diagrams
  - — Any integration pain points between the cloud and that require intervention, and what types of environments exist in the cloud (for example, sandbox, pilot, production)
- Draft a detailed cutover plan that outlines contingencies in the event of system blackouts.
- Establish a full understanding of vendor support for administrators, the ticket-resolution process, and the escalation path once cutover has completed.

The ten steps of a successful cloud migration

Cloud migration encompasses the following ten steps:

1. Gather functional and technical requirements as well as use cases for the new platform.
2. Vet and prioritize requirements and use cases.
3. Evaluate the cloud market, comparing your organization's requirements to the vendor's offerings.
4. Select the optimal vendor.
5. Staff your cloud-implementation team.
6. Create a detailed project plan for implementation.
7. Train new users and administrators on the new platform.
8. Complete the cloud migration.
9. Define the operational model for product-release cycles and issue management.
10. Conduct cloud vendor new code releases and applicable regression testing.

Getting the most from your cloud vendor

As with any external vendor, cloud vendors must be managed. In our experience, L&D organizations typically face two common challenges in migrating their operations to the cloud and operating post-implementation. You can overcome these challenges without significant disruption by taking the appropriate actions.

Vendors typically create product road maps based on their own needs rather than on customer requests. When vendors determine the timing and new functionality of upgrades, L&D organizations often receive product enhancements that they don't need or want. You do have a way to influence future releases, however: most L&D cloud vendors have client steering committees that determine customer needs and provide input on product updates. By joining this governing body, you can work with other members—especially companies with heavy investments in the vendor—to influence product development.

New product releases, bug fixes, and other enhancements can cause unintended issues. The best way to mitigate potential problems is to understand your vendor's development-release process. Verify the testing of new code, the timing of its release, and the steps the vendor has taken to prevent any bugs. Further, defining your vendor's response to regression bugs in code releases, including how the vendor partners with companies to support testing and resolve issues, makes it possible to collaborate and problem solve with vendors before the new code is rolled out.

Managing your cloud vendor post-implementation

Tech companies such as Facebook, Google, Netflix, and Spotify have set a high bar for content, and your learners will expect your cloud vendor to meet it. To maximize the potential of your cloud solutions, partner with your vendor to innovate in the following areas:

- *Personalization.* First and foremost, cloud content needs to be completely relevant to the learner; the more relevant the content, the more likely your learners are to engage with it. Advanced integrations support better, more meaningful learning, so plan to integrate your content with HR systems and others.

- *Mobile first.* Workers are increasingly learning on the go, so any customization should ensure that users can access content on their mobile devices.

- *Optimized for search.* Just as learners want content to be relevant, they expect it to be easy to find. To meet these expectations, organize your data in uniform taxonomies so that your vendor's search-engine software can index it successfully.

- *Predictive.* Access to your organization's data helps cloud vendors use artificial intelligence and machine learning to anticipate learner needs and skill gaps. L&D functions should partner with their cloud vendor to provide as much data on their workforce as is legally permissible.

- *Ease of integration and aggregation.* Cloud solutions need to interact with one another across multiple clouds, so your vendor's systems must be able to accommodate application programming interfaces (APIs). Integrating on-premises platforms with the cloud can also be made more secure and seamless through a single-sign-on authentication service.

■ ■ ■

Cloud-based learning technologies are here to stay and taking over the L&D industry. Companies with comprehensive, forward-thinking learning-technology strategies—those that are based on business and learner needs—will prove the most successful in the long run. By contrast, organizations that choose to continue with custom development and on-premises servers will create barriers to keeping learners engaged. They will also incur increasing costs due to development and maintenance fees.

L&D organizations can no longer ignore the cloud. It is most cost-effective and efficient way to stay at the forefront of learning innovation. For your employees, the cloud can deliver the best possible learning experience—not only fueling their personal growth, but also ensuring that your company is best positioned for the demands of the ever-changing technological landscape.

Of course, the cloud is only a tool that can enable an effective strategy. Without a well-thought-out plan and a strategic approach to cloud migration, your company's learners will not reap the rewards of an efficient and engaging learning experience. ■

[1] In the simplest terms, companies can purchase a particular portion of a vendor's server capacity and its respective proprietary learning software.

Biographies

Editor

Based in the Amsterdam office, **Nick van Dam** is a partner, global chief learning officer (CLO), and client adviser at McKinsey. He is an internationally recognized thought leader, adviser, researcher, author, and speaker on corporate learning and leadership development. Over the course of his professional career, Nick has served more than 100 clients around the world. He is also a professor at IE University (Madrid) and Nyenrode (Amsterdam), and an adjunct professor at the University of Pennsylvania, where he works with candidates in the executive doctoral program for CLOs. Prior to joining McKinsey, he was partner, global CLO, and director of human capital for Deloitte. Nick has written articles for various publications and has been quoted by *Financial Times, Wall Street Journal, Fortune Magazine, Business Week, India Times, Information Week, Management Consulting, CLO Magazine*, and *TD Magazine*. He has authored and coauthored more than 25 books and numerous articles on innovations in learning and leadership development. Under the patrons of the European Parliament Federal Ministry of Education & Research, he received the 2013 Leonardo European Corporate Learning Award for shaping the future of organizational learning and leadership development. He is the founder of the e-learning for kids foundation, which has provided digital lessons for more than 20 million underprivileged elementary school children.

Authors

Based in the Southern California office, **Mary Andrade** is the director of McKinsey's Learning Design and Development Center of Excellence. She is pioneering 21st-century learning methodologies, approaches, and design for McKinsey and the learning industry. She is an authored, experienced learning professional with a 20-year track record of success in creating learning curricula, applying innovative design and development techniques, and delivering solutions to large organizations deploying at scale. She has written articles for *TD Magazine, Chief Learning Officer*, and *The Pfeiffer Annual*.

Based in the Melbourne office, **Maria Eugenia Arias** is a leadership, learning, and culture senior expert adviser. She is responsible for coaching programs for McKinsey partners (new partner coaching and senior coaching). On the client side, she works with executive teams and boards on issues of governance, alignment, leadership development, and performance transformation. This work often involves coaching individuals and teams. She played a key role in developing knowledge on top-team effectiveness and family-owned businesses at McKinsey. Before joining McKinsey, Maria Eugenia taught at INSEAD, INCAE (the leading business school in Latin America), and Mount Eliza Business School (Australia). She is the author of papers and cases addressing development challenges and articles on managerial practices, skills, and HR issues.

Carissa Bell is a learning solutions manager based out of McKinsey's Atlanta office who leads McKinsey's Learning Administration Solutions and Tools team. She has more than 18 years of experience in the professional services consulting industry and is a strategic leader of Global Learning Management System implementations and management of cloud-based learning platforms.

Kim Blank is a McKinsey alumni consultant. She has worked with McKinsey Learning on their global site strategy. Prior to this role, she worked as a full-time consultant for McKinsey & Company, consulting with companies in the nonprofit, media, and financial services industries. She is also actively involved in several local and governmental organizations that support public education.

Based in McKinsey's Amsterdam office, **Jacqueline Brassey** is responsible for leadership development and learning for the senior partners globally, as well as a client adviser. She is also an assistant professor at Tilburg University in the Netherlands, specializing in HR and leadership-development research; faculty at the master-class program learning-and-development leadership of Nyenrode Business Universiteit; and a member of the supervisory board of Save the Children in the Netherlands. Jacqui brings about 20 years of professional experience in HR and leadership development. She has coauthored nearly ten books and articles in the area of organizational behavior and leadership development.

Janine Carboni is a senior specialist in learning delivery in McKinsey's Stamford office. In this role, she manages on-site logistics and daily operations at McKinsey's North America Learning Center, which serves nearly 5,000 learners and faculty each year for in-person professional programs. With more than 20 years of experience in event management and on-site delivery, Janine finds her passion in the detailed work of bringing people together.

Lisa Christensen is a senior learning expert in McKinsey's San Francisco office. An expert in design, Lisa leads many of McKinsey's learning innovations, including the design of McKinsey's new One Firm Onboarding journey. Before joining McKinsey, Lisa worked across sectors helping clients develop learning strategy and interactive learner experiences. In addition to her design expertise, Lisa is an accomplished facilitator. She is the coauthor of several articles on ready-to-work learning experiences and simulation design.

Katie Coates is a senior learning manager with McKinsey, leading learning and leadership development for 12,000 non-client-facing professionals. She has more than 25 years of experience in learning and talent development in financial and professional services and is currently pursuing a PhD in Human Development at Fielding Graduate University. Katie has authored chapters in *The E-Learning Fieldbook* (McGraw Hill) and *Next Learning Unwrapped* (Lulu Publishing).

Based in the Atlanta office, **Tonya Corley** is McKinsey's director of Digital Learning Platforms and Solutions for the global firm. In this role she provides thought leadership and operational oversight to drive McKinsey's digital learning vision and technology road map. Tonya has more than 17 years of experience with innovative learning-solutions implementation, with a keen eye toward learner-experience impact.

Sara Diniz is a senior learning manager based in McKinsey's Houston office. Over the past couple of years, she has focused her time developing McKinsey's consultant learning journeys as well as shaping McKinsey's learning strategy. Sara spent the previous decade building iconic brands and high-performance organizations at Procter & Gamble (Always, Gillette, Pantene, Venus, and Wella). She started her career as a consultant with the Boston Consulting Group. She holds an MBA from Harvard and a BA in Chinese studies from UC Berkeley.

Based in the Stamford office, **Gina Fine** is McKinsey's director of learning delivery, leading the deployment of the firm's learning-development programs globally. In this role she oversees the delivery of the Global Learning curriculum of in-person and distance offerings. She also leads analytics and financial-management processes for McKinsey's Global Learning function. Before joining McKinsey, Gina was a partner at Accenture who worked to improve the efficiency and effectiveness of corporations' HR processes and systems. Gina is a member of several industry organizations and has presented at major conferences, including Future Workplace and Masie Learning.

Karen Freeman is a senior portfolio manager in McKinsey's Washington, DC, office. She is responsible for learning for New Ventures, McKinsey's innovation engine with 2,500 colleagues pioneering asset-based consulting. Prior to joining McKinsey, she was head of learning and development at CEB (now Gartner). While at CEB, she coauthored several *Harvard Business Review* articles, including "To keep your customers, keep it simple" and "Stop trying to delight your customers." She also led the team that developed the Challenger sales model and was a principal contributor to the book *The Challenger Sale*.

Stephanie Gabriels is a learning design manager in McKinsey's New York office. As a member of the Design and Development Center of Excellence, her role is leading the day to day of innovative learning projects. Her expertise is the result of 16 years designing and developing effective learning experiences for a wide range of audiences and settings, from operational-excellence digital learning to blended-learning programs for executives. She is the recipient of a 2017 Brandon Hall Group Excellence in Leadership Development Silver Award.

Sarah Gisser is a senior learning portfolio manager in McKinsey's Minneapolis office, leading learning-and-development initiatives that support the firm's partners and senior partners. In this role, she shapes innovative, practical, and varied approaches that keep the McKinsey's senior leaders at the top of their game and the forefront of their profession. Sarah's 20-plus-year career blends extensive experience in learning and development, consumer insights, and management consulting. Sarah also served on the faculty at the University of Minnesota's Carlson School of Management from 2012 to 2016.

Terrence Hackett is a senior learning expert in McKinsey's Chicago office and designs learning programs for McKinsey partners around the globe. Prior to his ongoing 17-year career in corporate learning, he designed award-winning educational software for schools. He is a long-time tutor, a published author and speaker on learning, and the author of *On the Edge: A Memoir*, a book about a Chicago teen's journey from homelessness to prison to a nationally recognized speaker on the topic of personal transformation.

Gene Kuo serves as director of consultant leadership development at McKinsey. Based out of Houston, Gene has global responsibility for the end-to-end leadership development curricula and journeys of McKinsey's prepartner client-service professionals. A former management consultant, Gene has more than a decade of experience in the learning-and-development field. He has particularly keen interests in the areas of leadership development in young, high-potential individuals; electronic performance support; and learning analytics.

Duncan Larkin leads the Digital Learning Innovation team at McKinsey. He is based out of the Philadelphia office and is a founding member of the Digital Learning Consortium. Duncan has authored three books and is a frequent speaker about innovation topics at various learning conferences.

Maeve Lucey is a learning delivery manager in McKinsey's Stamford office, where she helps enable the delivery of the firm's in-person and digital programs. Maeve embraced digital learning in its infancy—both designing and developing digital-learning programs, as well as providing coaching on effective ways to create and deploy engaging digital programs. Maeve has more than 20 years of experience in adult learning, in both the business and academic worlds.

Barbara Matthews is a learning manager in McKinsey's Sacramento office. She has 20 years of experience designing learning solutions to help solve strategic business issues in a variety of industries, including retail, finance, healthcare, professional services, and education. In her current role, she is responsible for Global Learning solutions related to change initiatives at McKinsey.

Karen J. Merry is a senior learning solutions expert in McKinsey's Houston office, where she leads learning strategy discussions and conceptual design considerations for McKinsey professionals in the oil and gas; pharmaceuticals and medical products; travel, transport, and logistics; health and human services;

and insurance industry portfolios. Karen has more than 20 years of experience in architecting strategic learning solutions for a variety of organizations and industries, including early-mid tenure capability-building programs, petrotechnical-resource entry programs for Most of World graduates, and learning strategy proposals for oil-and-gas concessions. Karen holds an M.Ed. in instructional systems technology from Indiana University, with an emphasis in training and development, and a BS in media communications and technology from East Stroudsburg University.

Based in Atlanta, **Larry Murphy** is McKinsey's director of Partner Learning and Development. In that role, he leads a team of colleagues in setting and implementing McKinsey's investments in the ongoing development of its partners and senior partners globally.

Based in the Chicago office, **Stephanie Nadda** is a digital learning technologies manager in one of Global Learning's center of excellence teams: Digital Learning Platforms and Solutions. Stephanie leads the strategy, operations, and project management office for the group. She joined McKinsey in November 2015 after leading her own consulting practice, which specialized in learning technologies, for 12 years. Stephanie has deep expertise in learning systems, as well as program and project management, and she has worked hard to collaborate closely with IT throughout her career. Stephanie has spoken at the HR Technology conference and ATD's Techknowledge conference. She coauthored the white paper "Enabling a culture of formal learning: A new LMS for the NCAA."

Nick Pappas is McKinsey's digital learning innovation R&D lead, based out of Chicago. Nick is responsible for running research and experimentation at the forefront of digital-learning technology to develop relevant use cases that significantly enhance the learning experience. Prior to joining McKinsey, Nick served as the director of technology for SpotMe, a mobile-app start-up.

James Pritchard is a digital solutions manager in McKinsey's New York office. As part of the Digital Platform Innovation team, he is responsible for evaluating and launching new learning tools and platforms. He has also led the custom development of McKinsey's personalized learning-journey portal, serving as a product owner and content developer. He received an MFA in fiction writing from New York University and a BS in management science and engineering from Stanford University.

Ron Rabin is a learning design manager in McKinsey's Seattle office. A former software developer and IT architect, he loves to work at the intersection of technology and learning. Prior to joining McKinsey, Ron was a senior learning technologist at the Center for Creative Leadership and lead designer and educational technologist at IBM's Center for Advanced Learning.

Brodie Riordan is a manager of Partner Learning and Development in McKinsey's Washington, DC, office. Brodie is deeply passionate about performance and potential, feedback, coaching, and leadership development. She has published more than two dozen journal articles, books, and book chapters on these topics, including the book *Using Feedback in Organizational Consulting* (under her maiden name, Jane Brodie Gregory). Brodie has a PhD in industrial/organizational psychology and is certified by the International Coach Federation.

John Sangimino is a senior learning solutions expert in McKinsey's Chicago office. In this role he works with McKinsey practices to develop learning strategies and solutions that drive deep performance change. John has more than 25 years of experience leading the development of learning programs and solutions for global clients.

Lois Schaub is a senior learning analytics specialist in McKinsey's Stamford office. In this role she develops metrics and data visualizations to help measure the impact of—and continuously improve—learning programs and journeys. Before joining McKinsey, Lois worked with K–12 teachers and administrators to maximize the use of data to improve student achievement.

Janice Steffen is a senior manager, learning design in McKinsey's Denver office. In this role she provides thought leadership and operational management for McKinsey's learning design solutions and resources. She is a seasoned expert in change management, team management, leadership development, and learning and organizational development strategies. Janice has previously published work in *Training Magazine*.

Based in Chicago, **Allison Stevenson** is Kirkland & Ellis's global director of legal education and development, leading attorney learning and development across the firm. In this role she has an impact on attorney growth through innovative solutions, managing continuing legal education tracking, accreditation, compliance, and reporting firm-wide. Allison is the former director of change management and strategic communications for McKinsey's learning function, where she led the global communication and engagement strategy for firm learning. Allison is an executive leader with more than 17 years of management and consulting experience in organizational change, learning strategy, and operational excellence across a wide range of enterprises.

Allison Thom is a senior learning portfolio manager in McKinsey's Stamford office. She manages the *Developing Every Day, Everywhere* portfolio, which is focused on learning that happens outside of the formal classroom through digital learning, learning on teams, coaching, and many other opportunities to learn. She also leads efforts to collaborate with McKinsey's offices worldwide to support them in the learning they offer locally and improve sharing of best practices on learning and development.

Gina Webster is a learning manager in McKinsey's New York office. She leads distance and digital learning globally for the Operations Practice and manages a portfolio of core ops in-person training programs, focused on lean and transformation topics.

Based in the Atlanta office, **Ashley Williams** is chief learning officer (CLO) for McKinsey Academy, which supports clients in building capabilities at scale. In this role, Ashley is helping McKinsey Academy scale the learning experience design and execution capabilities, counseling clients as they build capabilities in transformational environments, developing thought leadership on topics across capability building, and growing and innovating the McKinsey Academy curricula and offerings. Prior to McKinsey Academy, Ashley spent more than ten years in Learning at McKinsey, including as deputy CLO, where she helped lead several transformations and key innovations for McKinsey Learning.

Cathy Wright leads McKinsey's global Knowledge Management and Dissemination function, which oversees the systems for creating, managing, and disseminating knowledge internally as well as directly to clients. Her specific areas of expertise include knowledge strategy, theme identification, curation, knowledge systems, knowledge governance and culture, external knowledge dissemination, and measuring knowledge impact. Cathy joined McKinsey in 2001 as a consultant and then became a knowledge manager and expert in the Marketing and Sales Practice. From 2008 to 2014, Cathy led Visa Inc.'s marketing consulting and research functions. She has an MBA from the Wharton School at the University of Pennsylvania and a BA from the University of California, Santa Cruz.

www.ingramcontent.com/pod-product-compliance
Lightning Source LLC
Chambersburg PA
CBHW020357100426
42812CB00001B/99
9780692150818